THE RISE OF CHRISTIAN CONSCIENCE

The Rise of Christian Conscience

The Emergence of a Dramatic Renewal Movement in the Church Today

Edited by Jim Wallis

1817

Harper & Row, Publishers, San Francisco

Cambridge, Hagerstown, New York, Philadelphia, Washington
London, Mexico City, São Paulo, Singapore, Sydney

FIRST EDITION

Library of Congress Cataloging-in-Publication Data

The Rise of Christian Conscience.

Includes index.
1. Christianity and justice.   2. Christianity and politics.   3. Conscience—Religious aspects—Christianity.   I. Wallis, Jim.
BR115.J8R57   1987   269   86-45076
ISBN 0-06-069052-6 (pbk.)

---

87   88   89   90   91   MPC   10   9   8   7   6   5   4   3   2   1

For Allan Boesak of South Africa and Karl Gaspar of the Philippines, two dear friends who have helped to teach me the meaning of both conscience and hope.

CONTENTS

EPILOGUE: HOPE

PREFACE

When Roy M. Carlisle of Harper & Row San Francisco asked me to do a book about the new movements of conscience arising within the churches, I told him that no one person could or should write it. Rather it is a story of faith best told by the many people involved in those movements. I agreed to edit the book, gathering visions, testimonies, and reflections that comprise the many faces of a growing movement of faith and courage. *The Rise of Christian Conscience* tells the many stories and, through them, a single story of spiritual renewal and political hope in the United States.

I'm thankful to Roy for the encouragement, support, and practical help he provided. Joyce Hollyday gave good advice on the selection of material, and Sandra Shenk-Lapp and Joe Lynch were a great help in the editing. Sally Peterson typed much of the material in preparation for editing, and Steve McKindley-Ward assisted with publishing tasks. The real credit for the completion of this project goes to Karen Lattea, who served as managing editor and principal copy editor of the book. It was the deep partnership between Karen and me that really produced this book. Her characteristic competence and companionship throughout the effort made the work an enjoyable task.

The strength of this book is in the stories it contains and the commitments of the people who have written the articles or are interviewed. Special thanks go to each of the contributors. Most of this material was originally published in *Sojourners* magazine.

The Rise of Christian Conscience points to the possibility of a different future beyond the circumstances we now endure. For that, we should all be thankful.

Jim Wallis

FOREWORD
Daniel Berrigan, S.J.

The essays that follow are offered as reports from the ramparts where, in a manner of speaking, their authors have stood and withstood for a matter of years. Understandably, the mood of the writing is both grateful and chastened. All of the authors have felt the rigors of the times, whether in urban ghettos or out, in courts or out, in jail or out. In the church, God be praised—but not out.

In the church. And that, as the poem goes, has made all the difference.

Such things as are going on in the church! The pain and high spirits attendant on changing the face of things. And in the process, as most would confess with a sigh, changing one's own face as well. Even undergoing healing perhaps, along with its fevers and chills. And hoping with all one's hope that the same healing might touch on the deep illnesses that afflict all.

And then there's that distressful matter of the law. A touchy subject indeed, taken seriously almost nowhere—except in the church.

I reflect on that "taken seriously." What I mean is, taken biblically.

The opposite of this? Perhaps taken obsessively, taken idolatrously, taken inhumanly. Taken piecemeal, taken frivolously, taken vengefully.

The law, the sticking point of Reagan's petrified America. A culture stuck, literally, in the law. What a curious pivot of history we spin on, what astonishing contradictions arise. We live in an atmosphere in which law and order have become a sacred shibboleth, unexamined, self-justifying, defining all else, self-propagating, increasingly isolating Americans, rendering their government intemperate, apt for sudden spasms of recrimination.

The question arises: what conceivable benefit has this obsession with law and order bestowed on people?

It is a lonely business playing God. Running the world. Telling the world off. Might above right. Americans are at once guardians of the law and snootily above it. The government has become a law unto itself, the law an internal combustion machine churning away. The courts have never been busier, yet they have never offered less of justice, equity, light, or heat. The citizens are edgy and contentious; each, it appears, has rights and grievances—but only someone else has obligations.

Strangely to behold, the culture of the law is at the same time lawless. The law-abiding and the lawless are one and the same. Citizens are stuck in a profound spiritual schizophrenia. They are obsessed with rights of property, having and getting, personal security. A veritable chasm opens between mine and thine. And the same people are utterly contemptuous of international law, that feeble instrument assaying timidly and inchoatively to protect human and civil rights across the world. No part of this! More, these people are equally contemptuous in the face of domestic law, as this would, however feebly, protect human and civil rights of the poor or minorities or the "undocumented."

It is precisely at this point that the essays of this book intervene in a saving way. The book is like a wedge thrust in the teeth of a falling portcullis. It is a feeble wedge, admittedly, one that can impede only a measure of damage; but still in such times any slight edge offers hope. For the law as presently envisioned, formulated, pushed, and administered in America literally and mercilessly descends, crushes all who impede, subverts conscience, and both creates and condemns victims.

The law needs not law enforcement. The law needs salvation—from itself.

The ironclad claims of the law, its hold over humans, its conspiracy with death and sin, its pettiness and pretension, its hypocrisy, its subversion of faith—long ago these were analyzed, exposed, and condemned by Paul and his Lord.

The law is the omni-Mafia of history; it fronts for crime. The law crushes the powerless and holds the powerful unaccountable. The law kills—conscience first of all. The law creates and maintains a system of misery, exclusion, and mindless violence. The law holds property sacred and refugees, the poor, and the powerless of no account. So reads the scriptural indictment. So, it might be added, is Scripture constantly verified in the events of the times. *Tolle et lege*. Let the literate read, book and event.

As this book goes to print, the law has shown its true face once more. And its tooth and claw. Legally, as they say (high crime is always legal), a group of church sanctuary workers has been convicted. Under the law.

Futility is matched by pretension. The law that presumes to speak the last word, to crown civilization, to be wise and humane and simpatico with the best in us, to sustain the weak and curb the powerful—that law after centuries in the cockpit of history (the law of capitalism, of Marxism, of revolution, of kings and shahs and juntas and God knows what)—that law has yet to speak (or indeed give ear to) a word that liberates.

Who of us could point to a government anywhere in the world, whose laws achieve economic justice, whose prisons are empty, whose women and gays and minorities are equals, whose leadership speaks to each and all a word of truth? Have human laws ever liberated their people? Indeed liberation comes invariably from a far different source—not the high places of the powerful but from the victims. From such as Archbishop Romero:

> Christ invites us not to fear persecution, because those who are committed to the poor must risk the same fate as the poor, and in El Salvador we know what the fate of the poor signifies: to disappear, to be tortured, to be captive, and to be found dead.

A word of hope spoken, appropriately enough, not by the law or lawgivers or prosecutors or law professors or judges. Nor, it goes without saying, by presidents or kings. A word spoken, strangely enough, by the celebrated victim of the aforesaid eminences.

The word of hope, both the saying and the hearing, belongs to those who confront the law for the sake of the living. In America, that word belongs to the sanctuary movement, the witnesses for peace, the Plowshares prisoners, those who resist South African policy and practice, the draft refusers. But the same word is spoken also, could they but hear it, to the venerable self-victimized custodians of the law.

Most of those who report in these pages have stood in the courts, endured hearing their vocations derided and criminalized by pharisees and publicans alike. As the book goes to press, the Silo Plowshares resisters face trial. Times of life and death, powerful times. The law of God confronts the lawlessness of power. The last word, the word that vindicates the powerless and indicts the powerful, is yet to be spoken; it will most certainly be spoken by others than judges and prosecutors. Cold comfort, but Christian. The judges also will be judged.

Are we to think of Paul's condemnation of the law as a word that has changed things? Is the law once and for all reproved, reformed, pro people, in right relation to the end time and the justice of God? Hardly. We have only to look seriously at the law of the land. Totally politicized, totally apolitical, it does as it pleases, favors whom it will. The law of prestigitators, chameleons. Tighten the clutch of law, violate the law. A law-enforcing culture, a law-condemning culture. Punish violators ever more seriously! And then contempt for the World Court, for the sovereignty of legitimate governments, for control of the military by the civilian head of state—indeed and in sum, contempt for international law, for the Constitution itself.

One's first instinct is compassion. How victimized Americans are, how conned, how lied to, how kept off balance, how trivialized, how subject to scandal in the biblical sense. To have the law deified, even as it is defied. And in the process, how the sense of humanity is eroded, the sense of human measure so grievously inflated.

And then a second sense—danger. Americans are dangerous. To lose one's bearings in a traditional sense can awaken only pity in others—as long indeed as the lost one is accounted harmless, a kind of village character, a mildly diseased mind in a community of the healthy. Such a one can be borne with, can be even a grace.

But the present case is something else. Americans are armed to the teeth. They are also isolated from the common sense of the world, even as they are determined to be the decisive voice in the affairs of the world. There is the stuff of tragedy here, of finality, of doom.

The mitigations are slight, but they may well be crucial to the world and to America. They are told of in this book. Courage and prayer and the counterarmament of the Spirit, which makes for steadfastness. And then also the sanity we name biblical literacy. A true sense of the law, conveyed by the One we name both Compassionate and Judge of the living.

Will something of social salvation come of it all? Of outcome in any large sense, we know next to nothing. Our friends, resisters, defendants, prisoners—their best efforts seem to offer a pitifully meagre outcome. And yet perhaps the question is still lodged in a bad perspective. "Discerning the times" is a biblical task, they are telling us. The people of this book are telling us about a new (and very old) sense of time, something about a "meantime."

Ours is a time of no great achievement except in the most frivolous and questionable realms of technology and military muscle. Indeed, the supposition goes, what other achievement is worthwhile?

It is a time like wet concrete underfoot; and we, slogging through, are half stuck; the concrete hardens behind us. Most Americans are cut off from a past that might shed light or grant a vatic word. Ahead of us, a vast concrete wasteland; we have no clear sense of a future emerging, of relief, intervention, or vision. Indeed, the only future offered is a more horrid version of the past: permanent hardened terror.

Meantime the work goes on, in spite of all. Those who discern the times, improvise, do what can be done, make do, in a time like the catch of a breath.

Something is in the air, something ominous, even ruinous, but indistinct, undefined, unresolved. The god named nemesis takes no clear form; it's cloudy, menacing, a vague thunder nearing. The grandiose technology is a mockery; it turns against the promethean artificers in a spasm of doom. No one is exempt, even the immortals.

Still, in spite of all, something else is in the air. There does come a measure of light, and a voice. It is not generally perceived or heard, but no matter (or at least, not the point). The common understanding, strange as it seems at first sight, seems to be something like this. It is not the responsibility of those who strike the flame or tell the truth to gain a following, to win a hearing. In a final sense (and in such times no other sense is helpful), they have only to persevere in the task that makes all the difference. Do the good for the sake of the good and pay up. Resist evil, succor the helpless. Do not kill, do not remain silent in the face of crime. Stand where the violence is worst, say no, go to court, go to prison.

They know the task by heart; they are doing it. We are their debtors in a double sense: for the doing and the telling.

INTRODUCTION:
The Rise of Christian Conscience
Jim Wallis

At a 1984 gathering of two hundred top military leaders at the National War College, a revealing statement was made: "The greatest challenge to all that we do now comes from within the churches." The speaker was a high-ranking general who went on to say, "A whole new way of thinking is developing in the churches, and we have to know what to do with it."

In April 1985 Langhorne A. Motley, then Assistant Secretary of State for Inter-American Affairs, said, "Taking on the churches is really tough. We don't normally think of them as political opponents, so we don't know how to handle them. . . . It has to be a kid-glove kind of thing. They are really formidable."

A year later the U.S. government tried to crack down on churches offering sanctuary to Central American refugees. Eleven priests, ministers, and lay people representing thousands of sanctuary workers from coast to coast were tried in Tucson, Arizona. Eight of these eleven church workers were convicted of conspiracy or other substantive counts, but that hasn't diminished their conviction and commitment to the sanctuary movement. They intend to appeal the court decision.

The U.S. government prosecutors admitted during the trial to sending paid agents into church meetings, worship services, and Bible study groups to gather information. And during the government's court case, two church denominations, the Presbyterian church (U.S.A.) and the Lutheran church, sued the U.S. government to put an end to illegal infiltration of churches and religious organizations.

Other signs of official concern about the new stirrings in the churches are also evident. The government now has "liaisons" assigned to the various churches who monitor and maintain close contact with the peace activities of the different denominations. Bishops and other church leaders are receiving almost weekly mailings from the White House and government agencies defending policies related to Central America, nuclear weapons, and domestic priorities. Some have received personal visits from special government emissaries to "explain" administration policies.

Christian activists are reporting incidents of surveillance, break-ins, and even infiltration. The Internal Revenue Service is cracking down on war-tax resisters, and stiffer sentences are being given to those who commit nonviolent civil disobedience in protest of the arms race and U.S. war policies.

New executive orders and legislative proposals have resulted in the lifting of restrictions on government intelligence agencies, the promise of harsh measures against dissenters, and a threat to constitutional rights. One recent proposal in Congress even suggested capital punishment for crimes of "treason," a word that history has shown extremely vulnerable to changing political definitions. In her nationally televised speech at the 1984 Republican National Convention in Dallas, former United Nations Ambassador Jeane Kirkpatrick said that those who disagree with U.S. military and foreign policy should not be tolerated.

The government's allies on the political Right have their own part to play. Right-wing groups have become revitalized in the last several years. Even those never before taken seriously are now basking in the light of new credibility and prominence. The Right is demonstrating a confident militance and has taken the offensive against those who would question U.S. foreign and domestic behavior, accusing them of being Marxist and pro-Soviet.

A rigorous campaign of distortion and slander is now under way, aimed at discrediting those individuals, groups, publications, and churches who dare to dissent from official ideology and policy. The Right is especially afraid of such religiously based dissent. An independent movement of conscience whose cry for justice and appeal for peace is rooted in the Bible rather than political ideology is the hardest to discredit, ignore, or accuse of communist sympathies.

Historically, the political authorities have shown more awareness of the gospel's threat to established power than have the believers. Indeed, it was the ruling authorities of Jesus' day, more than his disciples, who were the most keenly aware of the political danger he posed. Ironically, it was the religious and political rulers who put Jesus to death who remembered and feared the promise of his resurrection, not his followers, who forgot and fled. And today the powers-that-be and their religious coconspirators have reason to be afraid of what is happening in the churches.

The renewal of Christian conscience is now a worldwide phenomenon. In Latin America bishops and priests used to be the honored guests at the tables of the rich; now many have become the companions of the poor. The clergy used to bless political prisoners before their executions; now priests, lay church leaders, and even bishops have become political prisoners themselves, and many have been killed or have disappeared. At popular liturgies, names such as that of murdered El Salvadoran Archbishop Oscar Romero and countless other Christian martyrs are raised up and the people respond, *"Presente"*—meaning "they are with us." The faith of ordinary people, gathered together into hundreds of thousands of base communities, now fuels the engine of change in Latin America and is renewing the face of the church.

Karl Gaspar, while a political prisoner in the Philippines, wrote letters from his jail cell that read like modern-day prison epistles. And in Poland and El Salvador, priests murdered by government security forces are found at the bottom of reservoirs and ravines. Small groups of Christians working for peace meet and pray on both sides of the Berlin Wall.

Religious dissidents—Christians and Jews—suffer courageously in the Soviet Union. In South Africa a "confessing church" is emerging with Christians such as Dutch Reformed Church minister Allan Boesak and Archbishop Desmond Tutu leading the people's struggle for freedom against apartheid. Even in highly secularized Western Europe, the threat of nuclear war is sparking religious renewal and revitalization in the churches. Some peace groups in West Germany have published the Sermon on the Mount in their daily newspapers, leading to the first real discussion in many years of the meaning of Jesus' teaching.

In the United States, a new "peace church" is emerging that spans virtually every denomination, confession, and constituency. The threat of nuclear war has raised, for an increasing number of Christians, not only the question of survival, but a crisis of faith.

The nation's reliance on weapons capable of mass destruction and its expressed willingness to use them have become a profoundly theological and spiritual issue for the churches. For many, the heart of the matter is the idolatry, blasphemy, and heresy of nuclear weapons. The old distinctions between pacifists and "just war" adherents are breaking down and giving way to a "new abolitionist movement"—a commitment to abolish nuclear weapons rooted in the imperatives of faith.

Most of the major church bodies and bishops' conferences have made statements against nuclear weapons and the spiraling arms race, some of them quite strong. Most of the denominations now have task forces and active programs in peacemaking. At the congregational and parish level, Bible study, prayer, discussion, and action are taking place around the nuclear question literally all across the country.

The movement can best be seen working at the grass-roots level. The train that carries warheads from the Pantex bomb factory near Amarillo, Texas, to deployment sites around the country once traveled unnoticed and unhindered. That was before the Nuclear Train Campaign, which is conducted by the Agape Community along the tracks. Now, whenever the Nuclear Train moves, a national network of prayer and action springs to life with vigils along its route. Wherever the train goes, it is tracked, met, and blocked by thousands of people, mostly religious, offering prayers of resistance.

Similarly, fewer and fewer of the nation's nuclear facilities and military bases that have operated quietly in U.S. communities are spared the regular presence of Christians and other nonviolent protesters, especially at special days and seasons in the church's liturgical calendar. The geography of worship and prayer is being relocated, moving beyond the confines of church sanctuaries and crossing the lines, fences, and boundaries that read "No Trespass." By so doing, the evil being done in secret at such places is being exposed to the light of public scrutiny, the light of conscience, and the light of God.

The time-honored practice of nonviolent protest and civil disobedience, so deeply rooted in both our biblical and democratic traditions, is being recovered in our nuclear age, and many Christians are going to jail for the sake of peace. One recent count of those arrested for nuclear protest in one year alone tallied five thousand, and the majority of them were Christians. Vigils, public liturgies and prayer services, symbolic actions, war-tax resistance, direct-action campaigns, courtrooms, and jail cells are becoming a part of the church's life.

Who is involved? At the heart of the new Christian peace movement are religious sisters and priests, Baptist ministers, Episcopal doctors, Pentecostal truck drivers, Catholic bishops and police officers, evangelical mothers, United Methodist school teachers, Presbyterian businesspeople, and Lutheran farmers. I remember the Peace Pentecost events here in Washington in May 1983. On Pentecost Monday, which turned out to be the day the issue of MX missiles came to the floor of Congress for debate, 242 Christians were arrested while they prayed for peace in the Capitol Rotunda. It was the largest mass arrest in Washington, D.C., since during the Vietnam War. The beautiful singing and prayers that began with three thousand people in the National Cathedral the night before continued into the Rotunda and then the D.C. jail.

The next day in court was a memorable experience as all those arrested were arraigned and testified to the faith that compelled them to act. The judge later said it was the hardest day of his legal career. A German psychiatrist said she had learned from the Nuremberg trials after World War II that there comes a time when Christians must simply stand up and say no. A mother made a plea for her children and for other people's children. A Southern Baptist minister simply said, "Jesus is Lord," and then sat down. Baptist ministers often say those words, of course, but the place and circumstances in which they were spoken made all the difference.

The widening war in Central America has also sparked Christian conscience. Many thousands of U.S. Christians have traveled to Nicaragua, El Salvador, Honduras, and Guatemala to see for themselves what is happening. They have come home with a very different picture from the one painted by the U.S. government, and other U.S. citizens have now heard their stories. More and more U.S. church people now believe the testimony of their denomination missionaries and other Christians in the region and the reports of their own church delegations instead of the official statements of the State Department and the distortions of the mainstream media. Out of such firsthand exposure, personal involvement, and mounting concern over U.S. policy, a number of bold initiatives have been undertaken.

The Witness for Peace in Nicaragua began as a risky experiment in nonviolence and has become a powerful venture of faith and prayer. Approximately fifteen hundred U.S. citizens, mostly religious people, have traveled to the war zones of Nicaragua to stand with the people under attack by the *contras,* to pray for peace, and to present an obstacle to the U.S.-sponsored war.

In Nicaragua, the Witness for Peace offers a direct challenge to the U.S.-backed *contra* violence as North American lives are put alongside Nicaraguan lives in places of great danger. Witness for Peace gives a clear message to the Nicaraguan people who are suffering so much: many U.S. citizens do not support the war being waged against them.

In the United States, the Witness for Peace has brought home a steady stream of changed people who are now eyewitnesses to the consequences of U.S.-inspired terrorism against the people of Nicaragua. Witness for Peace volunteers always come back deeply touched by what they have seen and experienced. The stories that each has to tell give a human face to the suffering caused by U.S. policies.

North Americans are risking their lives in Nicaraguan war zones for the sake of peace, and a clear signal is being sent to the U.S. government. The waiting list for volunteers is still long; there are teams from every region of the country. The Witness for Peace has been sounded as an altar call throughout U.S. churches, and all who respond are being converted to a deeper faith.

The sanctuary movement has also spread throughout the country, opening both U.S. doors and hearts to Central American refugees fleeing tyranny and violence. At least three hundred churches have become havens of rest and sanctuary for El Salvadoran and Guatemalan refugees whose lives are in danger from their own governments.

To harbor these strangers and sojourners is very consistent with the best of biblical and church tradition, but it is done in open defiance of U.S. government law and policies toward Central America. An underground and overground railroad has developed around the country, with churches and Christian communities as the points of hospitality along the way, to carry refugees to safety and freedom. The process of deciding whether or not to become a sanctuary church in disobedience to the law has been a cause of real transformation in many congregations.

As with the Witness for Peace, it is the personal relationships established between North Americans and Central Americans that give the sanctuary movement its real force and motivating power. The government has already arrested and convicted U.S. church workers for giving refugees safe passage, but the churches are standing firm.

The Pledge of Resistance grows directly out of all this activity and helps tie it all together. It is a "contingency plan" in the event of a U.S. invasion in Central America. Similar to other initiatives, the Pledge of Resistance originated in a retreat that brought together Christian peacemakers for Bible study and prayer. The Pledge of Resistance calls for protest and nonviolent civil disobedience on a massive scale at Congressional field offices, federal buildings, and military installations if the U.S. government invades or significantly escalates its military intervention in Central America.

Literally tens of thousands of U.S. citizens from the religious community, peace movement, Central America solidarity networks, and labor and civic groups have already signed the Pledge. The hope is that the existence of such a plan and the willingness to carry it out might prevent an invasion and help end U.S. military intervention in the region. But if the U.S. government decides to invade Central America, it will have to put tens of thousands of its own citizens in jail. That is the promise.

It is always appropriate for the religious community and people of conscience to try to prevent bloodshed and needless human suffering. It is in this spirit that the Pledge of Resistance, the sanctuary movement, and Witness for Peace are offered. They are acts of faith and conscience, developed not on behalf of any government, party, or ideology, but carried out on behalf of the victims of violence, in defense of justice, and in pursuit of peace.

The Free South Africa Movement has also sparked the conscience of people across the country. The tactics of nonviolent protest and civil disobedience are being reinvigorated by the Free South Africa Movement, led by much of the same leadership that introduced them more than twenty years ago during the civil rights movement. The list of those arrested at vigils in front of the South African Embassy in Washington, D.C., includes members of Congress, labor leaders, and representatives from the civil rights movement, the peace movement, the women's movement, and the religious community.

Never has the apartheid regime of South Africa been so directly challenged from within the United States. Pressure is mounting on the White House to change its failed policy of "constructive engagement." It now appears that the energy to act against the evil of South Africa's racist system existed just below the surface and needed a catalyst to ignite it. The awarding of the Nobel Peace Prize to Desmond Tutu, the repressive brutality of the South African regime, and the leadership of the Free South Africa Movement have provided the spark. The movement promises to renew the power and possibilities of nonviolent direct action on many fronts and establish crucial bridges across racial lines and between key constituencies.

The face of Jesus is being rediscovered not only among the poor of Central America, South Africa, and the Philippines, but also right here at home. All across the United States, the "misery index" is rising. In our inner cities and rural areas, the poor swell in numbers and cry out in distress. The government's policy toward the poor is now one of official abandonment. Those least able to defend themselves will bear the burden of budget cutting and deficit reductions.

But everywhere you look, Christians and churches are feeding the hungry, sheltering the homeless, ministering to the sick, organizing with the disenfranchised, visiting the prisoners, and advocating justice for the oppressed. Wherever there are works of mercy and acts of justice, Christians are in the midst of them. The faithful persistence of Christians like Dorothy Day and the Catholic Worker is bearing much fruit. In many places Christians are finally beginning to heed the gospel message to bring good news to the poor and the warning that we will be judged by how we treat the "least of these."

The energy and passion of Christians have also been at the heart of the opposition to abortion on demand. While it is true that much of the antiabortion movement has been tied to the reactionary political agenda of the religious Right and to antifeminist forces, a new call is emerging for a consistent prolife ethic.

The selective morality of both the Right and the Left is being challenged by a new prolife stance that calls for the defense of human life wherever it is threatened, from the beginning to the end of the life cycle. Thus the rights of women and the unborn, the rejection of nuclear weapons, opposition to military intervention in Central America, the defense of the poor, and the pursuit of economic justice all form a "seamless garment" on behalf of human life.

Christians are also providing leadership in restoring the integrity of family life and personal values as both have broken down in the larger society. In a time of sexual confusion and brokenness, many are beginning to see the relevance and wholeness of marital fidelity, personal commitment, and mutual respect. And equality between women and men in the family, the workplace, and the church is being upheld by more and more Christians as essential to the biblical vision of justice. Some still use the word "family" to support patterns of patriarchy and the oppression of women, but many other Christians are pioneering new family patterns based on partnership and shared responsibility.

As all of these developments suggest, the churches in the United States are going through a fundamental transformation. The changes under way are motivated by faith, formed by conscience, and rooted in the Bible.

The rise of Christian conscience couldn't be more timely. The political conservatism also on the rise is harsh and cruel. Its spiritual companion is a rampant self-interest.

The policies of the Reagan administration ignore the needs of the poor, and whole sections of the country and sectors of the population are in grave danger of simply being abandoned. The development of a growing urban under-class and the near extinction of the small farmer are but two examples.

The United States is also witnessing an escalation in white racism, which is surfacing with renewed strength and boldness. The masses of black Americans still suffer in the prison of poverty, while the White House turns back the clock on the pursuit of civil rights. The status of women is insecure as well, with powerful forces, both ideological and economic, seeking to push women back into old molds and patterns.

The arms race rushes on as the production of even more dangerous nuclear weapons and increased military spending wipe out the remnants of already gutted social programs. Military interventionism has become a way of life, especially in Central America, and the projection of American power to protect American interests has completely super-seded any concern for human rights in the conduct of U.S. foreign policy.

The moral failure of liberalism has greatly added to the present crisis. Liberalism has abandoned the realm of faith, family, and personal values and has thus become increasingly distant from the ways that ordinary people live their day-to-day lives. The militant secularism and moral rootlessness of the liberal establishment have contributed to cultural and spiritual degeneration.

Liberals have preferred bureaucracy to democracy, dependency to justice, power to genuine participation. Their economic solutions are old and tired and ultimately tied to the same basic assumptions on which conservative economic thinking is based. In foreign policy, liberals have accommodated to militarism, anticommunism, and narrow self-interest; their proposals just suggest a little less of all these than their opponents' proposals.

Conservatism now appeals to the country's worst instincts, preju-dices, and fears, while liberalism struggles to hide the fact that it has no real alternative. Both offer only technical solutions to problems rather than human ones.

On the global scene, the Left has failed to keep its promises, produced a rigid ideology, and sacrificed human freedom in the process. The Right has descended to new levels of brutality and has piled the corpses of its victims as high as its worst Communist counterparts. Both right- and left-wing regimes show a remarkable similarity in their willingness to violate human rights when it suits their purposes and to subordinate persons to causes.

The resurgence of religious fundamentalism around the world has often made matters worse by offering religious sanction to war and terrorism, racism and sexism, the suppression of freedom and the abuse of human rights, and the domination of the rich over the poor. From the holy war crusades of the Iranian Ayatollehs to the nuclear Armageddon theology of the American religious Right, the danger of such fundamentalist nationalism is increasingly clear.

In striking contrast, the rise of Christian conscience around the world is a search for social, political, and economic alternatives based on more human values than the solutions offered by the present ideological competitors. That search moves beyond the old polarities of right, left, and center and drives to the spiritual and political core of our problems. New ideas, needed dissent, and an alternative vision are now coming from religious communities around the world.

In the United States, the new movement of Christian conscience has a number of distinguishing characteristics. First, Christian conscience is politically independent. It is neither right nor left, neither liberal nor conservative. It defies categorization by traditional labels and is not ideologically predictable.

For example, Christians opposed to U.S. nuclear policy and interventionism in Central America may seem to agree with the Left. But those same Christians may differ sharply with the Left over issues such as abortion, sexual morality, and the ethics of violence. Christians may have conservative personal and family values but disagree completely with conservatives on the role of women, the solutions to racism, or the value of economic success. Christian conscience doesn't distinguish between violations of human rights under right-wing military dictatorships or left-wing totalitarian governments.

Second, Christian conscience is especially sensitive to those who are the victims of the prevailing social order: the poor, the marginalized, the political prisoners, the oppressed race or class, women, the ethnic minority—these are the ones Christians should be particularly attentive to in any society. Christians must see the view from the outside, learn the perspective from the bottom, hear the voices of the forgotten ones. Since all systems have their victims, none will respond enthusiastically to the exercise of Christian conscience on behalf of the victims.

Third, Christian conscience has deep spiritual roots. It is grounded in the Scriptures, which do not change but are always new. The life rhythm of reflection, prayer, and action is essential to the exercise of Christian conscience. Without the river of faith to refresh and replenish it, Christian conscience can easily dry up into rigid self-righteousness. The rediscovery of the Bible, the return to prayer, and the recovery of the spiritual life are at the center of the new movement of Christian conscience.

What does the future hold? A movement of Christian conscience could spark the conscience of a nation and lead to changes beyond our imagination. It has happened before. Christians were at the center of the abolitionist movement, the movement for women's suffrage, and the civil rights struggle. It could happen again.

The rise of Christian conscience could provoke persecution, as has happened in other parts of the world. The conversion of the churches to the side of the poor and the cause of peace has often led to attacks on the church from governments set up to protect wealth and power.

That has been the experience of the church in the Third World. However, through this trial by fire, the faith of Third World churches has been strengthened. Similarly, the official persecution of the churches in Eastern-bloc countries has not crushed people's faith but rather has led to overflowing and flourishing congregations. The experience of official repression and persecution of Christian dissidents may become our own in the days ahead.

It will take a much deeper moral confrontation between conscience and power to make the real issues clear in our own country. This growing movement in the church may be forging the "creative tension" of which both Mohandas Gandhi and Martin Luther King, Jr., often spoke. That will certainly mean sacrifice and suffering, but it may be the only thing that can open the door to real change.

A discernible movement from protest to resistance already exists in the churches. A new era of church–state relations in the United States may soon be upon us.

National church bodies are now seriously discussing the theological basis and spiritual imperative for civil disobedience. Issues such as war-tax resistance, prayerful trespass at nuclear facilities, sanctuary, non-violent resistance over Central America and South Africa, and non-registration for the draft are all pressing issues in many churches. It is likely that a whole series of church statements on civil disobedience will follow the many church statements on peace. The churches and the U.S. government seem headed toward deeper conflict over militarism, fundamental questions of justice, and respect for human life.

We are entering a time when faith will be needed to overcome fear, when deep spiritual roots will be necessary to endure setbacks, when hope will be required to move beyond despair, and when vision will be called for to look beyond the present and see new possibilities.

PART ONE

Signs of Conscience

THE BIG PICTURE:
Where We Are and How We Got Here
Danny Collum

Everyone knows that this is a tough time to be working for social change in these United States. But that is not because of any shortage of activity. In the last five years, millions of Americans have entered struggles for justice and peace in different ways and with different levels of commitment. Many of those people have become active for the first time through the explosions of concern around issues such as the nuclear arms race, the U.S. war in Central America, racism at home and abroad, and the assaults on women and the poor that have marked the Reagan era.

But all this activity has, frankly, done little or nothing to slow the juggernauts of war and injustice. We all know the litany of horrors–*contra* aid, Star Wars, rollbacks of civil rights for minorities and women, broken obligations to the poor and unemployed, and so on. The sad fact is that on every front progressive forces in the United States are meeting defeat, and for the most part we have no idea how to turn things around in the short term.

Vertigo in the Eighties

By now many of us are probably feeling that the political ground has shifted beneath our feet, and we're not sure how to walk on this new terrain. Vertigo and exhaustion could be considered the movement watchwords of the day. In such a time of disorientation and defeat, it can be expected that many who have joined the struggle in recent years will simply give up and go along.

Meeting defeat, however, does not have to mean being defeated. On one level that is simply an expression of the theological paradox that is at the heart of Christian faith: that Jesus–not in spite of, but because of, his abject and total defeat–is ultimately victorious over the powers of death. Part of the good news of the last five years is that a very large percentage of America's newly activated dissidents are people who believe that Christian paradox. These people have become politically active out of a living moral and religious commitment that, at its best, is independent from immediate prospects for success.

But for individual commitment, even more so a coherent movement, to survive a time like this requires more than religious enthusiasm or moral fervor. We also need a deeper, longer-term understanding about the nature of the struggle we're involved in and a bigger picture of how it is unfolding.

That is especially true today, because in fact the political ground has shifted beneath our feet in some very significant ways. The litany of evils that we often exhaust ourselves combatting are all merely symptomatic of a historic trend that is under way in U.S. political life.

In broad terms, our corporate elite is trying to recapture and reconsolidate the ground lost in the 1960s and 1970s to domestic reform and Third World revolution. The battlefields range from Central American villages and Geneva negotiating parlors to U.S. day-care centers, union picket lines, and the mass media. But they are all part of the same protracted war.

If our commitment is defined by a specific goal or issue, for instance, stopping the nuclear arms race or getting the United States out of Central America, then if the desired changes don't materialize, we can rightly consider ourselves defeated and our efforts futile. However, if we see each specific issue as part of an overall system of wealth and power and define our activism as part of a lifelong struggle to turn that system around, then, short of total nuclear war, there are no ultimate defeats or victories. There is only a succession of battles waged around different specific concerns at different times, all of which, successful or not, contribute in some way to what Dr. Martin Luther King, Jr., called, "That long and bitter, but beautiful, struggle for a new world."

The Nature of the Beast

It is certainly the case that the people who run America think globally and systematically about their course of action. They are, after all, sitting astride an empire that requires trade, raw materials, labor, and markets from across the planet. Protecting that economic reach, of course, requires a global projection of military power. And the maintenance of a global military capacity ultimately requires that the citizens of the mother country (that's you and me) be convinced, through a combination of material rewards and cultural conditioning, that the whole imperial enterprise is worth the cost.

Managing a project of such scope and magnitude obviously requires more than just crisis containment. It requires grand conceptual frameworks and imaginative ideological constructions that must constantly feed upon reams of data, multiple reams of analysis, constant probing of the popular psyche, and endless contingency plans.

Elite universities, corporate research departments, and a whole universe of think tanks work full time compiling, sifting, and shaping this official picture of the world. Then it trickles down to media professionals and politicians. Finally, at the other end of the process, there emerges a "consensus" regarding things like deregulation of natural gas prices or "democratic reform" in El Salvador.

Somehow the policies that come out of this process always seem to serve the interests of the corporate elite that set the agenda. The process by which policy is shaped and public consent manufactured is simply the natural interaction of economic interests, ideology, and raw coercive power through which rulers everywhere have always maintained their dominion.

For the first twenty years of the American empire, from 1945 to 1965, consolidation and management of the global system went pretty smoothly. The first step of the process was to create a permanent state of war with the Soviet Union and an omnipresent international communist threat. This was necessary to, in the famous words of the late Sen. Arthur Vandenburg, "scare the hell out of the American people" in order to ensure a war-weary public's acceptance of a permanent war economy, peacetime conscription, and an institutionalized nuclear threat. Anti-communism also provided the all-encompassing ideology needed to cloak the imperial project in the language of freedom and democracy.

After a brief period of political and cultural repression and retooling, the Cold War liberal consensus emerged unchallenged. That "consensus" delivered a period of unprecedented prosperity at home and a kind of global stability abroad built on nuclear terror and covert interventionism.

A symbiotic relationship existed between the "cold peace" and the boundless prosperity of that period. America's wealth depended on free access to the markets, labor, and raw materials of other countries. That required intervention against nationalist forces in the Third World. It was also necessary to neutralize the Soviet Union's potential as the only countervailing force, and the nuclear threat offered the only way to do that short of another exhausting world war.

The Revolution of Rising Expectations

But there were at least two glaring contradictions built into this strategy. In setting themselves against the nationalist aspirations of the Third World, our rulers were from the very beginning marching against the all but inevitable tide of history. That fact finally became evident in the villages of Vietnam. Meanwhile, on the home front, a generation of prosperity and the messianic Cold War rhetoric of freedom and democracy combined to create a revolution of rising expectations.

Black Americans were the first to recognize the gap between America's rhetoric and its actual behavior, perhaps because they were largely locked out of the nation's prosperity. When blacks began to demand that America's fabled freedom and wealth be extended to them, they also brought to the surface and galvanized the vague unease many young white people were feeling about American life.

In the early 1960s, these two forces already formed a powerful current of dissent centered around the demand that America deliver on its democratic promises. By 1965, when the United States began full-scale war in Vietnam, the currents of dissent had become a flood of outraged rebellion.

As it spread from blacks to draft-age youth, the nature of the protest deepened. A civil rights movement that started out demanding black voting rights in the South began to attack the legitimacy of a system that left almost all blacks everywhere economically disenfranchised. An antiwar movement that started out calling for negotiations and a bombing halt quickly realized that the United States was the aggressor in Vietnam. The demand for negotiations was replaced by a call for unilateral withdrawal, not just from Vietnam but from all of America's Third World fortresses.

In challenging an economic system ruled solely by private profit and denying America's right to project its military power anywhere in the world, the great social movements of the 1960s were taking on the most fundamental institutions and assumptions of the empire. And much of the movement's leadership was coming to see the inextricable connection between inequality at home and warfare abroad.

By 1975 America was a beleaguered and clearly declining empire.

The Vietnam War was lost and so was the myth of U.S. invincibility. OPEC (Organization of Petroleum Exporting Countries) was rewriting the ground rules of the international economy on terms decidedly unfavorable to the West, and suddenly the postwar resurrection of Japan and West Germany was beginning to challenge a U.S. economy weakened by the endless war. A corrupt president had been driven from office in humiliation. And the Watergate-related investigations had also exposed parts of the secret and undemocratic intertwining of government institutions, corporate wealth, and covert action by which the United States and much of the world had been ruled for thirty years.

The black and anti-war movements had been largely silenced by the death of Dr. King, the end of the draft, and concerted state repression. But the disruption they had created in the society continued to reverberate through the events of the next several years.

The ideological energy previously generated by America's "free world" crusade was utterly exhausted. Even U.S. citizens could no longer easily believe that America was a uniquely moral and democratic nation ordained by its very virtue to rule the world. When, in the waning days of his rule, Henry Kissinger tried to force a U.S. intervention in Angola, an outraged public and Congress flatly refused, ignoring all the "great man's" talk of oil supplies, shipping lanes, and strategic balance.

Yankees and Cowboys

Clearly, from the perspective of our ruling class, something had to be done to turn this receding tide. One answer was Jimmy Carter. To all appearances this relatively obscure Southern governor burst onto the national scene out of nowhere in the early months of 1976. But in fact he had been recruited to run for president by David Rockefeller himself in 1974. He was subsequently "created" as a national figure by appearing, for no apparently newsworthy reason, on the cover of *Time* magazine.

In Carter the Eastern-establishment elite saw a white Southerner who'd won strong black support in Georgia and could potentially ameliorate the dangerous anger and alienation of black America. It saw a man with fundamentally conservative economic views. Most important, in Carter the corporate kingmakers saw the morally serious Sunday school teacher who could conceivably make Americans again believe in the righteousness of their system.

As candidate and president, Carter became the vehicle for the sector of our ruling elite that considered it futile to try to turn back the economic and political shifts of the previous decade. Instead, they accepted an era of limits and sought to preserve the essentials of their wealth and power through pragmatic accommodation to the changed circumstances.

These old-money, Eastern-establishment "Yankees" tend to look at the world across the Atlantic Ocean, for a combination of financial, historical, and geographic reasons. They are the heirs of the great robber barons—Rockefeller, Carnegie, Morgan, Mellon, Harriman, et al.— whose fortunes were largely made in the nineteenth century. As a result, their financial and political destiny tends to be intertwined with the European colonial powers of that era.

Their dynasties, which began in oil, coal, railroads, shipping, and heavy industry, now form the backbone of the system of international finance. It is a world that revolves around New York, London, Paris, and Zurich; and in it the fate of Saigon had counted for very little except as an expensive and ultimately inconvenient symbol. The captains of finance yearned more for stability than for new conquests.

On the global stage, the Eastern elite's accommodation to the new realities was called trilateralism. Its basic principle was that Japan and Western Europe should be promoted to the status of senior partners roughly equal with the United States. Together the three capitalist superpowers could effectively manage the international economy and reach consensus positions on similar businesslike accommodations with the Soviet Union, China, and troublesome Third World populations.

In foreign policy Carter's establishment advisers counseled a program of moderately enlightened reform, including the much-vaunted human rights policy. Military aid was cut off to dictatorial regimes in Argentina, Chile, and Guatemala, while equally heinous crimes in more geopolitically significant places like Iran, the Philippines, and South Korea were ignored.

On the domestic side, there were institutional reforms like affirmative action and tougher business regulations. These were aimed at restoring confidence in the virtue of our foreign policies and defusing potentially volatile issues like women's rights, continuing racial discrimination, and growing environmental concern.

But the Carter-era program of accommodation and reform ran aground. That was partly a matter of Carter's incompetence and bad luck, but it also reflected the growing power of the new-money Sunbelt elite. Its still-expanding dynasties had mostly begun since the onset of World War II and tended to be based in minerals, construction, defense industries, agribusiness, the postwar suburban retail services boom, and electronics.

The members of this new "Cowboy" elite tended to look at the world across the Pacific, to the emerging economies and expanding markets of East Asia, which naturally caused them to be considerably less sanguine about the loss of Indochina and the rise of Japan than were the trilateralists. And their concentration in the Southwestern United States left them naturally more concerned about Latin America than were the Yankees.

But the key difference is that the Cowboy empires were still dynamic and in need of room to grow. They were inherently more interested in conquest than stability.

The Carter administration's acceptance of limits in the Third World, economic parity with the Japanese, and military parity with the Soviet Union was anathema not only to the Cowboys' vestigial Wild West ethos but to their concrete and immediate economic interests. Out of that combination, one can glimpse an ideological offensive emerging. And the Cowboys didn't need *Time* magazine to create their candidate; Hollywood had done it for them years before.

The constellation of forces that gathered to elect Ronald Reagan in 1980 could already be seen in skeletal form in the collection of Western millionaires and Far Right ideologues (then considered crackpots) who made up the Goldwater campaign of 1964. But in 1964 the as-yet-unnamed New Right was out of step with history. Its adherents insisted on seeing Communists at America's doorstep and rampant moral decay within, at a time when most Americans saw only clear skies and sunshine.

But despite Goldwater's humiliating defeat, the Far Right didn't give up or go away. It began painstakingly building its own institutions and cultivating its own new constituency in full confidence that, when the time was right, it would be ready to replace the weary Eastern establishment and the Democrats' badly frayed New Deal coalition.

With the generous financial support of men like Adolph Coors, Justin Dart, and the renegade Mellon in-law Richard Scaife, the New Right established its own network of think tanks and policy institutes like the Heritage Foundation, the Rocky Mountain Fund, and the Hoover Institute, with the latter even gaining a foothold at prestigious Stanford University. When they were still unwelcome and weak in the Republican establishment, New Right operatives like Richard Viguerie, Paul Weyrich, and Howard Phillips built their own political action committees to perform the traditional political party functions of candidate recruitment, campaign financing, and cadre training.

Through these institutions the New Right leaders uncovered and developed issues that conventional politicians were ignoring and that had the capacity to galvanize previously unidentified constituencies. Early in the Carter administration, the fruits of this work could already be seen in New Right agitation against the Panama Canal and SALT II treaties on the now-familiar theme that America was becoming "weak." They also saw the baby-boomers-having-babies mini-boom coming and were the first to adopt "family" and "family values" as effective political buzzwords.

But the greatest of these was abortion. The New Right recognized it as the kind of issue that can permanently alter the political landscape. The right-to-life issue peeled off a significant layer of formerly Democratic, white, working-class Catholics into the Republican column, and it cemented the New Right's profitable alliance with the TV preachers. Most important, it infused the New Right with the moral energy of one of this era's only genuine grass-roots social movements.

The New Right's electoral successes were built on cleverly crafted appeals to feelings of patriotism, love for family, and religious faith, which are natural and healthy parts of human life. But, in the wrong circumstances, those feelings can also be manifested as xenophobia, racism, and a violent terror of the dissenter or the "different."

While Reagan has worked the high road of lofty American values, his allies—including New Right members of Congress, TV preachers, and the "independent" New Right political action committees—have bulldozed their way down the low one with ads and speeches appealing to racism, subtle or otherwise, and to the most hateful sort of national chauvinism. In New Right rhetoric, it is common to identify dissent with terrorism, stir irrational fears of a unisex ERA future, and attack homosexuals in ways that border on incitement to violence.

But whether on the high road or the low, the purpose is the same. In essence the Reagan administration and its many allies have been redoing the task that was accomplished so well at the onset of the empire forty years ago: instilling national unity (i.e., stifling dissent), constructing a moral and ideological language and fervor around America's imperial mission, and using the Soviet threat to "scare the hell out of the American people." And beneath the rhetoric is the same long-term agenda of assuring the absolute right of corporations to do whatever they please to workers, farmers, communities, or the environment at home and their right to do business wherever they please abroad under the protective umbrella of U.S. military power.

America Is Back

To reassert the agenda of free enterprise and empire in an age of expensive energy, strong international economic competition, Soviet military parity, and still-proliferating Third World revolutions requires, as the saying goes, "hard choices." The first thing required to reconsolidate the empire in the 1980s is a lowering of the expectations that had been raised by the Third World revolutions and domestic social movements of the previous two decades.

In the international arena, that has meant firmly demonstrating that the United States has recovered from the Vietnam syndrome and is willing and able to use its military power to keep other countries from veering out of our political and economic influence. That was the point of the Lebanon disaster, the Grenada invasion, and is the point of the creeping entry into war against Nicaragua. The current administration campaign to win support for anticommunist "freedom fighters" around the world takes the interventionist policy one step further in attempting to actually roll back the changes that occurred from 1975 to 1979.

The drive for all-fronts military superiority over the Soviet Union is, of course, intimately related to this bring-back-Vietnam syndrome. By now the nuclear arms race and the U.S.–Soviet enmity have taken on a near-mythic life of their own. But it is still the case that the United States wants unchallenged superiority over the Soviets, including a nuclear first-strike capacity and Star Wars, not because our leaders especially want to incinerate the Soviet people, but because that capacity is considered an insurance policy against Soviet interference with our plans for the rest of the world.

With plans to use U.S. military power around the world also comes the need to ensure against undue interference from the American people. On that front, the Reagan administration has bypassed Congress and promulgated a series of executive orders broadening the power of federal agencies to act against domestic dissent.

The renewed U.S. militarist drive throughout the world is related in several ways to the domestic social and economic components of the New Right agenda. One of the most obvious and most important connections is the simple fact that when you allow military spending to absorb $300 billion a year from the federal budget, there is little left for things like preventing hunger, educating children, or providing health care.

But the Reagan administration hasn't begun rolling back government social services simply because of the defense budget. It is also doing this as a matter of principle. On one level, many of the Reaganauts do have a genuine, almost religious, faith in the myth of a free-market economy and the corollary doctrine that the market works best when the size and scope of government are reduced to a bare minimum. But at a deeper level, the shrinking of the social safety net is also a response to global economic and political changes.

Since it is becoming more difficult to extract profits abroad because of foreign competition and the occasional revolution, U.S. corporations need to wring more wealth from the domestic work force. When there is a comprehensive social welfare system, including decent supports for the unemployed, it is much easier for workers to demand better wages or working conditions and to take risks, like going on strike, to attain their demands. When the social supports are drastically curtailed and it becomes clear that it is every man, woman, and child for themselves, workers become more docile, and the unemployed become willing to accept the lowest-paying and most demeaning jobs.

Within this overall picture of lowering expectations lies the unique plight of the masses of blacks in America. The disenfranchisement of black Americans is so deeply rooted in our social, political, and economic institutions that it can't be redressed in any significant way without radically disrupting those institutions. Simply opening the way to decent jobs and adequate housing for the decimated urban black communities would require public intervention in the economy at a level that the most liberal corporation head would find intolerable. And that's not even considering the wholesale disruption of leadership elites in every area of society that would come with a just representation of blacks in their number.

Unlike its predecessors, the Reagan administration has faced this reality. As a result it has dispensed with the pretense of piecemeal reform and is seeking instead to forge a new business-oriented black leadership from the small number of blacks who made their way up in the 1970s.

Apparently the strategists of the Right hope that if the pool of future black leadership can be disconnected from the aspirations of black people as a whole, then those left at the bottom will remain disorganized and hence harmless in their discontent. In the interim, their proposals to deal with the immediate and potentially explosive problem of unemployed black youth is to lower the minimum wage and build more jails.

In a similar fashion, the shapers of the current offensive have perceived the long-term implications of feminism more astutely than did their moderate predecessors. By now feminism is much more than the National Organization for Women or the National Women's Political Caucus. It is a widespread consciousness among women in every sector of society that they have a right to full equality with men.

So far the organizational forms haven't caught up with the consciousness. But if they ever do, women's demand for full and equal participation in society would require, just as a beginning, changes in the organization and even the definition of work that would turn our economic institutions upside down. And the strategists of the Right see the fact, embedded in polling data though not yet translated into organized political reality, that women at every level of society place a much higher priority on creating a just and compassionate social order at home than on controlling other nations through the accumulation of military power.

The New Right has moved to counter the feminist threat through a variety of tactics. One is co-optation through tokenism. Ronald Reagan appointed the first female justice to the Supreme Court. It's in the history books, and the Republican Party can, and will, crow about it for the next twenty years. And with Transportation Secretary Elizabeth Dole waiting in the wings and Jeane Kirkpatrick cast as a female Kissinger, the Republicans have more women in positions of perceived prominence than do the Democrats. There are excellent odds that one of those women will be the 1988 vice-presidential nominee.

Meanwhile, the real agenda of the Reagan administration has been visible in the dismantling of affirmative action and the quiet gutting of government-supported programs, from job training to battered-women's shelters, that make possible women's independence. And down on the low road, Reagan's surrogates, including Vice President Bush and White House Chief of Staff Donald Regan, fan the flames of male backlash with rhetoric incorporating all the worst male stereotypes about women.

The Right has also been very successful in using the legitimate moral concern many people feel about abortion to counter the wider range of demands for women's rights. It is clear that politically the mainstream feminist organizations have made things much easier for their opponents by casting abortion-on-demand as their make-or-break litmus-test issue.

Moral Rearmament

The most important accomplishment in the reign of the Right thus far is not to be found in specific policy changes. In that regard they've won some and lost some. But their greatest success by their own estimate has been in changing the atmosphere in which political discussion is conducted. This can be seen in the fact that on every issue the leading Democratic 1988 presidential contenders are steadily inching their positions rightward.

The New Right forces have a comprehensive vision of America and its place in the world and articulate sweeping long-term goals. They unashamedly cast that social vision in the language of moral values and even religious faith. And they have the financial resources to get their message heard. As a result, they have tapped into the deep and legitimate need of the American people for a sense of direction, meaning, and commonly held values in public life.

The morality of the Right is often hypocritical at best and narrowly exclusivist and even theocratic at worst. But in the moral vacuum that U.S. politics has become, the appearance of people who seem to actually believe in something, regardless of the content of that belief, is enough to shift the center of debate.

That is so because liberalism, which constituted the political center of gravity for the last fifty years, has largely reduced public life to the value-free balancing of interest groups accomplished through self-perpetuating and faceless bureaucracies. As a result, there developed a widespread perception among ordinary citizens that America was simply adrift and that their values and aspirations didn't count for much anymore. That left a perfect opening for a political movement that says it will restore "traditional values" and for a president who says he seeks a "spiritual revival" in America.

The rise of politics rooted in people's cultural traditions and religious values is not simply, or even primarily, an American phenomenon. It is a global current that can be witnessed in Poland's Solidarity, the base communities of Latin America and the Philippines, and freedom churches of South Africa. Yet as the repression and bloodshed that have grown out of the Islamic revolution in Iran indicate, it is a phenomenon that exists for both good and ill. But in all these widely varying contexts, the common denominator that emerges is the failure of narrowly secular, technocratic political systems—whether communist or capitalist—to meet people's needs for justice and democracy.

In our own country, too, the phenomenon of "religious politics" cuts both ways. Jerry Falwell, Pat Robertson, and a host of others preach a religion of the state, lending the name of Jesus to the latest initiatives of the Reagan White House. At the same time, the most substantial opposition to the Reaganauts comes from people of faith.

Currently there are only two voices granted recognition by the mainstream media that are speaking unequivocally against the rightward tide. One is the National Conference of Catholic Bishops, and the other is the Baptist preacher-politician Jesse L. Jackson. In the real world, which usually lies beyond the view of the three networks, a significant body of Christians—black, white, and brown and across the denominational and theological spectrum—are going about the business of welcoming the stranger, feeding the hungry, making peace, and speaking prophetic truth against the powers that create oppression and war. In July 1985 an article in *The Nation*, a vehemently secular magazine, estimated that of all those involved in significant work for social change in the United States, at least two-thirds were working from a religious motivation.

Though it may not feel like it from day to day, we too are part of the big picture of where our country is going. Long-term political and economic reality seems to suggest that if America continues to define its national purpose as the accumulation of material wealth and domination of other nations, and if it continues to retrench, reconsolidate, and crack down every time that purpose is threatened, the end result would be either a disastrous war or the erosion of such democracy as we have.

If the United States is to turn from its present course, it must discover a sense of purpose, and even mission, other than accumulation and domination. We must begin to answer the old question of what kind of country this is going to be through such monumental challenges as extending the notions of democracy and equality, building a truly multiracial society, overcoming sexism, and developing a sustainable economics that serves our people and allows us to share our wealth responsibly with our neighbors. In the U.S. context, such a radical change of direction can only come as the result of a political movement strongly rooted in our best cultural and religious traditions.

Even within the harsh realities of the current political and cultural atmosphere, we should see ourselves and our commitments as among the possible seeds of such a movement. And, in that view, what's needed from us now is not just better legislative strategies or more creative demonstration scenarios. We also need much more than in recent years to find ways to address the cultural and spiritual assumptions that form the very foundation of our country's current direction.

Urgent struggles around life-and-death issues will continue. And we may very well continue to lose many of them. But if we believe in the God of history, we know that the results of our efforts are not in our hands anyhow. All we can do is speak and act as faithfully and wisely as we can and try to do so in ways that hold out the possibility of a new direction, should more people become ready to pursue one.

THE SANCTUARY MOVEMENT:
Conspiracy of Compassion
John Fife, Jim Corbett, Stacey Lynn Merkt,
and Philip Willis-Conger

On January 23, 1985, while the Inter-American Symposium on Sanctuary was taking place in Tucson, Arizona, John Fife, Jim Corbett, and Philip Willis-Conger were arraigned in the same city. They and thirteen other sanctuary workers had been charged with seventy-one counts, including conspiracy and harboring and transporting "illegal aliens." Evidence against them included tapes surreptitiously recorded by informants planted by the Immigration and Naturalization Service (INS).

Stacey Lynn Merkt has been arrested twice for her work in the sanctuary movement, serving a 179-day sentence for her later conviction. Charges involved transportation and conspiracy to transport Salvadoran refugees to the United States.

John Fife is pastor of Southside United Presbyterian Church in Tucson. Jim Corbett is a retired rancher. Philip Willis-Conger is former project director for the Tucson Ecumenical Council Task Force for Central America. And Stacey Lynn Merkt works with Central American refugees at Projecto Libertad in Texas.

As participants in the sanctuary symposium, Jim Wallis and Joyce Hollyday had the privilege of meeting and conducting the following interview with the four indicted church workers the day after the arraignment in Tucson.

—The Editor

Wallis and Hollyday: Could you talk about how your faith relates to the work you're doing, and particularly to your determination to continue doing the work in light of the threats you have received from the government?

Stacey Lynn Merkt: I think that I would start by saying that my faith is my work, and my work is my faith. I believe in the sanctity of life, and that has carried me through the last ten years or so.

It started out when I lived at Koinonia [in Americus, Georgia]. That's when I learned about living in community and about the social issues that we need to look at as Christians and as responsible persons today. More than that, I learned about the nitty-gritty of seeing Jesus reflected in the faces of my brothers and sisters. That is the essence of what faith is to me.

For me to start responding to the cry of the people in Central America meant that I had to start living and working and touching these people. When I went to work at Casa Romero, these people became more than names and numbers and faces and events. They became María, and José, and statistics became living flesh.

I just seek to be a person who lives what I believe and who lives what God has asked me to live. It's clear to me that God asks me to love. The greatest commandment is to love the Lord your God with all your heart, soul, and mind, and to love your neighbor as yourself. And my neighbor is a world community of persons. That means I have to offer food to the person who's hungry, clothes to the person who has no clothes; I have to welcome the stranger in my midst, and I have to work for the day when those needs, when those deprivations, those injustices won't be. It's an outpouring of myself more than anything else. I believe that I am to love, and in so doing here I am.

Philip Willis-Conger: I grew up in a church that was real concerned about the social gospel and talked about social justice. My parents had been missionaries in Latin America. In growing up I became conscious of some of the major social justice issues such as racism and U.S. imperialism.

I have a definite sense of what is right and wrong, and I believe that comes out of the very core of me, which is God-centered. If there are people out there suffering, I can't ignore them. My upbringing won't allow me to just close my eyes to that.

I'm inspired by the words of people around me and the faith I see in the refugees, the hope that comes out of the incredible suffering and incredible hardship that these refugees are experiencing. They are Christ crucified, and yet the hope is still alive and still there. That keeps me going; that is an important part of my faith.

Jim, could you tell us how the sanctuary movement got started and how you got involved in it?

Jim Corbett: How it got started? You'll have to consult Exodus on that. It's very important to realize that the sanctuary movement is not something that someone, somewhere, suddenly invented. It has been around better than three thousand years.

Those of us who are involved in the sanctuary movement have never, I think, really accurately anticipated what sanctuary would become when it was declared. It has been a process of discovery that doesn't seem to be over yet.

On May 4, 1981, a friend of mine was returning from Sonora [Mexico]. He had borrowed a van from me, and he picked up a hitchhiker in Nogales, Arizona, who was a Salvadoran, a refugee. At the roadblock just a little north of Nogales, this refugee was taken from him by the border patrol.

He returned the van that evening. Another friend was there, and we discussed what might happen to the Salvadoran refugee. I think the other friend may have been the one who had read an account of a planeload of Salvadoran deportees—deported from the United States—having been shot down right at the airport outside of San Salvador on arrival in December of 1980.

I'd been working prior to that with some seminomadic goat ranchers. I wasn't a Central America activist—I probably at that time could not have given the name of the bishop who had been murdered in El Salvador—but I had seen enough news that I knew that things were pretty bad, people were getting murdered. And that's where we left it that night.

But I woke up the next morning convinced that I really ought to find out where this guy was, what could be done for him. I was naive enough that the first thing I did was call the border patrol and then the INS and said, "You picked up a Salvadoran yesterday at a roadblock, and I want to find out whether there's anything I can do to help him." They said, "No, there's not, and you cannot even see him unless you have his name and are an authorized legal representative."

Well, my name is the same as the name of a former mayor of Tucson, now a judge, a person who is politically prominent here. So I found the name of the top people in the INS and called and said, "This is Jim Corbett here in Tucson. You picked up a Salvadoran at the Madera Canyon roadblock yesterday. I need to know his name and where you have him." The guy looked it up and told me.

He was in the Santa Cruz County Jail. Fr. Ricardo Alfred was suggested as someone to contact. I asked him if something could be done, and he got me a G-28 form, which establishes legal representation.

I took the G-28 and went down to the Santa Cruz County Jail and managed to talk my way in to see the refugee. I discovered there were more refugees there, and they in turn told me about other refugees who had been picked up at the same time or that they knew about, relatives, and women who were being held in another place. One woman they had heard about was being held more or less in isolation to try to break her, in the women's part of the Santa Cruz County Jail. About fifty in all had been caught in the previous few days.

The first step I took was to get that one G-28 signed and get out and get some more G-28s for these folks, these other refugees I'd run into. I went back to the Santa Cruz County Jail, but they had me wait and wait and wait, and it was getting close to the time I needed to rush back to file these things in Tucson. And so I said, "Look, when can I see those guys that I asked you about thirty minutes ago?"

"Oh, the border patrol came and got them thirty or forty minutes ago," they told me. "There's no way of telling where they've gone."

So then I had to start searching. I found one in south Tucson and the other one up in El Centro [refugee detention center in California]. I was starting to get an education about the border patrol and INS.

There was a Salvadoran with me [on a visit to El Centro] who had a little recorder, which I took from him. The recording would have indicated that they [INS] had systematically denied these people their legal rights. So they locked me in El Centro and said they wouldn't let me out if I didn't give up the tape. Eventually they called their supervisor, who apparently said, "You've got an American citizen in there. You better let him out."

By early June my wife and I had set up an apartment in our house where refugees could stay while they were doing their I-589s, their asylum applications. I got a call from one of the refugees, who by that time was in Phoenix, saying she had some relatives who had turned up on the other side of the border and were in trouble and didn't know what to do, and could I do something? I didn't know what I could do, but I went down on the other side at midnight and found them hiding under a house. I didn't know how to smuggle, but I got them through the fence.

I went over to visit the priest in Nogales, who is now indicted. He said, "There are refugees being held in the Nogales-Sonora Penitentiary. I give the Mass every Thursday, but they're held in a holding tank separately, and they have an urgent need regularly to contact relatives in the United States, relatives back in El Salvador, and so forth. If there was someone who could go in with me while I give the Mass and talk to these folks . . ."

So I was "Fr. Jaime" each Thursday. I'd go in and get letters to Central America and telephone numbers of relatives in Los Angeles. We distributed a sheet with my name and number on it, names of organizations giving legal services, and what their legal rights were if they got across the border in the United States. This evolved into an ongoing program. Phil inherited that.

Willis-Conger: The difference perhaps between some of our actions and those of other Americans is maybe only that we've been more persistent about it. It's all about responding to your neighbor, Christ in each one of us.

Corbett: The personal contact makes the difference. The first week after I learned about the refugee problem, I learned that there was a Salvadoran woman with a bullet in her, who was hiding out and needed a doctor but was afraid to get help. She'd been shot in El Salvador just a couple of weeks before, and the bullet was still in her. I just started calling doctors to see who was willing to risk license, prison, and so forth in order to let us know what to do about this woman.

That's how it was all along. We didn't ever organize by running around and asking, "Will you become an active member of this secret organization?" When someone is in need, a lot of people respond.

How and why did you get involved in the sanctuary movement, John?

John Fife: I think that what Jim has suggested has been common to all our experience. Our encounter with refugees has been the point at which we had to make some decision about whether we would turn our backs on this overwhelming need or meet that need. As soon as you begin that with one refugee, you begin to hear about others. When we started off, we didn't realize we were standing on the edge of a whirlpool that just drew us in as we began to see the life-or-death plight of the people of El Salvador and Guatemala.

That started for me when a professional *coyote* [smuggler] abandoned twenty-five or twenty-six Salvadorans in the desert west of here in the middle of the summer [of 1980]. Half of them died of dehydration in the desert, and the other half were picked up by the border patrol and brought to Tucson to be hospitalized. INS put a hold on them, so that as soon as they were released from the hospital, INS would put them in a detention center and start the deportation process.

Some immigration lawyers came to the churches and said, "We've been talking to these people, and they're terrified of being sent back to El Salvador. The churches need to help us."

At that point I couldn't have put El Salvador on a map. That encounter meant that I had to hear about death squads, and about churches being machine-gunned, and about priests being murdered. The real driver for me was the persecution of the church.

The only thing we could think to do was what I assume people of faith have always thought of first, and that is, "Let's pray." We said we'd start a prayer vigil for the people and the church of Central America. We'd do it every week, and we'd invite our congregations and others to come and join us. That's been going on for four years now; every week we meet to pray for the people of Central America. That became a gathering place where people who had bumped into refugees, or immigration lawyers who encountered them in the detention centers, would come, and we'd talk about the latest need and how the churches could start helping.

That went on until somewhere around April or May of 1981. Then the government's policy about the treatment of refugees changed. As we encountered that hardening of policy, it became clear that we couldn't do the work as individual congregations any longer.

We pulled together a meeting of people who were at that prayer vigil from different churches. We formed a task force under the Tucson Ecumenical Council—sixty-five Protestant and Roman Catholic churches—and said we're going to try to meet those needs. We entered into an agreement with a paralegal organization. The churches would raise money for bonds, try to meet the expenses of the paralegals, and they would do the work in the detention centers, filling out political asylum applications and filing I-589s.

The next step was to go to the regional detention center. We made an absolutely crazy decision at that point. I don't understand how rational people can sit down at a first meeting and say, "Okay, we're going to raise $35,000 in the next month, and $120,000 in collateral, and we're going to take a bunch of volunteers from Tucson and go over to California and bond out all the Salvadorans that need to be bonded out in one group a month from now." But we did it!

We raised that much money. Some people put up their homes as collateral. On one day we brought 140 Salvadorans and Guatemalans out of that detention center, and then said, "Now what do we do?"

We had this enormous social service responsibility to relocate people, to get them in touch with families if they had any, and bring them to Tucson and Los Angeles and put them in the churches. It took about a month before everybody was settled.

The paralegals went back to the detention center, and the government had another two hundred refugees. We obviously couldn't sustain that kind of effort or that kind of fund-raising, so we put together a long-range plan. We set a policy in place that we'd try to raise enough money in collateral to bond out ten people a week, those who had been in the detention center the longest. What we needed to do was give refugees who were under threat of deportation or in the detention center some sense of hope that if they held out, we'd get to them eventually. Hanging on in there was really tough, with the conditions in the detention centers and the harassment and coercion.

That effort continued for two years. And we've got somewhere around $750,000—just the churches in Tucson—in collateral, in bonds. We've been expending somewhere between $60,000 and $100,000 in legal defense efforts. And that effort goes on. So if you hear from INS that what those church people ought to do is try to work within the law first, we did it. And we did it with as much energy and imagination and creativity as we could.

At that point everything I was doing was very Presbyterian. Presbyterians understand legalities. We live and die by a book of order and legal procedures in our institutional life. I was doing everything possible within the bounds that had been set by government and culture to serve refugees.

Then Corbett started talking to me about theology and ethics. He said, "If you're really serious and you really think God is calling you to serve the needs of refugees, then you're working at their needs on the wrong end. After they're captured and in detention centers, the process of deportation is inevitable. All you can do is buy time." And he was right.

"If you really think that God is calling you to serve the needs of refugees," he said, "then you must meet their most critical and apparent need, which is to avoid capture and inevitable deportation and death." He was already doing it, helping people cross the border safely, bringing them to his home. When I first went to Corbett's house, he had twenty-one people living in one room.

At any rate, Corbett says to me, "We've filled up our house. I've got other Quakers' houses filled up in town. Can I bring people to your church? You're already keeping Salvadorans in your church that you've bonded out of detention centers." And I said, "Yeah, but that's legal." And he said, "Yeah, I know. Can I bring Salvadorans who are undocumented to your church?" I said, "Gee, Jim, I don't make the decisions around here, the elders of my church do. You'll have to ask them."

And we did. The elders and I sat down and spent about four hours discussing that question. I was real clear with them: "If the government catches us doing this, it's five years in prison for every refugee we bring in this church." They voted to do it.

Some of the refugees would come to worship on Sunday, and I'd introduce them to the congregation as we introduce all guests, telling their story briefly and saying to the congregation, "Your government says that these people are illegal aliens. It is your civic duty when you know about their status to turn them in to INS. What do you think the faith requires of you?" We'd just leave that question hanging Sunday after Sunday.

The congregation would take people home after church for dinner, call me up later that afternoon and say, "People can't live in a church; that's not a decent place for this family to live. They're going to stay with us for a while."

By the time the next critical step came, I was driving some refugees from the border up, and so were other members of my congregation. Other church people were involved with that whole work that has since come to be called the "underground railroad."

But we were all a bunch of amateurs. My training is in Bible and theology, not smuggling and covert activities. We did all the things we saw on television that we thought we were supposed to do. We had codes and code words, but it never worked out. We got a telegram in code from Corbett in Mexico one time, sat down with a whole group of us, and couldn't figure out what he wanted us to do. It took us two hours.

We got a very clear and direct message from INS and the border patrol, delivered from an INS attorney to one of the paralegals who was working with us. It said, "Look, we know what Corbett and Fife are up to. You tell them to stop it, or we'll have to arrest them." We sat around my living room saying, "What do we do now?" I said, "I can see the headlines in the paper now—'Presbyterian minister indicted for smuggling illegal aliens.'"

We couldn't stop. We'd already made the decision when we got involved in the whole effort that the life-or-death needs of the refugees overrode any other set of risks that we might encounter here in the United States. We came to the conclusion that the only other option we have is to give public witness to what we're doing, what the plight of the refugees is, and the faith basis for our actions.

And then the question came, "Well how do you do that?" Do you call a press conference and say, "Hey, we'd like to acknowledge that we've been smuggling people into this country for some time"? It didn't seem to make any sense.

Out of that discussion emerged the idea that what we're really doing is the ancient historic tradition of sanctuary in the church. We decided to publicly declare the church a sanctuary and publicly receive a refugee family into the sanctuary of the church. The only thing we could do was tell our story so that at least when they arrested us, they'd have to play on our turf. They would have to deal with the reasons why we did it. And the community and the church would have to deal with that too.

Then I left to make coffee, so they all decided that Southside Presbyterian Church ought to be the one to try it. But then we took about two months—December 1981 and January 1982—and we did Bible study, prayer, discussion, and agonizing over that two-month period. At a four-hour congregational meeting, we took a vote by secret ballot so nobody felt intimidated by anybody else. They voted to declare sanctuary. I think there were fifty-nine affirmative votes, with two negative votes and four abstentions.

Somebody at the congregational meeting said, "Why don't we ask other churches to do it, too?" And I said, "That's a good idea! Great idea!" We wrote a bunch of letters to churches across the country and said, "We're going to publicly receive a family into the sanctuary of the church at worship, and we've decided to do that on March 24, 1982. It's the anniversary of [Archbishop Oscar] Romero's assassination, and the attention of the church is going to be at least partially focused on Romero and Central America."

Four other congregations wrote back and said, "Yes, we'll do it on the same day." They were First Unitarian Church in Los Angeles; University Lutheran Chapel in San Francisco; Luther Place Memorial Church in Washington, D.C.; and an independent Bible Church in Long Island, New York.

Because we were public, more refugees knew there was a place where they could get help. So we were swamped at the border, and at the same time we were getting requests for information on sanctuary from all over the country. One of the groups that called was the Chicago Religious Task Force, and that relationship developed and the movement took off.

In 1982 I went to Central America for the first time and got converted. That's the only way I can describe it. I discovered a new way of reading Scripture, of seeing the community of faith under enormous pressure and persecution respond with courage and hope.

The refugees began to tell us about the *comunidades de base,* about their experience in the church in El Salvador and Guatemala, and the new spiritual vitality and strength that was being given to the people in Central America through their faith. My first sermon to the congregation when I came back began with: "This may come as a shock to you, but I have been converted to the Christian faith since I last was with you."

I think that part of what the sanctuary movement means in North America is that there are covenant communities, congregations who are being converted to the Christian faith, to that spiritual reformation that is now being brought to North America from Latin America and other parts of the world. I now am convinced that there is a genuine reformation, and it's going to change our world as much as the sixteenth-century Reformation changed our world.

You have all faced trial and some have been convicted. What are your reflections now?

Merkt: These days are showing us more clearly what it means to be a faithful person. I think we're all aware of what the cost is, but the reality of that becomes a little bit clearer as days go on. What I have learned from the people of Central America is that I believe in a God of love and of life and of faithfulness, and that means that I live each day, come what may.

I think so far as the sanctuary movement goes, everyone has been up front in saying that this [the indictments] can only strengthen and galvanize the response of everyone to meet the needs of the refugees both in El Salvador and here in the United States. I have also become aware that the "subversiveness" of the church that we have experienced through the eyes of the refugees from El Salvador has become more clearly what is happening here in the United States.

I also have been asked about the fears that one individual might have being in this seat. We as people of faith need to examine our fears in light of the stories of why the refugees come to us. If we don't take that small step and act regardless of our fears and regardless of whether or not we have courage, we'll never know what courage is. It is step by step and inch by inch that we struggle in our process to live out our faith.

In contrast to that word "fear," I try to look at hope. We are a community of people that God has mandated to act in a certain way—for the best interest of others and also to proclaim that we are a faithful people. Those are pretty powerful things.

Willis-Conger: For me it's been a deepening of faith and conviction. I know what's right, I started in the right direction, and it's the faith that keeps me going down the road that I've already started on.

The way that the government is going about attacking the church and attacking the refugees, they're making it easier for people to understand—by the fact that they infiltrated a church and that they've deceived us as to how they would deal with us. I think it means that the church under persecution is going to respond, and it means a lot of organizing and educating. The religious community—including the Jewish faith and people of conscience who wouldn't even consider themselves religious—is going to respond and is going to rise to the challenge. I see it happening already.

Corbett: We very quickly discovered in the process of declaring sanctuary that sanctuary is not a place, but that it's the protective community of a congregation of people with the persecuted. It has infinite dimensions.

What we're doing is called for in large measure by our place here on the border. There are all kinds of sanctuary congregations around the country who are discovering new dimensions of sanctuary outreach, of what is most appropriate for them in the way of entering into a protective community with the persecuted.

The sanctuary covenant group that formed in the [San Francisco] Bay area on March 24, 1982, instantly launched a program to maintain a protective presence in the refugee camps in Honduras. The Seattle covenant groups are trying to establish sister-congregation relationships with churches in El Salvador. The Madison [Wisconsin] covenant congregations have led in establishing a protective outreach to the border, especially to the Rio Grande Valley. I think we can be pretty confident that sanctuary will continue to be so dynamic that we'll be uncertain at any given moment what it's going to become.

What will be your response in light of the infiltration and deception by the government?

Fife: The refugees have set the agenda; their needs have set our agenda continuously since 1981, and I suspect that they will continue to do that. Depending on what our government decides to do in Central America, depending on what the death squads decide to do in Central America, and depending on what immigration officials decide to do on the border and in Tucson—that will set our agenda, and we'll just have to walk into it one day at a time. We have to struggle in the midst of those things that are out of our control to discover what it means to be faithful from day to day. I now understand that spiritually and emotionally.

I think the other thing we've discovered over the last three years is that we serve refugees more effectively the more we "testify to our faith" publicly. Clearly the government would like through intimidation and harassment, indictments, arrests—and now through placing spies and agents inside church worship services and Bible study groups with wiretaps and bugs—to drive us more and more into ourselves and our own little "trusted," close-knit organizations. I think we've got to resist all that. I think we've got to be more and more welcoming and open in our invitation to people to join us as a covenant community, and we have to be more and more public in our testimony and in our witness to what our faith is and what we believe.

And I think—I've learned this from a couple of people at Sojourners whom I have just now met—we need to understand what resistance is these days. We have to be more and more creative in finding ways in which the church community can actively resist the evil that is so pervasive around us. Central America and Central American refugees are only one facet of the call to resistance at this point, and Sojourners has helped us to understand that calling.

Willis-Conger: My concept of sanctuary is not just resisting, but a forward-moving, positive kind of thing where we're going out and doing justice as a community. And the reason we've survived here in Tucson is because we've been able to take the initiative instead of just resisting what the government's doing.

Corbett: We're discovering that while as individuals every one of us can make that choice to resist, if we are going to make that choice to do justice, we have to come together in community—and sanctuary takes that step. It's not a step that allows us to avoid that decision between resistance and collaboration, but it's a further awareness—that as communities provide sanctuary, or enter into protective community with the persecuted, the poor, the marginalized of the world, it may result in our becoming "illegals" along with the refugees.

Fife: I think we've all grown in understanding that sanctuary is what God created this world to be. Rev. Marta Benavides [of El Salvador] first told me what we really need to do is work with them to make Central America a sanctuary for Central Americans. Nuclear freeze people have come to me and said what we really need to do is make this earth a sanctuary from nuclear armaments.

I think sanctuary is beginning to capture people's spirits and imaginations. It is the way the church community can really be a covenant community and a way we can understand ourselves and our faith and our role in this world. I'm looking for the whole community gathered to put our souls to work in discovering just what that symbol can mean and how it can explode in our consciousness and lead us into all kinds of creative pilgrimages.

WITNESS FOR PEACE:
The Long Road to Jalapa
Joyce Hollyday

The sun pauses for a moment on the edge of the Honduran mountains that ring the tiny town. The market stands empty where earlier in the day onions were spread out over the ground and fresh rolls sold for pennies a bag. The bell in the church tower next to the community peace garden, which is dominated by a broad-leafed banana tree, gives forth a few rings, and the voices of children giving glory to Mary drift out of the church's windows. A rooster crows—they crow at all times of the day and night here—and a few dogs bark.

Someone once told me that Jalapa is "at the end of the world." It was meant as a compliment to the dusty, little Nicaraguan town, which exudes character and warmth to the peaceful stranger who comes to its isolated streets.

There is one telephone in Jalapa (it works most of the time), and transportation is mostly by foot, horse, or oxcart. Time seems to hide itself here; the community is called together to the church or the park, over which towers the emblem of Lions Club International, by a sound truck that roams the streets announcing the day's events: a town meeting, a children's rally, a funeral.

When the sun finally slips behind the mountains, stars pop out by the millions in Jalapa's sky. At night one can occasionally hear the call of a child, the clopping of a horse down a street, or if you're in the right part of town, the seemingly misplaced North American rock music filtering out of Sandra's Place. A report of gunfire now and then from the mountains reminds the town that all is not at peace in Jalapa.

Jalapa may seem like the end of the world to a foreigner's eye, but it is the center of the world for the people of Jalapa and the surrounding valley, which is the agricultural hub for all of northern Nicaragua. Ironically, by virtue of its isolation, the town has become the focus of attention from unwelcome intruders and their primary supporter, the United States government.

After the overthrow of the brutal U.S.-supported Nicaraguan dictator Anastasio Somoza in July 1979, the Sandinista leadership of the new government set free most of the members of Somoza's terrorist national guard. The former national guard made their way to the Honduran mountains on Nicaragua's northern border and began to plot a counter-revolution.

These counterrevolutionaries, or *contras*, have made repeated incursions into Nicaragua, employing the same methods of terror they used under Somoza. Located just six kilometers from the border on a peninsula of land that juts into Honduras, Jalapa has been an ideal target for the *contras* in their effort to capture a town and set up an independent territory with a provisional government. One of their strategies has been to cut off Jalapa by taking over the only access road the town has to the rest of Nicaragua.

Contra activity began in Jalapa in March 1982. The first evidence: numbers of people found beheaded outside their homes. Since that time there have been four major attempts to take Jalapa, and bands of the marauders continue to roam the hills spreading terror, using state-of-the-art camping equipment supplied by the CIA. For more than four years the *contras* have been unable to prevail militarily. Their most recent slogan: "We cannot win, but we can kill."

While the people of Jalapa have suffered terrible tragedies, crop production in this area has also suffered. The *contras* have focused on disrupting the harvest, and crops have sometimes been brought in under a rain of bullets. Because of the war, only 50 percent of the rice crop was planted in 1983, and losses between December 1982 and July 1983 amounted to more than $100 million in land, homes, storage barns, and crops.

North American Christians who visited the northern Nicaraguan frontier in April and July of 1983 found that while they were there, the *contra* incursions ceased. Townspeople in Jalapa attributed the cessation to the presence of the North Americans. Soon the idea emerged that a continuous presence of North Americans might inhibit *contra* activity and offer some protection for the people on Nicaragua's frontier. Turning a different kind of U.S. attention to Jalapa, U.S. Christians began to organize Witness for Peace. By early October 1983, plans were under way for a long-term team of four members to go to Jalapa, to prepare to receive rotating short-term teams of fifteen members who would go to Nicaragua every two weeks to pray and offer nonviolent resistance to U.S. policy against Nicaragua.

It is a long way to Jalapa, and for those of us who were part of the first short-term team to go, our journey began long before we arrived. In late November 1983, the team, representing a wide diversity of ages, occupations, church denominations, and geographical areas, converged on Washington, D.C. We gathered for a few days to get to know one another and share our fears and expectations about the uncertainties that lay ahead of us. We worshiped together and participated in role-plays in which we worked through possible scenarios we might face: the ambush of our bus on the road to Jalapa, the disappearance or death of one of our team members.

On the evening of Wednesday, November 30, before friends and family gathered in a Washington, D.C. church, members of the Witness for Peace steering and advisory committees, who had come from all over the country, placed white stoles over each of our shoulders at a commissioning service. The names of the long-term team members already in Nicaragua were read, and they too were "commissioned."

Songs and prayers were offered up, and Vincent Harding of Iliff Seminary in Denver placed Witness for Peace in the stream of history of nonviolent witness, speaking from the "cloud of witnesses" text in Hebrews 12. He sent us forward on our journey with the mandate, "Walk your talk."

On Thursday morning we held a press conference and prepared for our next day's departure. But that night we received word that our flight to Managua, Nicaragua, had been cancelled. We learned later that Daniel Ortega, Nicaragua's chief of state, had to fly to Ecuador for high-level talks. Since Nicaragua had no air force, no presidential "Air Force One" to carry him to such meetings, he had to borrow one of Nicaragua's two commercial airliners. The irony didn't escape us that this is the nation the Reagan administration accuses of being a military threat to the "free world."

An extra flight was scheduled Sunday to accommodate Friday's passengers, and we arrived in Nicaragua two days late—on the day that the Nicaraguan government set a date for elections in 1985, declared a general amnesty for *contras* outside Nicaragua, and set free 300 Miskito Indians who had been imprisoned in Managua following the "Red

Christmas" massacre of Sandinista soldiers by Miskitos in December 1981. These were hopeful signs to us, particularly the release of the Miskito prisoners, since the Sandinistas seem to have committed their most grievous abuses in their handling of the Miskito situation.

That night we attended a party with the released Miskitos and their families to celebrate their freedom. On Monday we held a press conference in Managua and received orientation to the Nicaraguan situation from CEPAD (the Evangelical Committee for Aid and Development).

Tuesday we arose well before dawn to begin our journey to Jalapa in a bus belonging to the Baptist College in Managua. We stopped for breakfast in the town of Esteli, about 150 kilometers north of Managua. We explained our mission to the proprietor of the restaurant, who thanked us and wished us well. As we left, we passed by a sign hung on his wall bearing another wish for us: "May the water that makes ditches in the street not make the same in your intestines."

We pushed north toward Jalapa and got as far as Ocotal, a town thirteen kilometers from the Honduran border and about sixty kilometers west of Jalapa. Upon arrival in Ocotal, we got word from local military officials that we could not go on to Jalapa; the *contras* had taken over a section of the road, and combat was taking place in an effort to reclaim it. This was the first time since June that the road had been closed.

We heard from the CEPAD representatives in Ocotal and the Maryknoll Sisters from the United States that the *contras* were within fifteen kilometers of Ocotal and that the town had been under alert the night before.

We held our first vigil that night in Ocotal. We began with a procession through three of Ocotal's *barrios,* and by the time we arrived at the town park, we had with us a crowd of four hundred people.

In the park we had an ecumenical service of song and prayer. David Gracie, an Episcopal chaplain at Temple University in Philadelphia, unfurled an American flag that was given to us by a supportive U.S. congressperson. He talked about his shame at what the U.S. government is doing against Nicaragua and explained that we were there to remember and uphold the best of the American tradition, which claims a commitment to justice and freedom.

Scripture was read, and, as is common in Latin America, the congregation was invited to offer its reflections on the readings. One woman, like many of the people we met in Nicaragua, apologized for her lack of education and then spoke eloquently about her faith. She is the mother of one of the martyrs in the revolutionary struggle to overthrow Somoza. She closed with gratitude for the current situation in her country: "Under Somoza we had no voice; but now we can speak."

We spent that night at the Baptist Church, which we shared with refugees who had fled their scattered mountain homes during attacks by the *contras*. Their presence, as well as the trenches dug in front of homes in Ocotal, reminded us that we were in a war zone. We heard gunshots that night and slept close to our "crash packs," small bags packed with our most essential items—passports, flashlights, water purification tablets, and antimalarial medication—that were easy to grab in case we needed to flee on sudden notice.

We felt very vulnerable that night, and I was conscious that we were making our way into this war zone armed with only gifts and prayers. I had with me letters from Sojourners Community and my family, including a rainbow painted by my young nephews and labeled "for God's promise of safekeeping."

I felt assurance in knowing that people in many places were focused on us. The Community of Celebration in Woodland Park, Colorado, had given us a candle to light every night; when we lit it, we would know that an identical candle was burning for us at their community and that a similar one was the center of a continuous prayer vigil at Sojourners. A member of our worshiping congregation at Sojourners gave me a beautiful necklace made of myrrh to carry until Jalapa as a reminder of her prayers and then give away. And the children back home in our community had hung a map of Nicaragua in one of our household's kitchens and were tracing our route as we traveled. I had warm thoughts of many people that night in a place very far from home.

By morning, the water that had been turned off throughout the town the night before because of a severe water shortage was not yet back on. We awoke early with Jalapa on our minds and washed our faces in a rain barrel outside the church. The refugee women already had firewood in their dome-shaped clay stove and were slapping out tortillas. They had fled with little more than the clothes on their backs, but they offered us coffee and tortillas, one of many examples we found in Nicaragua of profound graciousness and generosity in spite of meager resources.

By nine o'clock the road was open, and we were on the last leg of our journey to Jalapa. We had heard that vehicles on this road are often ambushed, and it was easy to see why. The road is narrow, rutted, and steep, and the first half of the journey was through dense underbrush.

We stopped at occasional military checkpoints to get news of the road ahead. We were told that a *contra* attack was expected on the road at noon. It was ten-thirty. We pushed on through the clouds of dust, some members of the team covering their faces with bandanas to keep from breathing the dust.

An open truck carrying some soldiers and a family caught up behind us. I could see a mother holding an infant with a bottle, and I thought how difficult it must be for them riding through this dust and how vulnerable they were.

About halfway to Jalapa the road opens out onto expansive fields of coffee, beans, and rice. Ambush is less likely on this part of the journey, but the Honduran mountains are visible and the road is within mortar range.

Women pounded laundry against rocks in the streams that flowed over the road and that made passage sometimes difficult for our bus. Cows wandered over the road, and scattered on both sides of us were small homes with orange clay-tile roofs. We saw an occasional homemade cross along the route, marking the site where someone had been killed.

A large cemetery marks the edge of Jalapa, row upon row of homemade crosses. A sign at the entrance to the town lists the names of Jalapa's martyrs fallen in combat or by *contra* attack. As our bus wound its way toward the center of town, the long-term team came out to greet us. We prayed together in thanks for our safe arrival and in expectation of the days ahead.

That evening in the park we held our first vigil in Jalapa. We stood with our Witness for Peace banner while a light rain fell. People from the town joined us, and one woman gave us each a gift of warm *ayote,* a piece of squash cooked with a sweet topping, which she served to us on broad leaves.

When we explained that we were the first of many teams that would continue to come to Jalapa as long as the war goes on, one of the townspeople said, "This is the kind of U.S. invasion we like!" We were touched that people who have suffered and sacrificed so much, who live daily with terror and fears, offered prayers of deep gratitude for us: "We are simple and humble people, but we know the sacrifice you are making. If everyone in the U.S. government were like you, we would not be suffering these aggressions."

Gratitude marked all their prayers. One mother prayed, "Thank you for the rice, the beans, the coffee. Protect the harvest. Protect the children." And one of our team members added, "May there be a harvest of peace."

After a long and dusty day, we felt settled and peaceful there in the park, warmly welcomed by the people we had traveled so far to meet, cleansed by the cool rain and the power of the worship. The peace was marred only by occasional reports of gunfire from the mountains.

The day begins in Jalapa when the sun appears. A bright green parrot hanging upside down from a branch of a dead tree argued in Spanish with a radio for dominance of the dawn.

We began our first day in Jalapa by asking the proprietor where we should go for shelter in case of an attack on the town. She nodded toward boards covering a large hole in her porch floor. Three of her children were swinging over the boards in a hammock, laughing and playing with masks.

Our first trip out from Jalapa was to La Estancia, a community a few kilometers away being created from displaced families who had lived scattered throughout the mountains. More than six hundred families have been made refugees in the Jalapa area by the raids of the *contras*. Some have had to resettle temporarily in old tobacco barns, while others are building permanent shelter in areas like La Estancia.

While there, we met Martita, a fifteen-day-old baby, and her mother, who had fled on foot from their home in the mountains just days before delivering her beautiful daughter. Her husband was fighting with the militia and had not yet seen his baby.

Another mother told how armed *contras* came to her home and took away her two sons and three sons-in-law. She heard gunshots and, when she went outside, found them all dead: "When my husband returned, we fled. But he is old, and there are no more males in our family. The *contras* have cut off our future."

It has been said that to understand Nicaragua, you must talk to the mothers. Through their tears of grief, we found the most profound understanding. Some of the mothers in Jalapa have established the Gallery of the Heroes and Martyrs, a house across from the church that displays pictures and stories of their slain sons. They understand the struggle and the political situation as well as anyone. One mother asked us, "Why should the United States attack us now? Before we didn't even have schools; we had to live like animals. The first thing the new government gave us was not arms but hospitals and a chance to read."

Another added, "The rich can still stay here, and the government is giving amnesty to those who fight against it—what other government would do this?" And still another: "We want peace; we don't want blood. But we must defend ourselves."

But mostly they speak about their children: "It is incomparable suffering for a mother to lose her child; we feel the loss of a child in our own flesh." The bond of mother and child was particularly poignant while we were in Jalapa, because we were there during the *Purisima,* the celebration of Mary. This festival, accompanied with processions and singing, is as important in Nicaragua as Christmas. It is a celebration of Mary, a remembrance of her bearing of Jesus and her giving him up to death. It is a passion with which the mothers of Nicaragua readily identify.

One of the most agonizing of the stories we were told came from a mother who had lived in Teotecacinte, located right on the Honduran border about fifteen kilometers northeast of Jalapa. The mother was preparing a meal when she was alerted of a *contra* attack. She sent her thirteen-year-old daughter to their underground shelter and was going to follow. But the girl remembered her puppy and ran off in search of it. When the mother got outside, her daughter was dead. She carried her body to the shelter, and it wasn't until she got inside that she realized the *contras* had decapitated her daughter with a mortar shell. This woman, like many of the others, broke into weeping as she finished her story.

The refugees, a reverent people who have a profound respect for life, spoke of the atrocities of the *contras* as "ingratitudes," the actions of men who feel no relationship with their sisters and brothers. One woman said they "act like tigers" and described atrocities she had witnessed: tongues cut out, eyes removed, spikes through limbs, facial skin cut and rolled back over the heads of victims, and gang rapes of women both young and old. Burying the remains of the dead is particularly important for these people who draw so much strength from the sacrifices of those who have given up their lives, but the *contras* often dismember bodies and scatter the pieces to prevent burial.

It is difficult to write down such stories; it was even more difficult to listen to them. But this is the reality of Nicaragua, and it must be known that the Reagan administration, which denounces terrorism in so many places, is sponsoring such terrorism against the civilians of Nicaragua.

Half of the population of Nicaragua is under fifteen years of age, so this war is a war against children. It seemed that we met most of the children of Jalapa—the exuberant and the serious ones, the many who saw us as a curiosity and gathered around us with endless questions or tugged at our banner and begged to help carry it, the sad ones who have been made orphans by the war.

And there were the sophisticated ones, like fourteen-year-old Isaac who, upon hearing of the Witness for Peace, decided to help form a "peace corps" of Nicaraguan teenagers to go to the United States to pray for peace. He spoke to our team and extended an invitation to the children of the United States to come to visit Nicaragua: "So that we can express solidarity with one another, let us have an exchange of children for peace." When we asked Isaac what he wants for his children when he has them, he replied, "I want my children not to be marginal."

At the close of our time at La Estancia we held a Mass. George Dyer, a member of the long-term team and a Dominican priest from Brownsville, Texas, began the Mass with, "I would like to invite the future of the community to come and gather around the table." The children came forward to the table that held the bread and wine and a brilliant red and yellow orchid.

But one of the children hung back. He was a thirteen-year-old who had captured our attention throughout our visit at La Estancia, perhaps because he looked so young and was carrying an automatic rifle almost as tall as he. We learned that members of the popular militia range in age from eleven to eighty.

We had asked Agenor earlier how he felt about carrying a gun, and he had answered proudly, "I'm glad that I can protect my family." But now, when the children were summoned forward, he was like thirteen-year-olds everywhere. He hesitated, not sure whether he was a child or an adult. Finally he came to stand at the edge of the circle of children. I thought what a terrible weight that gun was for him, a weight put on his back by a belligerent U.S. policy that is robbing parents of their children and children of their childhood.

December is a peak harvest month in Nicaragua. It is also a time of heightened *contra* activity because it is difficult for the Nicaraguan people to divide resources between defense and production, and abductions and assassinations are much easier when workers are scattered throughout the fields. Since one of the goals of Witness for Peace is to become involved in reconstructive work, in repairing damage done by the *contras* or aiding in work that has been disrupted, we volunteered to help with the coffee harvest.

We arose before dawn on Friday in order to be picked up in the park by a truck carrying workers to the coffee fields. The location of each day's work is kept secret to try to prevent the *contras* from discovering where the work brigades will be. But soon we got word that the truck would not be coming. By now we were used to changed plans and waited patiently for a new one. A popular Nicaraguan slogan had also become quite popular with us: *"Vamos a ver"* — "We shall see."

Soon we were piling in our bus and heading toward Teotecacinte, the border town that had been the site of the worst suffering in the last major attack in the Jalapa area and also an area of bean harvesting. When we had told our proprietor and others at our *pension* that we were going to Teotecacinte, they said, out of concern for our safety, that it was *"peligrosa"* — "dangerous." We explained that that's why we were going, to try to document *contra* activity and provide a continuous flow of information back to the United States about the tragedies in Nicaragua. We arrived at the edge of Teotecacinte and were told that we would not be able to help with the bean harvest. A group of fifteen-year-olds had become separated from their work brigade near the town—"*contra* country," the local people explained. The safety of the twenty-six youths was the primary concern in the little town that morning, and it seemed best not to send us out into the fields. We learned later that the youths were found and returned safely.

We could hear and see a plane flying over the Honduran mountains just ahead of us. Commercial planes arrive in Nicaragua only three times a week, so the sound of a plane in the air usually means that it is a reconnaissance or bomber plane from Honduras and causes a great stir among the people. We held a short vigil as close as we could get to the border and then, in commemoration of the birthplace of Witness for Peace, drove to the cornfield behind the school in Jalapa where the vigil by 150 North Americans was held in July 1983.

We had come to Jalapa to proclaim the value of all lives—Nicaraguan and North American—to repent and offer nonviolent resistance to U.S. policy, and to say that if our government continues to attack Nicaragua it will also have to attack its own citizens. We came with a promise to keep on coming until the U.S. war stops.

For Nicaraguans the struggle for peace and against U.S. dominance has gone on for decades. Sergio Lobo, a young man who works with the local government of reconstruction in Jalapa, shared with us our last night in Jalapa: "It will be a long struggle. Our children and their children will engage in the struggle. We encounter the question every day that this may be the day of our death. In the long road our people have traversed toward the luminous reality of liberation, many people have been left dead on the road. And many more will be left in the future. But in confronting the power of death every day we also confront the reality of definitive liberation with joy and hope. Our people are full of sadness for the death of their brothers and sisters, but we all hope because it is the future we are building."

Sergio, like many of the Nicaraguans we spoke to, made very clear that Nicaragua will not be another Grenada. If the United States invades Nicaragua, the fight will not be with just an army but with an entire population, and the casualties and suffering will be great. In the words of Sergio, "The people are capable of giving to the last drop of blood." This will to preserve their freedom, which has brought upon them such tragedy, is also the hope of Nicaragua.

On the day that we were to leave Jalapa, the road was again closed, but we heard that it might be open in two hours. That gave time for one last walk through Jalapa. I headed toward the entrance of the town. I had wanted since the day we arrived in this little out-of-the-way place to walk through its cemetery, perhaps because in Nicaragua death is so prevalent and the sacrifice of those who have given up their lives for freedom is so well remembered and drawn upon for strength.

The sun was just up, and the mist hung low on the simple crosses stuck in the thick grass. The mist brought to mind the image of the "cloud of witnesses," and I felt quite literally surrounded by them in this quiet place. There was an enveloping stillness, and then a giggle. A young girl carrying a water jar appeared, and then another and another behind her.

They were sisters, they explained, with eleven children in their family. "I'll go get the rest," the oldest one said, and she skipped off. They came like a parade, each with a jar, the youngest, a three-year-old, with a small tin can.

There's a well in the center of the cemetery, I learned. And the children begin every day carrying the water they will need for that day. A well of life in the center of so much death. And before me, the future of the community, who draw life from both the well and the cemetery crosses, who understand the struggle.

My musings were interrupted by the sight of our bus turning the bend by the sign of the martyrs. The road was open, and we were on our way home. I had left the myrrh necklace with Maria, one of the mothers who runs the gallery of the martyrs and the giver of *ayote* our first night in

Jalapa. I was carrying home with me a handmade Christmas card from her with a fervent plea for peace in the world.

Because transportation is infrequent on the road, a young mother asked if she could get a ride with us as far as Esteli, where she was going to visit her twelve-year-old son in the hospital. As the bus started up, she looked lovingly at the seven-month-old son on her lap and asked Phyllis Taylor, a nurse from Philadelphia, and Grace Gyori, a former Presbyterian missionary from Chicago, if they would take Ricardo with them back to the United States.

"But wouldn't it be hard for you to be separated from him?" Grace asked.

"Yes, but I will follow," she replied. "I will come as soon as I can."

"But there are problems in the United States, too."

She began to weep softly. "But at least there is no war. Please take him to safety. I don't want him to grow up in a war."

We stopped then at a military checkpoint and were told that there was mortar fire on the road ahead of us. It was too late to turn back, and we were instructed to drive as fast as we possibly could to Ocotal. We couldn't imagine how Gonzalo, our driver, could drive any faster on the narrow, winding road, but we took off again leaving a large cloud of dust. One of the team grabbed our Witness for Peace flag and thrust it out a window, and we all listened for mortar fire.

My attention went to Ricardo's mother, who had become quite carsick. Kathy Breen, a religious sister from Manhasset, New York, kept an arm around her and offered comfort. Twenty-three-year-old Anita Bender from Philadelphia took Ricardo and cradled him in her arms while the bus bumped on.

I thought again of the words that traveled most through my thoughts in our time in Jalapa: fragility and vulnerability. We saw it in the revolution. We saw it in the children.

As we pulled safely into Ocotal and whispered prayers of gratitude, the faces flashed again through my mind: Martita, Isaac, the orphans, the young ones with guns, the children in the cemetery. The ones who ask not to be marginal, who ask simply to have a future.

I remembered the plea of one mother: "Please ask your government to stop. If they had any degree of mercy, they would stop this war. If they could hear the mothers, then maybe they would stop."

Hear then the mothers—and the children, and the others. There is tenderness in this war zone, and laughter and love. And unless we do all that we can to stop the U.S. war against Nicaragua, the laughter will die.

WITNESS FOR PEACE:
A Venture of Faith and Prayer
Jim Wallis

I remember my first trip to Nicaragua in December of 1982, as a member of a delegation of evangelical church leaders. I was full of questions. The reports in the United States were so conflicting and confusing, I really didn't know what to believe about the young government.

We were invited by evangelical church leaders in Nicaragua to come and see the situation for ourselves. We talked to all sides—government officials and opposition press, priests from the "popular church" and the Roman Catholic hierarchy, evangelical pastors and laypersons who thought they could work with the Sandinistas and those who were suspicious, old people and young people, the poor and the middle class.

It was very obvious that a dramatic change had taken place in July of 1979 and that the country was in the process of being transformed. It was also clear that those benefiting most from the changes were the poor, who in Nicaragua constituted the majority. The middle class was divided and much more dubious about the changes. But even the Sandinistas' opponents did not deny the tremendous strides already made in health care, literacy, and nutrition.

The U.S.-backed *contra* war was still "covert," but it had been made public with a cover story in *Newsweek* a few months before. The U.S. ambassador lied to us about it, and I was suspicious about our conversations with persons at the opposition newspaper *La Prensa* and at the archbishop's office who claimed to know nothing about the covert war. At the same time, I was not comfortable with the level of Sandinista press censorship, despite their reminder that even the United States had resorted to such measures in times of crisis and that the CIA had used the opposition press to help overthrow elected governments in Chile and Guatemala.

The issue that most troubled me was the mistreatment of the Miskito Indians by the Nicaraguan government. Listening to the Spanish-speaking government representatives and even to Spanish-speaking church leaders talk about the "Miskito problem" reminded me of white liberals in the United States talking about the "black problem." I knew I needed to talk to some Miskito Indian leaders directly.

I did, and I learned about the history of racism in Nicaragua, of the domination of the Indian minority by the Spanish-speaking majority. Young Sandinista soldiers had committed serious abuses against the Miskito people as the *contra* war entered ancestral Indian territory. The Miskito leaders regarded the conflict as a historic Nicaraguan problem and not particularly a Sandinista one and were working to help reconcile the situation. They pleaded with us not to let our government exploit the racial tension for its own ends.

A year later I was on the first Witness for Peace short-term team and saw the war firsthand. The suffering of Nicaraguan civilians due to *contra* terror on the northern frontier affected me deeply.

But I was also concerned with how Nicaragua was being militarized in response to the U.S.-sponsored invasion and the threat of a more direct attack from its powerful neighbor to the north. Every Nicaraguan knows the history of the U.S. Marines in their country, and they were getting ready for any possibility. Urgent domestic needs were being sacrificed for military preparedness.

Every Witness for Peace volunteer can tell stories of terror, torture, rape, pillage, and murder carried out by the *contras*. This mercenary army, created and sustained by the U.S. government and orchestrated by the CIA, engages in a consistent pattern of savage terrorism to which we have been eyewitnesses and which international human rights groups have thoroughly documented.

Witness for Peace has been undertaken by North American Christians who believe that U.S. policy toward Nicaragua is simply wrong and is only making the situation there much worse. It is an attempt to focus conscience in a way that is politically costly to U.S. policy against Nicaragua. Some of us are sympathetic to the goals and accomplishments of the government in Managua. Some of us have real concerns and disagreements with the directions of Sandinista policy. Most of us have both supportive and critical feelings toward the Nicaraguan government, but all of us believe that the positive forces in Nicaragua deserve our nurture and support. We are convinced that the hostility of the U.S. government will only strengthen the forces in Nicaragua that tend toward ideological rigidity and military solutions.

All those involved in Witness for Peace are committed to maintaining a posture of political independence in this project. We share a primary concern for the victims of military violence in the area. Nonviolence in word and deed is our central operating principle.

At an even deeper level, we are motivated by strong biblical convictions and by a faith in the God who demonstrates a special love and care for the poor and defenseless. We enter into this witness as an act of faith and a work of prayer. Because Witness for Peace in Nicaragua places people in life-threatening situations, the unity, strength, and courage required comes from being firmly grounded in faith and prayer.

While begun by Christians and strong in its Christian identity, Witness for Peace welcomes those of other faith traditions who would join hands with us and with the Nicaraguan people in this action for peace. We act in response to a clear invitation from Nicaraguan Christians, brothers and sisters who are also deeply rooted in biblical faith. Many of us in the North American churches believe that our bonds and fellowship in the body of Christ are stronger even than our national loyalties.

We believe that U.S. intervention in Nicaragua and elsewhere is contrary to the witness of Scripture and the best of American values of democracy. We enter into Witness for Peace in Nicaragua because faith compels us to.

By our visible presence in Nicaragua, we seek to protect innocent civilians who have been made victims of the military violence being sponsored by our government. Because the U.S. government is carrying out a violent and destructive policy toward Nicaragua, North Americans have a right and responsibility to be there to offer a different kind of presence. Our hope is that Witness for Peace might help save lives, urge the U.S. government to reexamine and change its policy toward Nicaragua, and provide access to eyewitness reports of the consequences of the U.S. *contra* war.

Since the founding of Witness for Peace in 1983, I have watched Nicaragua suffer from an increasing economic crisis and hardening internal policies in response to the U.S.-sponsored war. Through economic strangulation, diplomatic isolation, and military aggression, the U.S. government has pushed Nicaragua into a closer relationship with the Soviet bloc. That has been deliberate, in my opinion, so as to create a self-fulfilling prophecy—try to make Nicaragua become what you already say it is so that later, in hindsight, you can justify what you've done to it.

In Washington the administration has succeeded in virtually ending any rational discussion on Nicaragua. The rhetoric in the White House and Congress and in the media about Nicaragua has become overwhelming. The Reagan administration proudly proclaims a victory in its propaganda war by saying that Nicaragua has no friends left.

Well, that is not true. There are still many of us, especially in the churches, who have developed a deep friendship with the people of Nicaragua. We are not uncritical of the Nicaraguan government nor have we ever been; true friends are not uncritical. Developments in Nicaragua concern us greatly, but it is difficult to know how and when and where to express those concerns when you know that your government will use them as further justification for its intervention in Nicaragua. It is hard to talk honestly about Nicaragua when the U.S. government is openly lying about everything in Nicaragua.

Yet friendship requires us to express our concern over human rights, states of emergency, abuse of Indian minorities, militarization, and closer ties to the Soviets. We know that the U.S. government in reality cares nothing about all these issues. They are only useful as pretexts for intervention and eventually for invasion. Nicaragua has a far better human rights record than our Salvadoran and Guatemalan allies who have murdered thousands of their own people, created military police states and death squads, persecuted the church, crushed political opposition, wiped out indigenous Indian populations, and tortured, raped, and mutilated the innocent. What the United States does care about is regaining the political and economic control of Nicaragua that it lost in 1979.

The fundamental moral and political issue today concerning Nicaragua is U.S. intervention. That is the issue the U.S. government wants most to cover up and obscure by raising every other issue and creating an atmosphere of hysteria about Nicaragua. Nicaragua, like most nations after revolutions or great upheavals, has many problems (some inherited and some new), many obstacles to overcome, and many factions and conflicts over class, race, ideology, ego, and personality.

Real friends of Nicaragua should be deeply concerned about the solutions to those problems, the surmounting of those obstacles, and the peaceful resolution of those conflicts. But there is no problem in Nicaragua that justifies the intervention of the United States. Nicaragua has the sovereign right to determine its own destiny without interference from the foreign government that has for so long dominated its history.

No matter what course Nicaragua chooses for its own internal development, the United States has absolutely no right to intervene in its affairs. And no matter what criticisms we may have of Nicaraguan choices, we in the United States who are friends of Nicaragua will defend its right to choose its own path and will stand in the way of our own government's violent attempts to control its course.

THE FREE SOUTH AFRICA
MOVEMENT: Dismantling Apartheid

Walter Fauntroy

Walter Fauntroy represents the District of Columbia in the U.S. House of Representatives and is pastor of New Bethel Baptist Church in Washington, D.C. He has long been a leading figure in the black freedom movement. Fauntroy was a close associate of Dr. Martin Luther King, Jr., and a leader in the Southern Christian Leadership Conference founded by King.

Since entering Congress, Fauntroy has also continued his involvement in nonelectoral activities. In 1981 he was arrested with a group seeking to block the opening of a toxic waste dump in a poor and primarily black county in South Carolina. In 1983 he was the primary organizer of the Twentieth Anniversary March on Washington for Jobs, Peace, and Freedom.

On November 21, 1984, Fauntroy, Randall Robinson, director of TransAfrica, and U.S. Civil Rights Commission member Mary Frances Berry were arrested in a sit-in at the South African Embassy in Washington. That action sparked what has now become a nationwide campaign of nonviolent direct action against apartheid and U.S. policy in South Africa. On December 13, 1984, Jim Wallis and Danny Collum visited Fauntroy at his congressional office to discuss the development of the Free South Africa Movement and his involvement in it.

—The Editor

Wallis and Collum: The news of your arrest as part of a sit-in at the South African Embassy came as a very pleasant Thanksgiving Day surprise to many of us. Could you tell us about the sequence of events that led to that action and the subsequent Free South Africa campaign?

Walter Fauntroy: What happened on November 21 probably had its beginning back in 1982 when Coretta Scott King talked to me about the twentieth anniversary of the March on Washington and the need for a coalition of conscience like the one that had moved the nation twenty years before to deal with basic problems—segregation and discrimination—that confronted us at that time. I have been working for several years building what I call the black leadership family by pulling together the heads of about 150 national black organizations to put together a plan for our own survival, unity, and progress. I saw this twentieth anniversary as a means of implementing the plan.

Our plan, announced at the beginning of the Reagan era, was to do four things. The first was to go on the defense against cuts in those programs that improve the quality of life for American people and blacks in particular. Second, going on the offense, we aimed to come up with constructive alternatives to the Reagan policies that were being advocated. Third, we planned to organize ourselves in about 115 congressional districts where blacks are more than 20 percent of the population and could influence the work of those members of Congress. And finally, we aimed to reach out in coalition with others whose interests coincide with ours.

So I began to work on putting together the twentieth anniversary of the March on Washington. We pulled together not only the church, civil rights, and labor groups that organized with us in the sixties, but we expanded to include movements that have developed since that time: peace activists, environmentalists, the Hispanic movement, and the women's rights movement. We fashioned a masterful exercise of the First Amendment right to peaceful assembly to petition government for redress of grievances of about five hundred thousand people here.

We identified fourteen pieces of legislation we resolved to work on as a coalition of conscience over the 1983–84 year. Among them was the Hawkins Community Renewal and Full Employment Act that we got passed in the House, but not in the Senate. We also worked on the Martin Luther King Holiday Bill and the Gray Amendment to ban new investments by American corporations in South Africa. We worked on those, contacting the elements of the coalition, urging them to call their members of Congress, saying, "If you can't vote for this, we can't vote for you in November."

As a result, we got the Gray Amendment passed in the House, but we failed in the Senate because the president intervened and told his Republican-controlled Senate that he did not wish to have this alteration to his policies of constructive engagement.

We took that loss but determined to work in the traditional process— the electoral process—to try to change priorities from 1985 on. So we took some of the coalition of conscience into the Rainbow Coalition working around Jesse Jackson to raise these sharp issues of domestic and international problems. But because the majority of the American people were feeling better about themselves four years after Reagan started, because they were spending borrowed money, deficit money that had been built up, Reagan won.

Clearly, there was little hope of our being able to affect policy over the next four years through the traditional means, that is, political action. The founding fathers were wise enough to recognize that in our democracy there might come times when the political process would not function for those who had legitimate grievances and could not get them addressed. So they set aside a second means of affecting public policy, and that was the First Amendment right of peaceful assembly and the right to petition government for redress of grievances. It became very clear to us that that perhaps was the option we had to take.

It had worked before at a time when most of us wanted to affect public policy on "white only" signs across the South. Then we could not do that using traditional means, because we couldn't vote. We were beaten and maimed and killed and our organizers were brutalized for trying to get us the vote. Faced with that, faced with the failure of the courts to address our problem across the board, we then entered First Amendment politics—what we called the politics of creative tension.

We had demonstrations; we marched; we went to jail in order to raise our issue to the level where it pricked the conscience of the body politic. And on July 2, 1964, the body politic, in a bill called the Civil Rights Bill of 1964, translated what they believed into public policy and practice.

We could then move into traditional means of influencing public policy. After we got the Voting Rights Act passed, there was no need to demonstrate in the streets for Head Start programs, because we had developed political clout with new registrars to influence public decisions. We did not have to work for the Great Society programs. And we did not even have to work in the streets for the Humphrey-Hawkins Full Employment Bill or for the housing programs. Therefore, what issue should we address?

We were on the brink, on the threshold of historic polarization in the country pursuant to the elections of 1984, and the South African issue presented us a clear opportunity to reassemble a coalition of conscience around something with which most people have to agree. Then I was approached by Randall Robinson, the head of TransAfrica, what we in the black community consider black America's lobby on Africa and the

Caribbean. And as I am president of the National Black Leadership Roundtable, which holds together all the heads of national black organizations, we decided to launch something.

We chose November 21 because it's a down time for the media. We had to keep rather quiet, because we would not have been allowed in the embassy if they had had any idea what we were going to do. We went in and talked about policy options in South Africa. Eleanor Holmes-Norton, who is a professor of law at Georgetown [University] and head of the EEO [Equal Employment Opportunity] Commission, left the meeting to inform demonstrators outside and the press that we were going to sit-in.

The press eventually called the ambassador at the embassy to ask how the sit-in was going. He said there was no sit-in, that we were sitting there having a very enjoyable conversation. He said, "If it weren't so funny, I'd laugh about it." When he'd finished laughing, we shook our heads and said, "Yes, we're here to stay until you call Pretoria [South Africa] and tell them we'll leave when we get four things: release of all those who have been arrested this year; release of long-term prisoners who had been legitimate leaders of the black African people in South Africa; the start of good-faith negotiations with that leadership toward dismantling apartheid and writing a new constitution; and a change in our country's policy." Well, shortly after, they arrested us and took us out of there.

To understand precisely what happened you have to know that it is our view that this country's policy of constructive engagement—which is all carrot and no stick—released South Africa to become more brutal in its four stated objectives: to destroy the liberation movement; to co-opt those leaders in South Africa they can; to repress those whom they can't co-opt; and to prepare for total warfare, both economic and military.

Encouraged by this country's constructive engagement policies, they began undeclared wars on Angola, Mozambique, and Zambia, where freedom fighters had camps and were training to conduct sabotage forays into South Africa. When the South African army invaded Angola, the United States was the only nation to veto the resolution condemning the South African government for that action. Then they bombed Mozambique into submission and on March 16, 1984, forced the government to sign a treaty with South Africa in which they agreed not to allow the liberation forces to organize and strike South Africa from there. Having stonewalled in Namibia, having gotten things under military control with the help of $23 million in purchases—that Reagan allowed—from the U.S. government, they then turned on their second objective—to co-opt those whom they could and to repress those whom they could not.

Their first repression attempt was in February 1984 when the South African students recognized that they could not prepare for violent war, but they could go into nonviolent conflict. They had demonstrations against the inferior schools in which they are trained to work in the mines or in the factories while the minority white students are trained to manage the economy and run the government. As the result of their protest, 134 were gunned down, and the students' leaders were arrested.

Then, in order to co-opt as many as they could, the South African government came up with a proposal for a new form of government that would create a parliament for the 1.3 million "coloreds," or mixed-race people, and 800,000 Asians, but nothing for the black 72 percent of the population. When mixed-race leaders and Asian community leaders rejected that proposal and began organizing a boycott of the election, they turned out to be very successful. Eighty percent of the mixed-race people refused to vote; 70 percent of the Asians did not turn out. And as a result, again, the government arrested all of the leaders and said that if they raised their heads by any means of protest they would be arrested without charge and detained without trial.

Then black labor union leaders and the black student leaders who were still out and the black township leaders in outrage decided, though we cannot fight, while America is voting on Reagan, we will be voting with our feet. We will not go to work. A million of them stayed away November 5 and 6 from the factories, the mines, and the fields. The heartland of South Africa, the Transvaal province, was brought to a standstill. In response, the troops that had been deployed along the border, which were now no longer needed, were sent into the black townships arresting without charge and without trial every leader who had been identified. They ransacked the labor union office and imprisoned their leaders.

In short, Thanksgiving Day arrived, and it was clear that we had to do something here in the United States. People like me simply said enough is enough. If your policy now is to take any nonviolent leaders— be they black, mixed-race, or Asian—and imprison them without charge, take us too. So we offered ourselves, and you've seen the ground-swell of members of Congress, national leaders, black and white together, the labor movement, and others, all saying take us now, take us also. And the movement has just begun; we're going to go through several more phases.

Our purpose during this period is to educate the American people to the fact that apartheid in South Africa is not simply a system of social segregation that is repugnant to all decent thinking human beings, but, more important, it is a system of political domination for the purpose of economic exploitation. It is a system of labor control by which black South Africans are made available to the world as the cheapest labor source that can be found.

Those who have corporations and products to be made or money to be invested go there, where the average yield or return on a manufacturing investment is 25 percent, while around the world the average return is 18 percent. They come there to work the mines where the average return is 18 percent on an investment, while the average around the world is 12.6 percent.

George Wallace, the governor of Alabama, sent word to me that he supports the Free South Africa Movement. Why? Because at the port of Mobile, Alabama, where they build ships, they are importing steel from South Africa, while up the road in Birmingham, Alabama, they are closing down steel mills. They are importing coal from South Africa for the electric companies of the South, when up the road at Tuxedo Junction they have closed down coal mines in which there is the same kind of coal.

The system of apartheid and labor control, the passbooks and denial of citizenship rights, and the relegation of blacks to only 13 percent of the land—the most barren and unproductive land in the country—all operate to provide people who will work for $80 a month in a mine or $140 a month in a factory. If you send ambassadors and representatives to consulates around the world where economic activity is vibrant—whether it is in Houston or Mobile or Boston or New York or Los Angeles—and appeal to businesses that are operating there to relocate their facilities to South Africa, then no job is safe anywhere in the world so long as South Africa is not free.

You have set off a spark in this country that is enormous. Did you expect the breadth and depth of response? Are you surprised by it? How do you feel about the response and what is your sense about why it has been so widespread?

Of course I am delighted by it. What surprised me was the sense of frustration and anxiety on the part of people who are concerned about environmental issues, about peace, about the economy, who voted against Reagan out of a depth of understanding of the way he was moving the country, and who need some beginning point for awakening the American people to what is going on.

What also has surprised me has been the extent to which the labor movement responded; the leaders of that movement offered themselves for arrest at the South African Embassy. Steelworkers in Birmingham had been told they lost their jobs because of affirmative action and Equal Employment Opportunity. The workers are now saying that is not the issue; it is the South Africans getting into our pockets.

I am determined we are going to win this. We are going to get into the pockets of those who are getting into our pockets by a variety of means, and we are going to win.

You mentioned earlier that this is a beginning in terms of the Free South Africa Movement and several phases are to come. Would you elaborate on that?

First we must get the consciousness raised, so people begin to ask why leaders like that are going to jail. Then people are going to start asking what they can do.

Well, everybody can't get arrested; we don't want but one or two a day to get arrested. What you can do is go to any bank that's selling Krugerrands [South African coins], which make up 50 percent of all the exports to come out of South Africa, and tell them "either you stop selling them or we will withdraw our money from your bank." The result will be that within a few months you will see signs in banks around this country: "We do not sell Krugerrands." That's going to hit them in the pocket in South Africa.

We are going to identify some multinational corporations that may be based here that are exploiting South Africa's cheap labor system and are making good returns. We are going to ask not only that we selectively patronize them, but we will ask others to join us—those of conscience in England, in France, in West Germany, in the Netherlands, and from everywhere else where people want to free the world of this guaranteed cheap labor that is a threat to anybody who wants to work elsewhere. And I think that any of the multinationals in South Africa for that purpose are going to think about disinvestment.

We are going to continue to press cities that have pension funds to withdraw them from companies investing in South Africa. I think as we raise the issue of the $8 billion invested by stockholders in this country, individuals will feel pressure to disinvest.

I think those pressures helped move a president from saying, "I am not going to meet with Mr. Tutu" to then meeting with him, and then saying, "I am not going to change my policies" and coming out the next day and telling the country a lie: "I got eleven people released," a bold misrepresentation of whose political pressure actually did get them released. And then after thirty-five Republicans who are conservative say, "Look, it's us who are in trouble, so you'd better change." Then Reagan says, "Well, you know I said yesterday that my policies were working. I must admit today that constructive engagement, quiet diplomacy, doesn't always work. You have to judge your allies, and so I am judging today. Apartheid is bad; please change it." That's what he's saying today.

Before long he'll be saying he thinks it's a good idea to pass the Gray Amendment because Mr. Heinz, his blocker in the Senate from Pennsylvania, now has pressure from steelworkers in Pittsburgh, and Homestead, and Johnstown, workers who had thought that South Africa was the colored people's problem, who now understand that their jobs went there.

What I now predict is that just as 1865 was the year that came time to end the system of slavery in America, just as 1945 became the time to end the Nazi tyranny, 1985 will be the year that will begin to end apartheid in South Africa.

You mentioned the divestment of U.S. corporations that do business there as one of the goals. A lot of people say that the divestment strategy won't work, that it doesn't have the leverage to move the South African government. The other line of attack is that all it does is take away jobs from black South Africans and make them more miserable than they already are.

I am sure they said that to William Lloyd Garrison: "I know you want to abolish slavery, but what would these people do if we didn't feed them, didn't provide them with meaningful work. They're happy; hear them singing in the fields." It's the same thing that I am sure they said to the founding fathers here. "It is better to pay the tax than to be without their trade. They made this country. So taxation without representation is not too bad when you think about it." And so they're saying that about South Africa now.

But what are the facts? First of all, divestment by this country alone will not work, although we are South Africa's number-one trading partner. A change in South Africa will only happen when people of conscience around the world decide this is a threat to all of us. The pressure will come, and that's why we will be internationalizing the movement very soon. So it can't work alone, but we are building a coalition of conscience—nationwide and internationally based not only on moral outrage but on self-interest.

Second, the United States has been subjected to a massive propaganda campaign over the last five or six years by the South African government because we are its number-one trading partner. A lot of the investment of capital—some $3.8 billion in direct loans from banks—comes from Chase Manhattan, Citicorp, First Boston, Continental Illinois, Morgan Guaranty Trust, and Ritter-Peabody. All these banks are investing and South Africa doesn't want them to feel the pressure of "extremists" who have been saying South Africa is mean and bad. So the government there has suggested that the people are happy. They have begun bringing nice little choirs of South African children to sing "Jesus loves me" on television. That's a very interesting attack but it won't work.

You are a member of the Congress and a minister of the gospel. What word to Christians do you have? Why should Christians see this as an issue they should become involved in?

It is a matter of personal salvation. When this warfare of life is over, and all of us have got to go—we can't stay here always—the Lord is not going to ask us how many songs we sang in church, how often we went to church, whether we wore designer clothes when we went, whether we rode around in a Mercedes. But the question will be, when I was hungry did you feed me? When I was thirsty did you give me something to drink? When I was sick and imprisoned in South Africa did you come to see about me? And the Lord's answer to us will be, inasmuch as you didn't join the Free South Africa Movement in 1985 when I was trying to declare good news to twenty-five million exploited poor people, you did it not unto me.

Some would ask why you are going out and violating the laws since you are a man who makes laws. How can you make laws and break laws at the same time?

Because I am fortunate enough to live in a country that allows, by its First Amendment, the right of any citizen to peacefully assemble and petition and, in fact, to break a law so long as they are prepared to suffer the consequences. We broke the law; we are prepared to suffer the consequences.

But the South African Embassy knows that. They will not put me on trial because people would be educated by what I would set as my defense.

After I had been arrested, I went into the cell block and some angry young black men asked me what in the world I was doing here for some damned South Africans when people need jobs in the United States. And then I sat down with them for about an hour and explained that there are no jobs here because cars that used to be made here, steel that used to be made here, rubber that used to be made here, is now made there. And they said, "I'm ready to join the movement when I come out." The South African government didn't want that explanation to be made in a trial. And it's not my fault that they won't put me on trial for having broken the law.

As I told President [Lyndon] Johnson at the critical point in the [civil rights] movement, "The Lord is my shepherd. God is not a Democrat; he is not a Republican; he is not a conservative; he is not a liberal; he is not black or white; God is the reward of them that diligently seek him." My responsibility as a minister is to declare good news to the poor. In fact, I am anointed—as is every Christian—to do that.

THE FREE SOUTH AFRICA
MOVEMENT: On Behalf of Millions
Desmond Tutu

This interview with Archbishop Desmond Tutu was conducted by Jim Wallis on December 24, 1984. The sermon excerpt that follows was preached by Tutu at the Washington Cathedral in Washington, D.C., on December 2, 1984.

—The Editor

Jim Wallis: You are a Christian and a minister of the gospel. You are also a leader of the freedom movement in South Africa. How is your faith brought to bear in this struggle?

Tutu: If it weren't for faith, I would have given up long ago. I am certain lots of us would have been hate-filled and bitter. For me the Scriptures have become more and more thoroughly relevant to our situation. They speak of a God who, when you worship him, turns you around to be concerned for your neighbor. He does not tolerate a relationship with himself that excludes your neighbor.

It is the horizontal dimension that makes our faith so thoroughly subversive in a situation of oppression and injustice. It speaks of the infinite value of human persons. We count for God because he treated us lovingly. Each one of us is the object of the divine love as if we were the only person around. We are created in God's image and, therefore, each one of us is held to be a representative, a viceroy of God.

In the middle of our faith is the death and resurrection. Nothing could have been more hopeless than Good Friday—but then Easter happened, and forever we have to become prisoners of hope.

You and others in South Africa have called apartheid, and the church's acceptance of it, a heresy. Why do you use that language?

This ideology, this policy is not just wrong; it is not just one that causes pain to people. Apartheid denies essential aspects of our faith. And we have to speak of it in religious terms, not just political terms because it has been buttressed by others, or they have sought to buttress it, to justify it, on biblical grounds.

For instance, apartheid says what makes us valuable in the sight of God is a biological attribute, and by that criterion it talks about something that cannot be universal. If your value depends on something like the color of your skin, it means that not everybody can have the same value.

That is contrary—totally contrary—to the Scriptures, which say our value is because we are created in the image of God.

Apartheid says that we are created for separation; the Scriptures say "Rubbish." We are created for unity, for fellowship, for communion. Apartheid says that people are fundamentally irreconcilable; the Scriptures know nothing of this. It is denying what we might call the central work of Christ: attaining reconciliation. God was concerned with reconciling the world to himself.

Apartheid goes on to inflict an unnecessary and unjust suffering and misery on God's children just because they are black. Therefore, we are calling on Christians to say that they oppose this not for political reasons, not even for economic reasons, not even for the fact that they are worried that human beings are made to suffer—but because the people supporting this are behaving in an unChristian way.

You speak of a "confessing" movement. What does that mean?

I don't think the "Confessing Church" is something that emerges in a conscious kind of way. You don't sit down and say, "Now, you guys, we are going to become the Confessing Church." It is something that is almost forced on you by the situation, where you say that if you deny these aspects of the faith, you cannot really say you belong to the church of God.

And we are not saying it in any self-righteous kind of way. We are saying we are trying to be as true to the imperatives of the gospel as we can. And almost always it will expose you to suffering, to ridicule, and to worse.

What gives you the confidence to say, "We shall be free"? Where do you find hope?

The primary source of it is God our Lord. If after the horrible event of Good Friday, when even the physical nature seemed to mourn, and darkness covered the earth—if after that you see the glorious resurrection, what can ever be worse than that moment? And what can ever again make you doubt that if God be for us, who can be against us? If that has happened, what can ever again separate us from the love of God?

But I have to underline the effect of the church. It is a tremendous thing to come to the church and be upheld by the love and the caring of our brothers and sisters throughout the world. I mean, there would have been—there are—many moments when we are feeling despondent.

But you can't remain despondent when you are told by someone who leads a life of solitary prayer in the woods in California, "I pray for you every day of my life. My day starts at 2 A.M." I mean, how can you? What chance does the South African government stand? There is just no hope for them. And they really ought to listen to us when we say, "We are asking you to join the winning side."

When we say we are on the winning side, it isn't that God is on our side because we are good; it is because he is that kind of God.

Do you have a message for us here, for our struggle?

Well, the main one is to thank you very much for caring. It means a great deal to those who are oppressed to know that they aren't alone. And never, never let anyone tell you that what you are doing is insignificant.

Let them know that the sea is made up of drops of water. There is no way in which injustice can ever prevail over goodness. Love must always prevail over hate.

And know that we have the wonderful privilege of being fellow workers with God and, therefore, we will know that we are part of an enterprise that can never fail. God bless you very much.

Sermon

This service is in thanksgiving to God. I want to add my own thanks to you. We Christians believe that in becoming a Christian you become a member of the body of Christ and part of a worldwide fellowship. You have brothers and sisters scattered over the face of the earth.

We know, too, that we are by our humanity members of the human family and thereby have sisters and brothers in many lands. And we know in our experience what it has meant to be upheld by the love and prayers and the concern of so many around the world. It has been almost a physical sensation, this being borne up by those fervent prayers.

Sometimes you may feel sorry for us being in the kind of situation in which we are. Yet I think perhaps the proper attitude ought to be one of envy, for I think it is far easier to be a Christian, a person of belief and faith, in South Africa than it is here. For the issues in South Africa are so obviously clear; you are either for apartheid or against it.

In many respects it has very little to do with personal courage. People say, "Hah! Did you hear what Desmond Tutu said to the government of South Africa? He said to them, 'Hey, when you take on the South African churches, know that you are taking on the church of God. And do you know what has happened to those who have done so in the past? They have bitten the dust, and bitten it ignominiously!'"

No, friend, it has very little to do with personal freedom, personal courage. We are able to witness in South Africa as we do because you are faithful in your witness where you are.

Sometimes you may not feel like praying because your prayers are insipid. There is a dryness, and God seems miles and miles away. But because you are faithful, you say to God, "I want to pray, and I will offer you these thirty minutes, God, even if it means fighting these awkward distractions for a few minutes."

And because you are faithful, someone in South Africa suddenly receives an excess of grace; inexplicably it appears. Perhaps he is in a solitary confinement cell; perhaps he is being tortured. And instead of being hate-filled and embittered, he is able to say, "You know, father, when these men are applying their third-degree methods on you, you look on them and say, 'These are God's children and they are behaving like animals. They need us to help them recover the humanity they have lost.'" How is that possible except that you here have prayed him into that state of grace?

Another man's home is going to be demolished tomorrow. He's part of a community that is going to be uprooted because it does not fit into the ideological map of apartheid. The churches and the clinics and the schools in the community have already been demolished. The water supply has been stopped. The bus service to the nearest town is interrupted so that, as the government puts it, "The people will move voluntarily."

And this man, whose home is going to be demolished tomorrow, sets out to pray incredibly. He says, "God, thank you for loving us." How can that be except that you here have prayed him into that state of grace?

We know, too, that the highest levels of prayer are reached when we no longer have to use so many words. And so the words that I bring, "thank you," are shot through and through with ineffable emotion. And know that I speak on behalf of millions.

I know that I speak on behalf of a man who was sentenced to twelve years in prison for a political offense. He appealed his conviction and sentence, and the South African Council of Churches, through your prayers and financial support, was able to fund his appeal. And he won. The sentence and the conviction were crushed.

He would like to be here to thank you on his own behalf that he is not languishing in some maximum-security prison in South Africa for twelve years. His wife would like to be here to thank you that she is not alone for twelve years. His children would like to come and say, "Thank you, for our daddy is with us."

We thank you for caring and for incarnating that caring in such a costly way. Many of those for whom such actions have a greater significance are voiceless. You may not hear how they feel, but I was sent here to tell you that whatever you do to protest this evil system does not go without notice amongst those for whom it is being done. So, thank you.

God is good. God gave us the Nobel Peace Prize, and let us say firmly that it is not given as a personal distinction to Desmond Tutu. This award is for all of us, all of us committed to the struggle for justice and peace and reconciliation.

We thank God who says, "This is my world and I'm in charge." Just when the powers of evil seem to be on the rampage, God says, "I just want to show you who is boss around here." And here is the prize, a vindication for the work of the South African Council of Churches and those associated with it, a vindication for all who are committed to work for justice and peace.

Your cause will prevail. Your cause is just, your cause is right, and God enlists you and me and all of us to work together with him to change the evil of this world, to change its hurt, its antagonism, its anxieties, its poverty, its disease, its famines—to change all of this into the kingdom of shalom, of justice, and goodness and joy and laughter and compassion and caring and sharing.

And then we will see the kingdoms of this world transformed into the kingdom of our God, and he will reign forever and ever.

Amen.

THE NUCLEAR TRAIN CAMPAIGN:
Tracking and Resisting the Train
Jim Douglass

When the vigils by people of faith along the tracks of the train that carried assembled nuclear warheads began, the Department of Energy train was painted white and was referred to by vigilers as the White Train. The Department of Energy has since repainted the trains brown, maroon, and other colors, yet the efforts to oppose the transportation of nuclear warheads on these trains continue and are known as the Nuclear Train Campaign.

In May 1985, the U.S. government issued regulations making it a crime for persons with access to "Unclassified Controlled Nuclear Information" to pass certain information to others who are unauthorized to receive it. This kind of information sharing is foundational to the Nuclear Train Campaign. Penalties could include a fine of up to $100,000 as well as criminal charges.

—The Editor

W hen did we first see the White Train? Some of us feel we saw it first in Franz Jagerstatter's dream.

Jagerstatter was an Austrian peasant who refused to fight in Hitler's wars because he believed that the Nazi movement was anti-Christian. He was beheaded by the Nazis in 1943 and is now being considered for sainthood by the Catholic church.

The train Jagerstatter saw in a dream five years before his martyrdom (and which he wrote about shortly before his death) corresponded to the White Train that now passes our homes and explodes in our dreams:

At first I lay awake in my bed until almost midnight, unable to sleep, although I was not sick; I must have fallen asleep anyway. All of a sudden I saw a beautiful shining railroad train that circled around a mountain. Streams of children—and adults as well—rushed toward the train and could not be held back. . . . Then I heard a voice say to me: "This train is going to hell."

The train to hell in Jagerstatter's dream was a symbol of cooperation in the Nazi movement. Our White Train to hell is both symbol and reality: it contains the annihilation it symbolizes.

For the sake of his soul, Jagerstatter had to refuse to board his train to hell. For the sake of our souls and of life itself, we have to stop the White Train.

We began tracking the White Train, although we did not know it existed then, when we moved into our house alongside the railroad tracks entering the Trident submarine base at Bangor, Washington.

We saw the house by the tracks for the first time in 1977, while seeking a piece of land that could become Ground Zero Center for Nonviolent Action. The house we discovered by the tracks was too remote to serve as such a center, but it brought another possibility to mind. It stood on a hill overlooking the gate where railroad shipments enter the Trident base. By living in such a house one could, simply by being there, begin to break through the invisibility and silence of one critical means toward nuclear holocaust: the missile shipments that travel the United States by rail, analogous to the boxcars that moved unchallenged through Europe in the forties on the way to an earlier holocaust.

Through a series of miracles, Shelley, our son Thomas, and I moved into the house by the tracks four years later. The intervening time had been marked by my knocking on the door of the house every six months or so to ask if the couple living there ever planned to sell it, a friendly no always being the answer. Then one day I knocked on the door to no answer at all and saw through its window a house empty of both people and furniture. From that moment on, the miracles took over. Through the grace of God and the gifts of many wonderful friends, we were able to buy the house by the tracks and move into it in July 1981. At the same time the Agape Community was born.

We held a workshop at Ground Zero that month on "Christian Roots of Nonviolence" that included a pilgrimage around the fence of the base. It ended at the railroad tracks with a meditation on the trains entering Bangor and their parallel meaning to the trains entering Auschwitz and Buchenwald. As a part of the meditation we named some of the cities and towns along the tracks, as they wound their way up from Salt Lake City, near the Hercules Corporation, source of Trident's missile motor shipments. (At the time we knew nothing of the White Train's journeys to Bangor from the Texas Panhandle.) When we finished our litany of the tracks, we realized that most of the workshop participants lived along those same tracks.

We all recognized that this was one workshop whose community could truly be deepened in meaning by our going home and becoming an extended nonviolent community in our various towns along the Trident tracks. We decided to become the Agape Community and adopted a community statement which said in part: "We believe the spiritual force capable of both changing us and stopping the arms race is that of *agape:* the love of God operating in the human heart."

As we tracked and opposed Trident missile motor shipments through Utah, Idaho, Oregon, and Washington in 1981 and 1982, two truths found a special life in the Agape Community. The first is that evil, especially the systemic evil of a nuclear holocaust, does not like the light. The government and the railroads did their best to keep us from seeing the missile shipments. The second truth we experienced is that once evil is brought into the light, it can be overcome by God's love operating fearlessly in our lives.

Evil's power lies in darkness, our own darkness. Evil's power to destroy life itself comes from our denial of its presence and our refusal to take responsibility for it. The essence of our life-destroying evil lies in our unseen, unacknowledged cooperation with it. As we began to claim personal responsibility for the missile motor shipments and sought to express our love for the train employees, we experienced the faith to overcome the evil that was in us and on the trains: faith in the redeeming power of nonviolent love, faith in the cross. Our growing community of faith and nonviolent action made the tracks linking us a double symbol—not only of holocaust but of hope.

But we were about to experience a still deeper sense of both holocaust and hope along the tracks.

On December 8, 1982, I received a phone call from a reporter asking if we knew anything about a special train probably carrying nuclear warheads that was on its way to the Trident base. It had been spotted in Everett, Washington, two days before: an all-white, armored train, escorted by a security car traveling along highways.

I said we knew nothing of such a train. It bore no resemblance to the missile motor shipments that we witnessed going into the base every week. After the phone call I walked down our front steps to the tracks. I could see signs of unusual activity across the tracks at the base gate. More security cars than I had ever seen for an arriving train were parked inside and outside the gate, waiting for something. I went back in the house, loaded our camera with slide film, and came down the steps just in time to see the train approaching.

Perched outside the first Burlington Northern engine was a man, like a film director scanning his set. After the second engine came a string of all-white, heavily armored cars. Each of the two rail security cars had a high turret, like a tank's. Sandwiched between the security cars were eight middle cars, lower in height, white, and armored. The letters "ATMX" stood out on them. When the final security car came opposite me, the armored flaps on the side of the turret clanked open, and an object was extended in my direction.

The White Train passed by, a train to holocaust, and I remembered the train in Jagerstatter's dream: "This train is going to hell."

The White Train's December 8, 1982, arrival at Bangor moved us to two kinds of research. We went first to documents on hazardous rail shipments obtained from the Washington Utilities and Transportation Commission. They included correspondence from the Trident base that spoke of nuclear warheads that would be shipped to Bangor in specially designed "ATMX" rail cars. The warhead shipments would be in Department of Energy (DOE) trains (the letters "ATM" on the car stand for DOE's predecessor, the Atomic Energy Commission, and "X" simply means that the cars are not owned by a railroad) moving at a speed limit of thirty-five miles per hour, arriving at Bangor at a rate of two to three trains per year from an unspecified location in Texas. Given this rate of shipments and the rate of deployment of Trident submarines, we estimated that each White Train would carry between one hundred and two hundred hydrogen bombs, depending on its number of cars. We guessed the Texas source of the warhead shipments must be Amarillo, site of the Pantex plant, final assembly point for all U.S. nuclear warheads.

The second stage of our research was into railroad routes from Pantex to Bangor. A friend and railroad buff, Tom Rawson, drew up a likely rail route between Pantex and Bangor. We then sought old and new friends along this theoretical White Train route, sharing with them the Agape Community's vision of love toward the people on the trains and non-violent resistance to their nuclear cargoes. The community along the tracks grew, as we waited for the White Train to come out of its Bangor lair—and, we hoped, follow our route.

It did so on January 5, 1983, rolling past our house in the opposite direction. The fact that the White Train now had less security around it and was soon incorporated into a larger, faster freight train indicated it was probably empty on this return journey. As friends along the tracks monitored the train, we confirmed that it was traveling the route Tom

Rawson had drawn up, returning to Amarillo via Spokane, Denver, and Pueblo, until it was seen entering the Pantex plant the night of January 12 by Les Breeding of Northwest Texas Clergy and Laity Concerned.

"It was a haunting sight," said Les, "this white train moving slowly into the distance where amber lights were glowing with a light fog all around. It brought to mind a phantom train bound for Hades."

The White Train is the most concentrated symbol we have of the hell of nuclear war. It carries a world-destructive power within it, guarded by Department of Energy "couriers" who, according to a DOE spokesperson, are armed with machine guns, rifles, and hand grenades and are trained to shoot anyone who threatens the train. Yet there is another side to all this, as indicated by an experience Les Breeding had with the "phantom train bound for Hades."

On the night of January 12, Les had a unique, forty-five-minute conversation in the middle of the Amarillo switchyards with the head security guard of the White Train, prior to the train's final movement to Pantex. After this conversation Les lost the White Train when it moved out of the switchyards into darkness. He pursued it by car, discovering it again just outside Pantex. There was a tense moment when he drove up to the train, and a searchlight suddenly glared at his car. He got out of the car and heard the security guard say, "Hey, Les, is that you?"

At the heart of the greatest outward symbol we have of nuclear war, this train bearing instruments of hell, there is a human voice asking if we are there. The question destroys our sense of the train as absolute evil. There are people inside the train. We have to stop this White Train to hell, but we can stop it only through a truthful, loving process that affirms the sacredness of that life within it. The security guard and his question to us are at the center of the tracks campaign.

From January through March 1983, Agape Community contacts multiplied along the White Train route: in Colorado, Wyoming, Montana, Idaho, and Washington. In Missoula, Montana, Linda and George Greenwald and several friends held a weekly vigil by the tracks with a banner saying, "Silence is betrayal . . . the nuclear train passes thru this valley," which became a wire service photo and story in newspapers across the country. It helped inspire vigils in other places by the tracks. We shared information on the White Train in every town that we could reach along its tracks.

Then on the afternoon of March 18, 1983, we received an unexpected phone call from one of our new friends along the tracks, a woman in a town in Colorado. She said a friend of hers married to a railroad employee was told by her husband that he thought "your train" was just getting under way. We checked this report with friends in Amarillo, who confirmed the White Train's departure from there at 2:03 P.M. It was on its way to Bangor. The White Train odyssey of March 18 to 22, 1983, had begun.

The first group of vigilers to see the train were in La Junta, Colorado, at 11 P.M., March 18, in the middle of a snowstorm. They were confronted by several carloads of local police, who then lined the tracks as the train stopped there briefly. The La Junta group phoned up the line, and vigilers in other Colorado towns began to wait by the tracks in the darkness and snow.

During the next four days as the White Train made its way toward Bangor, vigils sprang up along its changing route like instant flowers by the tracks, seeded by the Agape Community's phone network. Vigils were held in thirty-five different towns and cities along its tracks. A number of these vigils were held along alternate routes to Bangor even after the White Train had been rerouted to avoid them, while about an equal number were created quickly on the new routes taken by the train.

Two people were arrested for approaching the train too closely in Denver, eight for kneeling on the tracks in front of it in Fort Collins, and six for attempting to sit in front of it at the Bangor gate. Thanks to the witness of these people and the hundreds who kept vigils and prayed along the tracks, the White Train may have become the most closely watched train in the world by the time it entered the Trident base on March 22, 1983.

In our house at the end of the line and in two other Ground Zero homes, our experience March 18 to 22, 1983, of extended community via telephone was overwhelming. We were on the phone continuously during the ninety-four hours of the train's journey: monitoring the train, updating vigilers up the line, sharing information with media, and meeting a series of people in the heartland of the United States whom I have never seen and will never forget. We experienced profoundly during those four days the capacity of "ordinary" people of faith to respond with nonviolent action to the nuclear threat, once they see a way.

We suggested three ways: to monitor the White Train by telling us and others up the line exactly when it went through their town, to hold a vigil by the tracks with their neighbors, and to tell their local newspaper what they were doing so that other neighbors would know. Their response in these ways to the White Train's passage through their communities broke open the silence and invisibility of this train to hell.

We have since learned from a Department of Energy statement that the White Train has been on the rails in this country for more than twenty years. The DOE and its two predecessor organizations, the Atomic Energy Commission (AEC) and the Energy Research and Development Administration (ERDA), have all used a special railcar fleet to transport nuclear weapons across the United States. Some of the original railcars have been modified and upgraded into the present White Train.

A question immediately presents itself: how did this train carrying holocaust weapons across the United States remain virtually invisible for more than twenty years until its March 1983 trip to the Trident base?

It is a question that brings other questions to mind: how did boxcars carrying millions of Jewish people across Europe in the 1940s remain invisible until after the victims had gone to their deaths? How did radiation victims of our nuclear testing remain invisible to us until recent years? Have we always known silently that the stark evil we open our eyes to opens an abyss in ourselves unless and until we open our hearts to faith?

When we monitored the White Train's return trip to Pantex April 11 to 15, 1983, we were startled by its traveling all the way east to Topeka, Kansas, before cutting back southwest to the Pantex plant. The government was willing to send the train far out of its way to avoid those places where it had met the most opposition going north. This pattern of governmental avoidance has continued to be true in the tracks campaign. The DOE now regularly avoids one entire troublesome state, Colorado, at the expense of rerouting the train through Kansas and Nebraska. The DOE command center for the White Train, located in a bunker at Kirtland Air Force Base in Albuquerque, New Mexico, regularly re-routes the train in progress onto whatever is perceived to be the track of least resistance.

The new route through Topeka prompted the Agape Community to invite friends in Kansas and Nebraska to join in the tracks campaign. Research into alternate routes has led to an expansion of the tracks campaign into every western state. The Agape Community and friends are now working along every possible railroad route from Pantex to Bangor to alert our neighbors to the possibility that the White Train might come their way.

On June 23, 1983, our knowledge of the White Train grew as the result of a subpoena issued by Denver judge Larry Lopez-Alexander ordering the Burlington Northern Railroad to turn over documents on the train to Bill Sulzman and Marshall Gourley, the two men arrested for approaching the train in Denver on March 19. Bill and Marshall had argued successfully before Judge Lopez-Alexander that such documents were necessary to their trial defense that the White Train was in violation of international law and that it was the train's criminal cargo, not they as people protesting it, that had no right to be there. The government, alarmed at the direction the case was taking, dropped the charges, but not before several revealing documents had been turned over by Burlington Northern.

The first of these documents includes the minutes of a meeting held in Denver on June 4, 1982, at which Peter Armstrong of the Department of Energy's Transportation Safeguards Division did a two-hour briefing for Burlington Northern personnel on the Bangor shipments. Concerning the contents of these shipments, Armstrong said their "uranium" was "not dangerous unless eaten or breathed." His comment on the shipments' "plutonium" was: "More potent than uranium, however considerable exposure required to be hazardous, keep upwind, stay away." The "high explosives" contained in the shipments he acknowledged as "very hazardous, especially if involved in a fire because they can become unstable (like crystal dynamite)."

DOE policy on demonstrations by the tracks, set forth in an April 7, 1983, "Personal and Confidential" letter from Burlington Northern executive T.C. Whitacre, is to keep the White Train "moving at all times including rerouting as necessary to avoid demonstrations or demonstrators." A public relations officer, J.D. Martin, adds more specifically in a memorandum to Burlington Northern Vice President W.L. Arntzen, "I would heartily endorse your thoughts on routing the next train differently; going through downtown Fort Collins is like crossing a stage for demonstrators."

According to the Whitacre letter, Burlington Northern is instructed by DOE to have railroad personnel on board the train "advise demonstrators that armed couriers are present and that these couriers will take appropriate action if the shipment itself is threatened."

The Whitacre letter also identifies state agencies as unwanted outsiders to DOE: "Would again mention that they do not want outsiders, including state agencies, etc., notified of the tentative operation of these trains or their location, etc., while in route."

During the next Pantex-to-Bangor shipment, August 13 to 17, 1983, DOE succeeded in its secrecy measures to such an extent that it managed to get a twenty-two-car White Train all the way to Elma, Washington (seventy miles short of Bangor), before it was seen by a member of the Agape Community. Because there had been no one in Amarillo watching Pantex on August 13, the train had departed in darkness and silence, and the Agape phone network had remained silent as the death train moved through its midst.

After the train's arrival August 17, a call went out from the Agape Community for a full-time White Train watcher in Amarillo. Word of this need was passed across the country by friends and on August 20 reached Hedy Sawadsky, who was then serving in the Pittsburgh Mennonite Church. After a period of discernment and preparation with friends in Colorado, she moved to Amarillo in September 1983 to follow the active, contemplative vocation of watching a train depart periodically with shipments of hydrogen bombs.

On October 11, 1983, Ground Zero was alerted by Hedy (and by Bill Sulzman, then visiting Hedy from Denver and watching the tracks with her) that the White Train had just departed on Santa Fe tracks heading northeast toward Oklahoma and Kansas. It was then that several other documents obtained in the Sulzman-Gourley court case became critically important. We knew from Burlington Northern memorandums that the White Train also went east, delivering nuclear warheads on a route we had traced to the Charleston Naval Weapons Station in South Carolina. We had alerted people in seven more states to that possibility.

As Hedy and Bill drove with the train up through Oklahoma and Kansas, and as others joined in the vigils and tracking, it soon became apparent that this White Train was in fact turning southeast and would go through Missouri, Arkansas, Tennessee, Mississippi, Alabama, Georgia, and South Carolina. Another chapter in tracking the White Train was beginning.

The government has shown signs of responding to the tracks campaign by means other than rerouting the White Train. The Department of Energy has now proposed regulations that would ban the publicizing of "Unclassified Controlled Nuclear Information" (UCNI), including the sharing of any information on the transportation of nuclear weapons. These proposed regulations bear a civil penalty of a $100,000 fine imposed by the Secretary of Energy and may include a criminal penalty as well. The crossroads which we may be approaching as a people is the incompatibility between a free society and the possession of nuclear weapons.

We remember again Franz Jagerstatter's train to hell and, more important, his refusal to board that train. His resistance to it was a choice of the kingdom of God. It is said that Jagerstatter's eyes shone with such joy and confidence in the hour before his death that the chaplain who visited him in prison was never able to forget that look.

Jagerstatter had to refuse to board his train to hell at the cost of his life, for the sake of life. Resisting that train to hell was identical with choosing the cross, and in it, the kingdom of God.

For us to reject hell, we have to stop the White Train, which not only symbolizes our cooperation with an ultimate evil but bears within its cars the annihilation of life itself. In being called to stop the White Train, we, like Jagerstatter, are being called to the cross and the kingdom.

The White Train can be stopped through education, reflection, and prayerful, nonviolent direct action: prayer vigils by the tracks, loving disobedience on the tracks, until there are more people on the tracks prepared to go to jail for peace than there are people to remove them or jails to contain them. Critical to this vision of stopping the White Train is a transforming love, *agape,* realized through prayer. Out of the White Train's trips toward total destruction has come the presence of people praying along the tracks, more and more people praying as the train passes, more and more considering that prayer of standing in front of the train. What we seek through *agape* is the conversion of ourselves, through the love of God transforming our hearts, so that we might realize a vision of active, contemplative peacemaking.

We remember the kingdom of God that shone from Jagerstatter's eyes in the hour before his death when he chose life. Out of the nightmare of a White Train to hell can come a realization of the kingdom of God. Now we are to choose.

ACTIONS AT WEAPONS FACILITIES:
A Theology of Trespass
Bill Kellermann

Warning!

On May 30, two persons were observed trying to look over the wall surrounding the concentration camp in Dachau. They were of course immediately arrested. They explained that they had been curious to see what the camp looked like inside. In order to give the opportunity to satisfy their curiosity they were detained overnight. It is hoped that their curiosity has now been satisfied in spite of this unforeseen measure.

We wish to still the curiosity of all those who might ignore the warning by informing them that in the future they will be given the opportunity of studying the camp from inside for longer than just one night.

All inquisitive persons are hereby warned once more.

In charge of the Supreme S.A. Command
Special Commissioner Friedriche
PUBLISHED IN DACHAU
JUNE 2, 1933

Who, in heaven's name, were these two people? It's tempting to wonder aloud. Were they just dear friends out for a walk and a talk only to happen upon some new construction along their old familiar road? Were they conscious political voyeurs looking to be titillated by the suffering of others? Or were they conscientious citizens, refusing from the "git go" to be good Germans? Were they perpetrators or bystanders, innocent or guilty?

Such questions one might contrive to answer with a short story, imagining the dialogue between the two and their angry captors. In my version of the story, these friends are local Christians. They took note in the newspaper last month about the opening of this curious facility in the suburbs. Already the thing has begun to haunt them, intruding on their conscience, their dreams, and now their conversation. They muster each other's courage, maybe even praying first. "Let's at least go look." And the visit, as the published report attests, is a real eye-opener.

When they are sent home chastised and duly intimidated, perhaps they pray some more. I suppose it's possible, in fact, that they went back again and suffered a solitary fate the papers neglect to report. In my fanciful version of events, they return (against all common logic) with a whole confessing congregation of sisters and brothers. I picture this crowd standing early one morning with candles along the stretch of fence, praying once more and looking deep into the barbed wire.

I knew a man once, as it happens, a Russian. His own memories were of Soviet fences and walls. He said, "If you want to deal with the nuclear arms race, the first thing you're going to have to come to grips with is barbed wire." That is a true saying. And I've often thought of it since.

Another friend of mine, Peter, who several years ago cut the fence at the Rocky Flats nuclear weapons plant and went in to pray, talks about barbed wire as an idol. If so, the cutting of the fence is a true act of iconoclasm.

Am I saying that barbed wire is more than barbed wire? Or fence more than fence? Of course not. But when the powers string it up, it gets charged with authority and fear. A circle of space is laid claim to.

The power of barbed wire is not so much in the physical barrier, but in the authority it defines and projects. The wire is revered as sacrosanct. It is a petty idol set up to mark and guard the threshold of profanely "sacred" space. Rituals of security and clearance attend it. We bow to its power by turning our heads. No looking or thinking or questioning beyond this point. The barrier is really to consciousness itself.

Among the political and theological issues here is the question of sovereignty. That barbed wire and the law that runs through it like an electrical charge are simply the front for bigger idols behind. The claim of the nuclear-armed powers is to more than just a circle of turf or even a realm of technology; the claim is to history itself. They pretend to direct it, manipulating events with the perpetual threat of death. They fiddle with the fate of the earth. Any challenge to those big claims will sooner (most likely) or later meet up with the lesser pretensions of barbed wire.

Recently a Methodist church in Detroit publicly declared its sanctuary a political refuge for resisters to draft registration. This declaration is simply an acknowledgment of what every act of Christian worship proclaims: that God is sovereign in our lives and in history. The claim of the church has been that when push comes to shove, the long arm of the law, or better, the reach of political authority, stops at the sanctuary door. A limit is affirmed.

All this comes back around to barbed wire because in recent years

Christians have more and more been taking their prayer and worship to the boundaries of nuclear weapons facilities. By this means the way of the cross is lifted up as a real alternative to the way of massive violence. Our stand on the question of security is clear: we celebrate the sovereignty of God in history over against the arrogant and truly blasphemous claims of the powers. Divine sovereignty is enacted in a liturgy of trespass. No legal right is being asserted as such; a holy truth is simply demonstrated.

A very good film came out a few years ago called *Day After Trinity* about physicist Robert Oppenheimer, the scientific city of Los Alamos, and the making of the first atomic bomb. The film tells the story of Oppenheimer, who was driven and single-minded in his preoccupation with the breakthroughs and necessities of building the bomb. The biographical account begins with his poetry and politics, passes through the scientific enthusiasm of the Los Alamos days, and ends showing him tragically broken (even his security clearance withdrawn) on the trash heap of the McCarthy attacks. It is, the filmmakers imply, a tragedy of classic proportions.

But we might be more precise. At one point, a young scientist reflects that Oppenheimer had made a "Faustian bargain" with the Pentagon's Gen. Groves, who was able to offer him all the resources in half the world to do history-making physics on a grand scale, in simple exchange for certain successful products. Oppenheimer delivers, it seems, heart and soul. With both political fervor and scientific fascination, he is captivated and captured. His personality changes. The metaphysical poet becomes the great administrator. His ego inflates. I hope I'm neither unkind nor unfair to say, at least on the evidence of the film, that this is a classic instance of possession in a very concrete and demystified sense.

This possession, be it moral, spiritual, or political, can happen to entire cities as well. The top secrecy of Los Alamos was a great barrier to the release of any news and information about what happened there, but that same security and secrecy was an even bigger barrier to the penetration of certain concerns into the premises. The New Mexico desert and another strand of barbed wire are the perfect elements for moral isolation.

Here again, I can't help picturing a handful of foolish American Christians trekking across the desert in their tennis shoes with a banner that says, "Stop!" and bearing leaflets that invite people to consider what they are doing and who will feel the fire of grand physics. Such a

Christian walk and prayer, regardless of liturgy or rite, may freely be called an exorcism. The intrusion of the simplest light is nothing less than the casting back or casting out of the power of dark.

It has been noted that with an amazing and unwitting consistency, people in recent years who have entered high-security nuclear weapons facilities for prayer and disarmament actions have commonly been instructed by the fifth chapter of Ephesians. They have attended there by way of preparation and meditation. The passage itself has become a source of light and a beacon to discernment. "Take no part in the unfruitful works of darkness, but instead expose them. For it is a shame even to speak of the things that they do in secret; but when anything is exposed by light it becomes visible, for anything that becomes visible is light" (Eph. 5:11–13).

Darkness: string up a circle of barbed wire and the most hideous crimes and horrifying weapons can be prepared and hidden within. Light: walk in, eyes and heart open. Look around. Pray, and maybe weep. Do the time.

Such deeds of worship and faithfulness are more often akin to holding a candle over the abyss than to lightning over the moral landscape (as we always wish). Still, if they are undertaken and offered in the gospel spirit, there is an element of exposure and true light, whether that can be readily calculated or not.

One element of exposure may come because trespass actions and their like yield some attention by the press. If the things they do in secret are mentioned in the headlines, all to the good. The papers might, thereby, fulfill some vocation to illuminate the truth, instead of aiding secrecy with silence. However, a caution is in order against measuring light by the column inch or confusing true illumination with news airtime. In the end this exposure runs quickly thin.

The public prayers of Christians are forever to God and not to the cameras. An action faithfully discerned and offered as a prayer, whether noticed by the media or not, may shed light that is unplanned, unexpected, and even unnoticed. More often than not, the light born to dark places comes back to the community of faith. It is among ourselves and the church that so much light is wanted.

Bishop Leroy Matthiesen of Texas, who several years ago urged members of his diocese to leave their work at the Pantex plant, has testified about this kind of unexpected light which brought his own awakening to the dark truth of the arms race. He explains that he used to drive regularly by the Pantex plant near Amarillo, where the components of all U.S. nuclear weapons are assembled. The facility is a mere four miles from St. Francis parish where he was pastor before becoming bishop.

He confesses to never thinking seriously about what went on inside. It just blended, for him, into the landscape of business-as-usual. It was just another fence on the treeless, wind-swept pasture and cropland of his parish. Then a handful of Christians early one morning transgressed that fence to pray inside, setting off an alarm and landing in jail for a year. It was as though a light went on for Bishop Matthiesen.

No one is talking here about credit or causality or even political effectiveness; there is simply a rejoicing in the work of the Spirit in and through events.

In speaking of the faith community, there is the suspicion that trespass turns quickly back on ourselves. One very tough question to be met here is the matter of secrecy in the movement. There are certain actions worthy of consideration, prayer, and embodied deed that do require an element of discretion simply to pull off. Surprise is a needful part of the entrance and the drama. The doves may need to operate with the craftiness of serpents. But (said with some trepidation) there is also a subtle temptation to draw our own circles of darkness. By justifiable degrees it's easy to mimic the masters of security, even to parody their rituals, drawing lines through the faith community.

The remedy for this temptation is not some absolute principle, Gandhian or otherwise. It has more to do with accountability to friends and community and, needless to say, the Lord of Light. It means a readiness to take the consequences—sticking around to take the heat with the light. There is a need, finally, to stand with our lives exposed.

We are not, ourselves, let it be remembered, the light. The preface to John's Gospel identifies the light with Christ Jesus. He is the one shining in the darkness and not overcome. It is abundantly clear that the light is not at all welcome in the world. He is not recognized or received, but hated and rejected. From the standpoint of the world and its claims, the incarnation is an intrusion, a divine incursion. It is, I suppose, a kind of cosmic trespass.

I am led to think of the way the New Testament speaks of the Lord's coming as a "thief in the night." The metaphor has always been troublesome to me. It evokes a little cringe. Our Lord the cat burglar. The point, of course, is the unexpected timing of things, but I suspect a further implication. Perhaps this glorified "breaking and entering" implies the breaking of our false securities. Our lives are penetrated and vulnerable. We are broken into. Here again, we find the truth sneaking in our back door.

The implication of every trespass action is the confession of our own vulnerability. People often cite (and often unfairly) the qualms that Dorothy Day reputedly had about the draft board break-in by the Catonsville Nine in 1968. Her sense of golden-rule nonviolence caused her to picture the same moral incursion into the front parlor of the Catholic Worker. I don't have the same qualms, but do regard the practical application as a spiritual insight. The Worker, of course, endured such intrusions (they poured in the front door) as part of its daily life.

Dan Berrigan, who was part of the Catonsville action, once told of being at the Pentagon with a symbolic action. A military officer stormed angrily up to him and said, "How would you like it if we did this at your house?" The implication that the Pentagon was his home is interesting in itself, but there is something provoking in the question. Berrigan, responding instinctively, promptly offered his address and said, "Why don't you come over for dinner and we'll talk?"

The practical flip side of trespass is hospitality. It is no coincidence that so many of those who cross lines open their front doors to the homeless and the stranger. And the spiritual flip side of climbing and cutting barbed wire is our own openness and vulnerability to truth.

In a liturgy of trespass we need to leave our arrogance behind. We are not the children of light facing off with the children of darkness. The sovereignty of God is not to be proclaimed as if it were really our own, as if it were a moral front, as if it were a theological extension of our certainties and claims.

God's sovereignty dictates our humility. It is practically another name for it. Before the barbed wire we need to pause, take a deep breath, and imagine that we may truly need to be forgiven for our trespass.

And then, with that freedom, in the end before God, we go ahead and act boldly. My prayer is that we do precisely that.

COMMUNITY WITH HOMELESS PEOPLE AND PRISONERS:
An Open Door in Atlanta
Joyce Hollyday

For poor people, the doors slam hard. In Atlanta, Georgia, two thousand men and women line up every day before dawn to wait for jobs handed out at the city's day-labor pools. By 7:30 A.M. they know what the day's prospects will be, and many wander off toward the city's soup kitchens.

Most have had doors shut in their faces all their lives: doors to education and jobs, access to good medical care and adequate financial support. And in increasing numbers they are being denied the most basic right of shelter.

As the homeless wander the streets of Atlanta with an aimless and cruel freedom, more than sixteen hundred men and women sit on death row in prisons across the United States. They are facing the final pronouncement that will shut them out of life itself.

The Open Door Community in Atlanta stands as a countersign to closed doors everywhere. Its name is an invitation and a reflection of a life marked by warm generosity. Compassion for those who have been locked out—the homeless—and those who have been locked in—the prisoners—gave birth to the Open Door Community and, with a strong reliance on God's grace, sustains its life.

On a chilly night in October 1984, the Open Door family—twenty-five resident guests, four resident partners and their two children, a handful of resident volunteers, and the evening's volunteer cooks—gathered around the dinner table. Joining hands, they thanked God for a partner's recovery from illness, prayed that people without homes would not be hurt by the oncoming cold, and asked that there would be no trouble in the soup kitchen lunch line the next day.

As the hands dropped, someone launched into singing "Happy Birthday to Y'All," in honor of three resident guests celebrating birthdays that week. And five-year-old Hannah and Christina ran from one to the next, offering birthday kisses to whiskered faces lit up with grins.

A rare collection of humanity shared the meal. Everyone carried a former identity: pastor, professor, and business owner mingled with carnival worker, wounded soldier, and alcoholic. What they had in common was that the Open Door had in some way transformed each of their lives.

Coleman Whatley, a veteran who suffered frostbite during World War II and cannot work, has been a resident guest for almost two years. He says of the Open Door, "We're all like sisters and brothers here," and of the resident guests, "We're the family too."

Coleman's medical records were lost at the veterans' hospital, so he is unable to receive benefits. He says he will move away if his benefits ever come through. "I'll let somebody else have the place I got, let another person have a chance like I had a chance. But I wouldn't ever forget the house. I'd come back and eat and so forth. This is the best place in the world here."

Carole Jordan, a resident guest who had recently been hit by a car, talked about the particular vulnerability and hardships for women who live on the streets. She shared her gratitude for a safe place to live and a loving environment without harsh regimentation.

She said the Open Door is "not just a physical environment, it's a spiritual environment, like a loving home. These people live like Christ did—surrounded by people who are sick, poor, and destitute. They live it, they don't just preach it."

It was a desire to live the gospel that took hold of the Open Door's founders eleven years ago and turned their lives upside down. In 1975 the first crack of light came, and eventually led to a door being flung wide open.

Ed Loring, a professor at Columbia Seminary in Decatur, Georgia, was called to pastor Clifton Presbyterian Church, a dying inner-city parish in Atlanta. Murphy Davis, also an ordained Presbyterian minister and Ed's wife, was in a Ph.D. program in church history at Emory University.

With the commitment and charisma that Ed brought to the work, young people soon flocked to the church and its life was revived. Though Murphy and Ed had never given Scripture or prayer much priority in their lives, they decided to begin a Sunday night Bible study at the church.

Their eyes began to open to new possibilities, and scriptures such as Isaiah 58:6–7—"Is this not the fast that I choose . . . to let the oppressed go free . . . to share your bread with the hungry; and bring the homeless poor into your house"—soon started to change their lives. They turned their backs on promising academic and ministerial careers to follow the gospel to new ground.

Rob and Carolyn Johnson were among those drawn to Clifton in search of a church community. Foundational to their individual lives and their marriage was a commitment to serve the poor, and they had worked for a number of years as social workers in Georgia and South Carolina. They had grown frustrated with the "professionalization" of ministry and social work and came to Clifton seeking a more faithful way to serve.

In the fall of 1978, Ed, Murphy, Carolyn, Rob, and a few other church members began to meet on Wednesday nights for supper, Bible study, and prayer at the Johnsons' apartment. This group came together after the larger Clifton congregation had been unsuccessful in attempting to focus its mission. For eight months the group focused on one central question: "God, what would you have us to do?"

The first answer to that prayer came, according to Ed, as "Cast our lives with the poor. We recognized then that the call to serve God is a call to serve the poor."

"How, God, how?" was the second question begging for an answer. On a January 1979 trip to the Maryhouse Catholic Worker in New York, Murphy and Ed were deeply touched by the generous and warm hospitality offered to the homeless people there. On the train returning to Atlanta, they tearfully read through *The Long Loneliness*, an autobiography of Dorothy Day, founder of the Catholic Worker movement. It was then that they embraced the call to hospitality.

Murphy and Ed shared the conviction with Carolyn and Rob, who responded with enthusiasm. They considered opening Clifton Church as an overnight shelter for homeless people, but decided by April 1979 that it "just wasn't practical." The church was too small, and the problems too big. Both Carolyn and Murphy were pregnant, and Rob needed back surgery. They decided they were going to "study the issue" for another year.

But as cold weather came on in the late fall, they felt compelled to open the church's doors to up to thirty homeless men on November 1, 1979.

They faced almost overwhelming odds. Hannah Loring-Davis was just ten days old when the shelter opened, and Christina Johnson was just a few months old. Rob was flat on his back following surgery a week before. Ed broke out in sores on his hands and face from all the cleaning up of the shelter he did with disinfectant.

They opened the shelter during the time that so many black Atlanta children were being murdered, and white people in a van trying to invite people off the street were greeted with the deepest suspicion. The first night they had only three people, and by the third day they were down to one.

But word soon got out on the street that there was a church serving good food, and the numbers swelled to capacity and beyond. The overnight guests enthusiastically pitched in with the work, and some of the burden began to be lifted.

Carolyn reflects that one of the strengths of the community is that "we've always started things before we're ready, and we always do a little more than we can." In their risk and sacrifice, the grace has always been given to them to find a way.

Two feelings grew over the next several months. The first was a deepening commitment between the two families that had begun the shelter. In July 1980 they went off together on retreat in North Carolina and wrote and signed a covenant, affirming their commitment to one another as the basis of their ministry. The Open Door was born.

The second feeling was a dissatisfaction with the limits of their ministry. The walk the homeless had to make from downtown to the church seemed to grow longer and further. Carolyn, Rob, Murphy, and Ed found it more and more painful to put the guests back on the streets and close the church door each morning. And many needs of the homeless still went unmet: simple needs like showers and clean clothing, as well as need for medical care or legal help in many cases.

The four discovered that Atlanta's population included four thousand homeless people, and that not one place existed for round-the-clock care and hospitality. Their desire to live with those they were serving intensified.

In February 1981, during days of prayer and reflection at the Trappist Monastery in Conyers, they decided to leave Clifton Church and find a place to develop a residential Christian community and house of hospitality. The decision felt very frightening, a choice to "put everything on the line." But for them it was the only choice.

After a long and frustrating search for a building to call home, they finally found a former Women's Union Mission at 910 Ponce de Leon Avenue. It had plenty of space for guests as well as the two families and was, according to Murphy, "clearly a gift of God."

The doors officially opened in joyful celebration on Christmas Day 1981. The chef of an exclusive Atlanta restaurant offered to cook Christmas dinner at the Open Door for one hundred people from off the streets. The meal was a gourmet feast including stuffed mushrooms, oysters and pecans, broccoli with Hollandaise sauce, and pumpkin pie with whipped cream. Murphy recalled the words of the Catholic Worker's Stanley Vishnewski, "Nothing is too good for the poor."

Since no one at the Open Door produces an income, such gifts— though not all quite so fancy—are important to the community's sustenance. The Trappists at the Conyers Monastery deliver two hundred loaves of freshly baked bread each week, and donations also come from the Atlanta food bank and the convention center; one thousand pieces of fried chicken after an insurance convention was a recent windfall.

Many professional people donate their services at the Open Door. Lawyers do advocacy work for the resident guests and others who come by to the monthly legal clinic. Once a month an ophthalmologist tests eyes and gives out used eyeglasses, offering clear vision to many for the first time. Art lessons are offered every other Saturday, and several resident guests participate in an Alcoholics Anonymous meeting, a rare and crucial gift for homeless people, many of whom battle alcoholism.

Perhaps the most unique ministry offered by the Open Door is that of Ann Connor, known as the "foot angel" among Atlanta's street people. Once a week Ann, a registered nurse, bathes and cares for the sore and blistered, sometimes bleeding and frostbitten feet of people who spend their lives walking miles and miles on concrete and asphalt, usually in shoes that don't fit.

Five days a week the clothes closet, organized by one of the resident guests, is open. People from the street can exchange their old clothing for a new set and get a hot shower. Lunch is served at the soup kitchen every day.

The various services of the Open Door have grown in response to the needs of Atlanta's poor people. A breakfast program was begun downtown at a day-labor center when Ed discovered that those who get jobs go off to a day's work on empty stomachs. When the Atlanta city government forced them to stop serving, they moved the daily breakfast to Butler Street Christian Methodist Episcopal Church.

Ed has spent many hours in Atlanta's day-labor centers talking with those who have been forced by desperation to wait for such work. Financial insecurity and exploitation are inherent in this system, in which companies pay the labor pools for work and they in turn hand out only minimum wage to the workers. The labor pools also often deduct fees for transportation to the work site.

The work, according to Ed, is always "the most difficult, dangerous, or demeaning," the kind of work permanent laborers will not do. He told stories of people he knew who worked three or four days at a time at an aerosol oven cleaner factory until their skin broke out in sores and burns from contact with acid, and of a man who fell from a dangerous bridge and broke his back. "It is worse than the slave market. At least slave owners had an economic investment in the flesh of the slave. There are so many people seeking work, it doesn't matter what happens to them."

While spending time at the day-labor centers and on the streets, Ed learned that most homeless people will spend some time in the city jail following arrest for public urination. Atlanta had no public toilets, and people were being arrested for something for which they had no alternative. The Open Door and the Atlanta Advocates for the Homeless, a group formed to address the needs of people on the streets, began a "toilet campaign" that generated a great deal of publicity around the city. The Advocates got the Atlanta city council to hold public hearings on public toilets. The group was asking for toilets in ten locations.

The downtown Atlanta business associates marshalled their top forces and came to the hearings armed with maps. Their arguments were that public toilets would make Atlanta a mecca for the homeless and raise criminal activity in the city, and that the city would lose convention business. Ed laughed as he pictured homeless people in Washington, D.C., saying to one another, "Hey, have you heard about Atlanta?"

On December 1, the night before the city council vote on toilets, twenty-five people spent the night on the steps of city hall in a twenty-four-hour fast and vigil. The Advocates won a small victory: one "experimental" Porta John in Plaza Park in the heart of downtown Atlanta. They were so pleased that they went to the park and took pictures. Murphy remarked, "Not everyone has pictures of a toilet in their family album!"

That same month Roosevelt Richardson, a man who lived on the street, suffered the freezing and loss of his legs after the day-labor center where he usually hung out closed one day due to snow. Twenty people froze to death over Christmas weekend.

The Atlanta Advocates for the Homeless put pressure on the city government to improve the day-labor pools. In April 1983, $100,000 of federal money had been received by Atlanta for renovations of day-labor centers, including the construction of showers and toilets. A year later construction still had not begun.

On June 8 Ed took a toilet to city hall and sat on it reading Scripture, promising to stay until the city government signed a contract to begin construction on a day-labor center toilet. Murphy led the singing at the demonstration, and Ed and two others were arrested and spent the weekend in jail. That same day a contract was signed.

Murphy described the scene at the trial. "First a city solicitor asked a friend if Ed always carries a toilet when he makes business calls. Then a city hall official began telling what happened: ' . . . and then two men came in carrying a commode.' The Harvard-educated judge interrupted, 'A *what*?!' and he responded, 'A toilet.' I thought the judge would die and fall off her bench." Ed added, "We're learning what it means to be fools for Jesus."

Ed considers it part of his spiritual discipline to go not only to the day-labor centers but also to other places in the city he considers "listening posts" for hearing the cries of the poor and the voice of God. "I go as a homeless person. I know that on one hand I can never be, and on the other hand I can experience the reality of the suffering of the poor."

He goes and sits at Grady Hospital with the lame, blind, and broken. He goes to the blood bank, where the ragged poor sell their blood plasma once a week for $10. He sits in municipal court, the public library, the soup kitchens, the park. He walks alongside those raiding dumpsters for aluminum cans to sell.

He considers the regular pilgrimage a Protestant version of the "stations of the cross." It is a journey into suffering, a reminder, an experience of Jesus.

Murphy does most of her listening in prison. She is founder of the Atlanta branch of Southern Prison Ministry. She found it difficult at first to get support for her work. "A lot of people told us that if we dropped prison work, we would get a lot more support for our work with the homeless. People think the hungry are deserving, but people on death row are criminals."

In her work Murphy is both a prophetic advocate and a pastor. In Georgia more than 100 people are under the death sentence. "I used to try to meet and keep up with everybody, but with more than a hundred, I can't know them all deeply." With the current resurgence in executions,

"We're forced into a crisis orientation. . . . about all I can see are those with active execution dates or those going to trial."

When an execution takes place, Murphy organizes press conferences, worship vigils, and statements from the religious community. "These feel like foolish, little efforts, but they just can't keep killing people without somebody saying something."

Murphy ministers to prisoners' families and helps facilitate family visits to both death-row prisoners and inmates at the women's prison. She is persistent, despite the fact that prison authorities do their best to make her work difficult.

She claims that the story of the widow and the judge in Luke 18 is "one of the most instructive in dealing with prisons. The judge cared nothing for God and had no regard for human beings. But it was more expedient to give the widow her rights than wear out. We have to go back and go back and go back and make a nuisance of ourselves or we'll never accomplish anything."

Most of all, Murphy upholds the humanity of the prisoners to a society that views them, like the homeless, as expendable. She emotionally told death-row stories, such as Billy Moore's first experience of Hannah: "Hannah had more murderers as friends than the usual baby. When she was six weeks old, I took her to meet Billy. He held her and rocked her and cried over her. Billy had a son he hadn't seen since his arrest. He told me that when he knew I would bring Hannah, every night before he went to sleep he practiced holding his pillow to be sure he would hold the baby just right."

The compassion and pain come through when Murphy recounts the candlelight vigils on execution days, the contacting of families and claiming of bodies. She described their first funeral for an execution victim. "When somebody has died in a terrible way, after living an oppressed life, the way you bury them becomes so very important. It's a way to claim dignity, a symbol of life, humanity, and community."

The connections between the prison work and advocacy for the homeless are often clear at the Open Door, but never so much so as in the case of Charlie Young. Charlie Young, part of the family at the Open Door, can often be found sorting donated clothes in the clothes closet. Another Charlie Young sits on death row and has been a long-time friend of the community. Murphy had his picture one day and was showing it at the Open Door. When Charlie at the Open Door saw it, he jumped up and down in the hallway shouting, "That's my son!" Until that moment none of the people at the Open Door had made the connection. Both Charlies had been placed under the death sentence by society—Charlie Sr. left to die slowly on the streets and Charlie Jr. facing execution. Both were finding a new chance at life through the efforts of the Open Door.

Worship serves as an anchor for the partners as resident guests and volunteers come and go. Some resident guests stay for short periods of time and others make the Open Door a more-or-less permanent home. Some move in after coming to the house for showers or food, and others have more dramatic entrances.

One of the guests lived for years in a cardboard box on the parking lot of a fancy Atlanta restaurant. When the restaurant decided to expand and needed his space, he was convicted of criminal trespass. He appeared before the same judge that tried Ed's toilet action and was "sentenced" to the Open Door.

For many of the resident guests, who have been battered by a society that deems them worthless, the Open Door is a new chance and an infusion of hope. But not all the people who come into contact with the community are appreciative. Two men who had been refused entry temporarily because they were drunk decided to take revenge. They called the Atlanta Fire Department and reported "a fire at 910 Ponce de Leon." Soon the whole block was ablaze with flashing red lights as hook and ladder trucks and rescue squad vehicles made their way to the "fire." This drama was repeated three times.

Guests who have to be asked to leave, usually for reasons of alcohol, are often invited back over and over again. Forgiveness flows freely— both ways. The partners freely admit that they have made mistakes in their efforts. "We represent people that God's been very patient with," reflected Ed. They are learning to build into their life the things that will sustain them over the long haul as they see the suffering of their friends mount, as the newness of community gets further and further away, and as they experience comings and goings among them.

Ed speaks of the call to live on two edges or "front lines." One front line is that of proximity to the poor. The other is confronting the attitudes of the rich. This second call is taking on new meaning as the Open Door faces the encroachment of wealth and business on its block.

"If we live in solidarity with the poor, we will have enemies, because the poor have enemies." Ed cautions that it would be easy to escape the responsibility to face the rich. "But the gospel calls us to be on the front lines of conflict. This is the point at which we make peace."

Murphy added, "It's a gift to be where we are. It doesn't feel like it a lot of the time, but we know it is."

The Open Door Community has been a gift and an invitation to many. On one wall of the dining room hangs a quote: "Christ is the head of this house, the chosen guest at every meal, the silent listener to every conversation." On the facing wall hang the words of a Scottish rune, which ends, "The Christ comes in the stranger's guise."

To share a meal or a conversation at the Open Door is to meet Christ in many forms. It is to understand suffering and hope. And as long as it is recognized that it is Christ who comes knocking, the door will always be open.

A CHRISTIAN FEMINIST PERSPECTIVE ON ABORTION:
To Preserve and Protect Life

Ginny Earnest Soley

For a people that identifies itself as a Christian and feminist people, a necessary backdrop to the abortion question is dealing with the reality of the oppression of women in our culture. We live in a society in which sexism is an institutionalized, systematic, all-pervasive reality. We live in a culture that is patriarchal, which means much more than the rule of husbands and fathers over women and children.

Patriarchy involves a very complex system of class and race and gender hierarchies. Patriarchy also involves the rule of colonizers over colonized people, landowners over land workers, and light-skinned people over dark-skinned people. A part of that is male control over women—their work, their bodies, and their children. It is important to realize that in the system of patriarchy, children are considered primarily the result of the male seed and are valued mostly for that reason.

It is also important to note that women in this culture do not have a monolithic experience. Women are members of different class and racial groups, and, as a result, they don't all share the same kind of struggle or the same kind of oppression. Some women in our culture, in fact, benefit from the system of patriarchy and are privileged under that system. For that reason we need to realize that when we talk of oppression, we are referring to some men and some women. That whole complex makes it difficult to make general statements, but we should not allow that to mask certain realities. In a patriarchal culture like ours, women as a class of people are oppressed.

To recognize that women are an oppressed class of people is a necessary step when we are talking about abortion, an issue that involves freedom and choice and justice. These are very, very important words and concepts to people who are oppressed.

In the United States, women are under-represented in all areas of government and in the legal system. The lawmakers are men, by and large. Women have the right to vote but are not elected or appointed to decision-making positions in any substantial numbers. The laws in this land reflect that reality. Our constitutional rights are not guaranteed as they are for some men.

In the area of education, the discrimination is obvious. Women's wage-earning potential is markedly different from that of men. White men, with the greatest wage-earning potential, earn close to twice as much money as black men, who are followed by white women, with black women earning the least in this country. Moreover, women, white and black, are relegated to what we might call job ghettos—areas of work that are mostly service-oriented and extensions of domestic work, such as child care and food services.

Many women live in relationships with men who are coercive, abusive, and hostile. In the culture at large, women are objectified as products, in the areas of prostitution and pornography, and as sales devices for everything from cars to alcohol to clothing. Women are exploited as workers, both in the labor force and at home.

It is also important to realize, although probably a little more difficult to understand, the way in which women are excluded from the myths and the symbol systems in our culture that make us less than fully human. That seems to indicate that we are less than full participants in human history.

One of the most obvious symbol systems from which women are excluded is language. We find ourselves excluded when, for example, "man" is meant to represent all humanity, and that has a strong impact on our psyches.

Given the realities of the oppression of women in our culture, it has been very difficult for many feminists to participate in the abortion debate and identify themselves as pro-life. Many people who participate in that debate from a pro-life position do not acknowledge the oppression of women in our culture or the rest of the world. Even though women live in the most unequal of circumstances, when it comes to the issue of abortion, women are assigned equal moral responsibility and are assumed to be equally empowered. That is a frustrating fact for many women and for many feminists.

In order to deal with abortion, we must deal with the reality of the oppression of women as a class of people within a patriarchal culture. From that perspective the question of abortion really becomes a question of justice. What does it mean to do justice? What does it mean to bring forth justice for women and their children?

This way of looking at abortion is characteristic of the liberal feminist perspective, which puts forth an agenda with which I am not in complete agreement. However, I am deeply grateful for the work that women have done through the centuries and continue to do toward its goals; it is because of that liberal feminist agenda that I have the right to vote and that many points of discrimination have been challenged, both legislatively and constitutionally.

The limitations of the liberal feminist agenda become particularly clear in relationship to moral issues. It attempts to deal with questions such as abortion in a moral vacuum. This agenda says that each individual has the right to determine for herself what is the path to fulfillment and happiness, and that somehow we do that apart from relationship with the rest of humanity. The focus is on the individual.

This kind of analysis leads feminists such as Betty Friedan—whom I greatly respect—to say that we've made great strides as women because now women as well as men have their fingers on the nuclear button. That perspective misses the moral question as to whether there ought to be a nuclear button. It basically says that whatever have been advantages for white, propertied men are desirable for everyone else.

When we look at the question of children, we realize that men have had great control over their time, money, career choices, and options for leisure because they have been free from the burden of responsibility for children. I don't mean at all to say that some men haven't chosen to be responsible for children; they have, but it has been a choice. It is equally true that many men haven't been responsible for the children they fathered and have, in fact, walked away from them. Many men, even when they have remained present, aren't responsible for children to the extent that women are.

Liberal feminism looks at this and says the problem is that women have been responsible for children and that burdening women solely with this responsibility is a way that men control women. The solution they arrive at is a logical one—that the way for women to gain greater freedom is to remove the responsibility for children, particularly children who are unplanned. In the framework of liberal feminism, it makes sense to assume that since men have had this option, women need the same option. It's a response that says that where there is inequality, women should gain equality.

The decision to abort a child is often seen as an issue of a woman's right to self-determination. The question of self-determination for women is an important one, because history has taught us that men, particularly when in positions of power, do not always have women's best interests at heart. When a woman is faced with an unplanned pregnancy, she is not likely to trust legislators. She is not likely to trust judges. She is often unable to trust a clergyman, and too often she doesn't trust her husband or male companion.

The particular and unique contribution of Christian feminism is to question two assumptions. The first assumption it questions is that the individual's self-interest is, in fact, the highest value. The second assumption it questions is the vision of justice that pits a woman's rights against a child's right to life, that forces us to see only one victim over and against another victim.

What we need to find is a way that is good for both mother and child. In the Christian worldview, the highest value extends beyond individual self-interest to what is good for the whole of the community. The responsibility for anything we do also extends beyond the individual to the whole of the community.

A Christian perspective, therefore, would broaden our circle of trust. It would say that as women we can depend on other people and that as Christians we intend to take responsibility for other people as well. It is very important that we not be naive about the real sufferings of women who face a crisis pregnancy and the possibility of raising a child without sufficient resources. As Christians we have the capacity to look at suffering and call it suffering, to look at pain and know that it is real pain and not blind ourselves to it.

It's important as well that we don't romanticize women who have abortions. Women don't have a monolithic experience in this culture, and women choose to have abortions out of a number of different contexts. But when we look at the question "What does justice require?" we need to look at the woman in the situation who is the most victimized, who has the fewest options, and apply our perspective on abortion to see if it bears up in that worst of circumstances. Then we ask the question, "What is an agenda for justice that would respond to her needs?"

Justice requires that all young men and women have good educational opportunities, that they have some hope for meaningful work in their lives, that they can expect to be paid a fair wage for the work that they do, that they be in situations that increase their sense of self-esteem and self-confidence. Justice requires that we work for healthier relationships between boys and girls, between men and women, relationships that are mutual and not coercive. At the same time, we should work against violence, the unilateral violence by men toward women.

Justice requires clear education about human sexuality, research for more safe and effective contraceptive methods, better prenatal and postnatal medical care, and support for women experiencing unplanned pregnancies. Justice requires support for family systems as well—for families who are trying to cope with a crisis pregnancy, for any man and woman who are trying to stay married in the midst of a difficult time, for people who have children with birth defects. It requires quality day care for children and adequate paternity and maternity leave.

When we look at this agenda for social change, we realize that it is overwhelming. We are far from having adequate support systems for women with crisis pregnancies. It is easy to see why people say that the simplest or easiest solution to an unplanned pregnancy is the solution of abortion—that the child not be born and that the young woman have the responsibility of that child taken from her.

But abortion leaves unaddressed the real issues and, in fact, adds a moral poverty to the physical poverty already present. It adds further psychological pain to the pain already suffered. We should not put women into a position without resources and then further damage them by encouraging abortions.

I believe that women are damaged by having abortions, psychologically, spiritually, and, often, physically. My word to women facing the difficult decision about abortion is not a word of condemnation but a word of encouragement that says that if we are really working at this together, we can do better. We don't have to settle for something that is life-destroying and painful.

We must be careful what we say to women who have had abortions and feel the guilt and the pain of that decision. What they need from Christians is a word of forgiveness. They need to be invited into a community that has room for them, to be encouraged to carry on with life, and to be healed.

From the words of the women interviewed in Linda Francke's book *The Ambivalence of Abortion*, it is clear that they were not people who had a number of positive options and, out of moral insensitivity, chose to have an abortion. They were often women who conceived the child in a very unhealthy, unstable relationship.

These women felt that they could not bear the responsibility of the child alone. They did not have confidence in themselves, and they also did not have confidence in the man with whom they were in relationship. Often they said, "He did not want me to have the child, so I had an abortion."

The sense that we get in reading their stories is that they are women who have had abortions against their better instincts, and they are suffering for it. Their better instincts were to preserve and protect life. I do not want to imply that women have inherently different instincts than men. But we live in a culture that intentionally numbs those life-preserving instincts in our future soldiers, generals, and corporate executives. I would suggest that the job of Christian feminism is not to numb those life-preserving instincts in women but to reawaken them in men and keep them alive in all of us.

Abortion is not a means of bringing about justice. Abortion is, finally, an act of giving in to despair. The decision to have an abortion reflects a woman's lack of confidence in herself. It means that she does not trust the man with whom she is in relationship. It means that she has no belief in long-lasting, long-term, stable relationships between men and women. In fact, it means that she has lost confidence in life itself.

By accepting the alternative of abortion as a society, we say that we don't intend to make any effort to bring about justice for women and that we don't intend to put forth any effort to guarantee a good life for children. The gospel challenges that despair with the declaration that life is essentially good, that God is still at work in the world bringing about redemption, and that healing and reconciliation are possible. As naive as it may sound in the face of overwhelming odds and very desperate situations, we need to speak of hope for the future and say that the lives of women and children can be lives of bearing good fruit, of justice, and of health and happiness.

Liberal feminists have stated that the problem lies in the fact that women have been responsible for children, and they have offered one solution: women should not have to be responsible for children. What Christian people need to say is that there is another solution: women and men can be responsible for children, and the community of faith can be responsible for children. But the society as a whole also can be made a place where children can be born and have a good life.

Children are a sign that life is still worthwhile. Accepting them into our lives is an act of faith. Protecting human life is a way of worshiping God, who is the creator and originator of life.

To destroy life in its very beginning is a statement that says there is no reason to have faith that life can work out for the good. It is a statement that life can't be fruitful and won't be worthwhile. That reflects a lack of trust and lack of faith in God and in what God has created and continues to redeem. I firmly believe that God intends that life be good and that all life be worth living.

THE CHALLENGE OF RACIAL
RECONCILIATION: In the Middle
Catherine Meeks

Catherine Meeks is an instructor and the director of Afro-American studies at Mercer University in Macon, Georgia. She is working on an interdisciplinary doctorate at Emory University in Atlanta, combining studies in Jungian psychology, women in West Africa, and Afro-American literature. Meeks was interviewed by Liane Rozzell in December 1985.

—The Editor

Liane Rozzell: *How did you first become involved in work on racism, and why do you continue?*

Catherine Meeks: The first time in my life that I realized race in America was something I had to address myself to was as a college student at Pepperdine University in Los Angeles. A sixteen-year-old boy named Larry was shot and killed on our campus by a campus security guard. This was in the mid-sixties when black people were very tired of having that kind of thing happen and having everybody say, "Well, isn't that too bad," and just go on about their business.

So we, as black students, waged a lot of protests around the whole event—how the funeral was handled, how the family was dealt with, and how the security guard was dealt with. Larry's death led to a time of questioning for me, a time of trying to figure out what kind of response I, as a Christian, should make in this situation.

I was a member of a black student organization, and I wanted to be really committed to it. But I also had a fairly strong and long-standing Christian commitment. I went to my church for advice, and their advice was that I should stay home until the whole situation got settled. To think that somebody who's supposed to be a Christian should run away from a situation where it looks like they could make a difference was appalling to me!

I was only twenty years old, working my way through school and trying to help take care of my sister, so it wasn't like I was "looking for a cause"; I was not. But somehow, in a way that wasn't completely thought out, I found myself at the house of the boy who got killed; I found myself talking to college administrators; I found myself in meetings with my peers in the black students' organization; I found myself in the white prayer group on campus. And in all these groups, we were talking about the situation and about what we should be doing. Somehow it became clear to me that as a black person I couldn't run away from those issues of racism and that my own well-being was mixed up in all of this.

While I was in college, I responded more out of passion and a sense of commitment to God. But looking back on those years now, I don't think I ever had a choice not to be involved. Even then I seemed to be geared toward reconciling. I was always trying to listen or to call people to look at both sides. And that's a lot of what I did during the events around Larry's death. By my mere involvement, I was forced to look into other points of view.

I was a scared, young woman from an Arkansas farm in the middle of a big problem on a campus in Los Angeles. I didn't have any idea what all that meant. I was just there. And in the middle. That was a funny place to be. And it's that funny place I've been in ever since.

I guess it wasn't until the mid-seventies that I started to really understand that racial reconciliation in America is an issue that black and white people have to confront personally, as an issue of wholeness. I suppose I could live my life saying, "I will never allow myself to try to understand white people. I will cut myself off from them. I will live my life as a black woman, and I'll just keep white people in boxes." But to do that means to keep myself cut off from a part of myself. And if white people do that about black people, I think the same is true: it keeps them cut off from a part of themselves.

For those of us who are Christians, I don't think we have any choice in the matter. I think God has made it clear that we're to be reconciled to God and each other. And if we're to be reconciled to each other, that includes everyone who happens to be in the world with us.

Reconciliation demands that you not take sides; it demands that you take a stand, I think—a stand that's maybe a merging of a lot of different pieces that represent several different kinds of philosophical stances. I think that one who chooses a road of reconciliation must be willing to look at more than one side of the coin.

Some people would say, "Racial reconciliation is fine and good, but black people need to get together and deal with their internalized racism and build a strong self-image apart from white people before they can enter a reconciliation process. And white people need to work at dealing with their racism before they go into a reconciliation process." How would you respond to that?

I think that's true. You have to have some sense of yourself before you're able to really call other people into accountability and get other people to deal with how they're responding to you. But I think we have to be very careful not to use that as an excuse for staying in our little pockets, safe and secure, and never dealing with the internal racial dynamics, either on the black side or the white side.

It seems to me that none of us is going to deal with racial dynamics unless we're forced to. And by interacting with one another, we are forced to confront some things we wouldn't otherwise deal with. I don't have to confront racism the same way if I'm dealing with another black person as I do if I'm dealing with a white person. Racial interrelatedness does, at least, present the issues to both sides.

What are some of the good experiences you've had during the time you've been involved in racial reconciliation?

The best experience occurred when I graduated from college and became part of a group called the Los Angeles Black and White Women's Camp-in Group. We were a group of community women and Pepperdine University women who decided to get together for a retreat in the summer of 1969 to have discussions about racial issues.

It grew out of a relationship between a white woman who was the dean of students at Pepperdine and a black woman who was very involved in Christian education in the city of Los Angeles. The friendship between those two women, and the vision they had for trying to call some black and white women together, arose out of the tensions that were occurring in the mid to late sixties and the early seventies.

Out of that summer meeting grew a group of women who have been meeting for about twenty years now. The group is made up of older women and younger women coming from different educational back-grounds. But the women in that group really have made some commitments to one another in trying to understand what it means to be black and what it means to be white.

There are also a lot of one-on-one experiences of seeing someone really be transformed. A couple of years ago, I was doing a three-day retreat for a group of Methodist women. The retreat wasn't particularly about race, but there's no way I can go into a retreat for three days and not talk about race relations when there are four hundred white women and I'm the only black person there.

I remember one woman whose husband was an employer with a large company, and a lot of his employees were black. She lived in an area where it would have been unheard of for her to have any kind of gathering, and invite the black employees to come be with the white ones. She had been really struggling with the idea of having some kind of party for her husband's employees. But her struggle was: was she going to invite everybody over or was she just going to invite the white people?

She said it never felt right for her just to invite the white people, but she wasn't sure if she had the courage to invite the blacks, too. And at the end of that weekend, she said, "Being here has helped me to come to terms with this, and I'm having this party and inviting all the folks who work for my husband."

You know, that was a little step. But I think that if there are going to be significant changes in this country, they're going to be made by common people, like that woman, who are not willing to accept that it's all right to keep doing things the same way they've been done for hundreds of years.

What are the things that discourage you the most in this work? What are the bad experiences you've had?

I'm fortunate in that most people who have been in audiences when I've spoken about race have been polite enough not to throw eggs at me. A few times I've had somebody walk out of a meeting, which is always a shocking experience. Sometimes I think, "Well, maybe they're going to the rest room or something." But a woman got up out of one meeting and yelled at me as she was going out. So, it was rather clear that she was leaving because of me, and it had nothing to do with her having to go to the rest room!

I have gotten anger from people in workshops, and sometimes folks come up to me to set me straight or to tell me how good they are. That's discouraging. I don't really know about the people who just leave and dismiss me without saying anything. But the folks who try to convince me how great, how liberal, and how open-minded they are discourage me even more than the angry people, because the angry people stand a better chance of making some changes.

It's the white people or the black people who say, "I never had any prejudice" who are frightening to me, because that's obviously not true.

They don't even know themselves well enough to know that they do have some prejudice. I don't think anyone can walk around in America without having some racial prejudices.

When I look at where we are in 1986 compared to where we were in 1955 or 1965, I get discouraged. In attitudes I don't think we've made any progress. Maybe we've made a bit of progress, but it's minimal. I think the systemic changes were made just because people were forced to make them by legal structures and not because people had any significant changes of heart.

When I look at the economic and spiritual conditions the majority of black people live in, I sometimes find myself close to despair. We had a big fanfare about racial equality, racial awareness, and black conscious-ness in the sixties and early seventies, and now people seem to think, "Well, we've done that, so we don't have to do anything else." Well, we *didn't* do it. We didn't do it then, and it's still yet to be done. The fact that we're sitting down as if we did it and we can rest now is disturbing to me.

I think young black folks, with their rage and their disillusionment with living in this culture, are going to force us to look at these issues again in a much more straightforward way. And I'm sorry about that, because I think we spent enough energy and blood in the sixties that we should never have to do that again. But we just don't learn from our history.

You have talked about the connection between racism and sexism. How have you experienced this connection?

It's a very profound connection, a connection that white people have a hard time making. Let me be more specific. It's a connection that white women have a hard time making, and it's a connection that black men have a hard time making, because it's not to either group's advantage to make the connection.

White women traditionally have wanted to say, "Because we under-stand sexism, we are not racist"—which is really a joke. Black men have said, "Because we know racism, we are not sexist"—which is equally a joke. And white men, of course, have just been racist and sexist, and they go on as if that's the way you're supposed to be.

For white women to say, "Sexism is really where we need to be focused, and this is what we need to be doing" is to ignore what black women have had to confront since the first black women set foot in this land. For black men to think that because they were enslaved and emasculated they somehow have an edge on oppression and therefore can't possibly be patriarchal and sexist is equally as crazy.

As with so many other things, it has fallen into the laps of black women to call attention to that connection between racism and sexism, because we are victimized on both sides of the coin. And as black women, we are left then to try to figure out what we're going to do about racism, what we're going to do about sexism, and who we're going to try to build coalitions with.

Our coalitions with white women have failed because white women won't acknowledge the whole of our problem. Yet they want our expertise and our energy to help them get something that they're not willing to share with us when they get it—the power that comes from being liberated.

We don't have any choice but to build coalitions with black men. They're part of our lives; it's not as if we can say, "Well, we don't want to have anything to do with you." So we have to try and figure out how to have relationships with the men who can't seem to see what they have done to us by not acknowledging their own sexism.

It leaves us in a funny position. I think it may force us as black women to finally come together as a group. I don't think black women are going to work all this out without building coalitions. But we must be sensitive as to whether or not folks we're working with are really willing to understand the whole of the problem. Sexist oppression, racist oppression, and classist oppression—all of it equals oppression, and you can't have integrity in your stand against oppressors without standing against all oppressors, wherever they happen to be.

I have an unmerciful analysis of the white women's movement, because I've been in conversations with white women who wanted me to take sides. They wanted me to take a stand on the side of fighting sexism and not to stand against both racism and sexism. They somehow wanted to associate fighting racism with patriarchy or with standing with men. That's the kind of split no black woman in her right mind can afford to make.

How do you explain what racism is and how it is that people are racist?

Racism is a combination of prejudice and power. You can be prejudiced, I think, and have no power. Some poor white person who has no education, no money, and hates black folks can do far less to me than a white person who is the manufacturer of a product or who runs a business.

Power is used to enforce your prejudice and to keep other people from realizing gains and rewards in the culture simply because of your prejudice against them. It's personal as well as systemic.

When white people say, "I'm not a racist," they think of themselves not as somebody who wants to abuse and misuse somebody else because of the color of their skin. The way the average white person participates in racism, even if they're not somebody who would condone it, is by enjoying the gains that have come in a society that is built on the backs of black people and by enjoying the economic and political power that has come to them because of the color of their skin. By accepting that power as a birthright, white people enjoy the benefits and rewards of what their racist forefathers left for them, even if they don't use their power to exploit other people.

As for prejudices, we cannot live in this country as blacks and whites without having some disregard, I think, toward one another, because it's just in the air. If you're black, you don't have to necessarily grow up hating white people, but you grow up knowing you're black, and with a sense that it means something different than if you're white.

Now what often happens with white people is that they grow up not really knowing or having to think about race. They grow up in a kind of "a-racial" atmosphere, and because they're in control of everything or their parents are powerful, they're not threatened, and they don't have to deal with racism. That person is not much less prejudiced than the one who grew up being told not to "sit down at the table with niggers." Both of them are equally a problem for me as a black woman, because if your racism is that unconscious, you're a problem; and if you consciously act negatively toward me, you're also a problem. So you don't get off the hook either way, as far as I'm concerned.

What can people do about their racism, whatever the combination of prejudice and power it happens to be?

They can start out by really trying to think about who they are and how they got to be that person. Then they can examine their attitudes toward everybody who happens to be different than them.

One of my friends told me that she never thought she was racist or prejudiced. She always thought she was open-minded and accepting of everybody, and for the most part she was. Then, all of a sudden, she came home hysterical after taking her son to school for the first day, because he was going to have a black teacher. Somewhere in her was a stereotype of what a black person is that characterized black people as inferior. She was appalled at herself, and, thank God, she was willing to confront that in herself. If white people want to deal with their prejudices and if black people want to deal with their prejudices, they need to have that kind of self-reflection.

What can people do about their prejudices? I think if people really get serious about this, they can refuse to live their lives in isolated, homogeneous groups. It's important to be willing to go into situations where you know you're going to find people of a different class, a different educational background, or a different race, whose philosophies are different. It's easier to be with people who are just like ourselves. But there's no reason in the world why you can't interact with people who have different political ideologies, different religions, and who have been socialized in different ways from you. Such interactions help you to catch glimpses of your prejudices and help you deal with them.

I once did an internship in a public hospital where I worked with cancer patients, some of whom were white, many of whom were black, and most of whom were poor. It forced me to look at and relate to a whole different kind of person from the graduate school crowd or the college teachers' crowd I'm used to. If we're serious in dealing with our prejudices, then we need to force ourselves out of our boxes.

But you can't go into this kind of process like it's a sightseeing trip. You've got to have openness and sensitivity; you have to be careful not to feel superior or be the one who's in control.

How does your doctoral dissertation relate to your work on racism and to your view of yourself as a black woman?

My dissertation is on black women and feminism. Its title is "The Mule of the World: A Jungian Investigation into the Afro-American Woman's Struggle Against Sexist Oppression." In the last five years, I've been studying Carl Jung, and my graduate work is focused on Jung and African culture and Afro-American culture. I'm looking to writers Zora Neale Hurston and Alice Walker, using them as examples of the evolution of consciousness in black women over a fifty-year period.

What I'm trying to do is a historical overview of what black women have been doing in their struggle against sexism. I'm trying to look at whether you can discover archetypes in the black woman's experience that are peculiar just to the black woman. And if so, what are they, and how have they fueled the black woman's struggle against sexism?

Black women have been talked about too much as stereotypes. We've been looked at as the matriarch or the mammy—the "earth mother." Or we're seen as the "loose woman" in high-heeled red shoes and a red dress—the harlot. There are other dimensions of our personalities that have never really been acknowledged. I don't think my dissertation will take care of the whole problem, but it's a beginning place.

The whole project has been one of enhancing my own journey, because at the bottom of all of this searching of Jung, black women, feminism, and Africa has been my own undying question about what it means to be a black woman in the world. It's been a continuation of a quest to understand myself better as a black woman and as a person of faith trying to journey through life with integrity.

If you find something that's true for you, a real temptation is to say, "Now I understand; I've got the puzzle figured out." Like they did in the Bible, you want to build a tabernacle, and you don't ever want to leave that spot—because we are all looking for security and a place to be comfortable.

But the better response is, "I see this little piece of the truth; it encourages me to keep looking—and to keep traveling." The kind of quest we're on will never end until we die. We don't ever "arrive"; we're always just on the way.

MARRIAGE AND PARENTING:
Discovering Mutuality
Rob and Ginny Earnest Soley

Ginny Earnest Soley and Rob Soley have been married for fifteen years and have two children, Annie and Jacob. Ginny and Rob experienced dramatic changes in their relationship and their view of the world when Christian faith and feminism entered their lives. They joined Sojourners Community in 1980.

Ginny is assistant pastoral coordinator of Sojourners Community and Rob is a teacher at Christian Family Montessori School in Mt. Rainier, Maryland, where Annie is a student. They were interviewed by Joyce Hollyday and Karen Lattea.
— The Editor

Hollyday and Lattea: As a starting point, would you explain what your marriage was like before you discovered feminism, and what assumptions you brought to your relationship with each other?

Ginny Earnest Soley: Rob and I grew up in Philadelphia in working-class families. We got married when we were fairly young, both in terms of experience and self-awareness. Rob had gone to college for a little while, but mostly to play soccer. I hadn't gone to school beyond high school. I think we came into our relationship without thinking through the questions and issues that a lot of people think through before they get married.

Rob Soley: We had, sort of by osmosis, learned from our families what marriage meant. We fell into the traditional roles for the environment we grew up in.

For example, in the beginning of our marriage, Ginny and I both worked full-time, but it was always Ginny's job to come home and cook and do the dishes. My big favor to her was that I read the newspaper in the kitchen, while she was doing the dinner dishes. That was just the norm. That was what we saw.

Ginny: I grew up with a strong sense that who I was in life was going to be determined by the man I married, that my own individual accomplishments were not particularly meaningful one way or the other. My mom felt that my hope for a good future was tied to my "catching" a man who was going to succeed. In her mind I passed up a lot of good opportunities and then married Rob, who I think I knew wasn't going to get wealthy and be successful in my mother's terms. It was almost as though I was choosing not to marry somebody who was going to take care of me the rest of my life.

Another important reflection on our relationship at the time is that I remember being afraid of Rob when we were dating and when we first got married. I don't know that I had any good reason to be afraid of him; I think that was just my attitude toward men and my posture in the world. I felt fairly powerless and vulnerable to whoever Rob turned out to be in our relationship. I remember not questioning decisions and not challenging him. My sense was that I was better off married than not married, but there was a difference of roles and an imbalance of power.

What brought about the change to a feminist perspective in your lives?

Rob: We started reading the Gospels together, and our religious selves came out of the closet. We had never talked about God because it was a taboo subject for me. We began to see in the Gospels and in Jesus an acceptance and a kind of love that we had never even thought possible. And I remember being really excited about that.

It had immediate implications in terms of how we treated each other. We weren't involved in the church, and we didn't know any other Christians. We had each other. So there was a kind of immediate application in our relationship of "Love your neighbor as yourself."

We also both decided to leave our jobs and go to Bethlehem, Pennsylvania, where we knew one Christian. He was starting an urban project for Christian street workers to reach out to the local kids in the urban part of Bethlehem. That was when the real work began in changing our relationship. We moved into a household with two single men.

Ginny: Wasn't it about eight single men?

Rob: The other two men had not lived away from home before, other than at college, and they had come from very traditional households like mine. Ginny and I had been married for less than a year when we moved into this house.

And in the outreach project, all the men were expected to do the street work. There was nothing for women to do except get coffee at meetings.

Ginny: The staff women in Young Life, the organization we were with, led songs and prepared meals for camping trips. Everything was based on the sexist assumption that the men take the lead and the women do the "behind the scenes" and support work.

We were in a region that was connected to New York City, and we had people from Chinatown, Yonkers, and the Bronx. They were working with issues of racism and with street gangs and poor people. So in our region, there was a concern for justice, but feminism hadn't quite hit yet.

At the same time, we were affected by the very conservative wing of the Presbyterian church, as represented by Bill Gothard. They said, "As long as you stay under your protective umbrella" in the hierarchy of authority, God will be faithful to you.

Rob: Gothard believed the hierarchy, or "chain of command," was a God-given thing, and the order was God, government, man, woman, child.

Ginny: I think we were experiencing the church in its initial stages of reaction to the secular feminist movement. For a long time, churches operated under the assumption of that hierarchy without articulating it. And when the secular feminist movement began to question some of that, the church responded by taking hold of and making that hierarchy of authority a very clear part of its theology.

Upon becoming a Christian, for the first time in my life I really took myself seriously and looked at who I was and at my gifts and my potential. I had always thought that I wasn't a smart person, and I didn't do very much reading. All of a sudden, I wanted to read everything I could get my hands on, and I started wondering exactly what it was that God would call me to. It was an exciting time for me, having that sense of self-worth and enthusiasm about my own life. But the message I got from the other Christians we were involved with was, "Your role is to be supportive in your relationship to Rob. Your role will be to have children." I experienced a lot of frustration and dealt with that for a long time just inside myself.

Rob: Occasionally Ginny would emotionally burst because of the stuff that was going on around the house and the organization. I was confused by it, because the feminist conversion had not happened yet. We hadn't consciously applied the gospel to that specific part of our lives. We tried to change a few practical things, but without really understanding what was going on. For a couple years, we went on like that, trying to change the symptoms rather than the actual problem.

Then we joined the Presbyterian church, and it happened, obviously not a coincidence, that we met Brenda Biggs, a radical feminist who was becoming a Christian but was not giving up feminism. She instinctively knew that they should go together somehow.

Ginny: She was an incredible influence for both of us at that time. She articulated what I had been feeling for three years but didn't have any words for. It was just rage. And she came along and said, "You're feeling angry because you're in an organization that has relegated you to doing office work and getting coffee, and your gifts obviously show that you could do more. You're angry because you're living in a house with three men who basically think they're doing you a favor if they wash their own underwear." It was both exciting and frightening to have that validated by another person.

I think I experienced a lot of what other women experience: resistance. We say, "Oh no, your analysis can't be quite right. The men in my life have my best interests at heart."

But Brenda encouraged me in ways that nobody in my life up to that point had ever done. The whole time we had been involved with Young Life, people would say to Rob, "You're a very talented, gifted person. Why don't you go to school? Why don't you get your master's degree? Why don't you go into ministry?" But nobody ever tried to empower me in that same way. Brenda was an extremely empowering force in my life, and she almost single-handedly convinced me to go to college.

Brenda and I went to the first Evangelical Women's Caucus that was held here in Washington, D.C. The first evening Virginia Mollenkott gave the keynote address. I didn't sleep the whole night afterward. It was one of the most exciting things I'd ever heard. Basically her message was that God intends for all of us to be free, both God's sons and God's daughters. And her invitation was, if we truly believe and trust in the God of the Bible, we will be willing to look fearlessly at what's there and what the tradition of the church has been. We will be able to call injustice injustice, and oppression oppression. Then we can move on from there, knowing that God is finally leading us all to freedom. That turned my world upside down.

When I got home I decided I didn't want to talk to anybody about the conference until I'd reread the Gospels. So I sat down every night for about a week and read through them. It felt important to me to look to the person of Jesus, to see if indeed his message was a message of liberation.

After I saw that confirmed in the radical nature of who Jesus was and what was at the heart of the gospel, I felt almost as though there was a call for me to teach that. I started a women's Bible study with a lot of the women who went to our church, and in a somewhat halting, inarticulate way, I began to challenge the Gothard hierarchy teaching.

The next stage we went through was when we both went to college. Rob went to Moravian College and majored in religion, and I went to Cedarcrest College and majored in art.

I think it was necessary for us to go through a time when I identified myself primarily outside of the relationship. We lived fairly separate lives for a while. We were both going to school full-time and working part-time. There wasn't a lot of time to be together.

In some ways I risked our relationship, because I made a conscious choice to put myself and the development of my gifts and working on my sense of self before anything else. That is another juncture at which the process of liberation is really frightening for women, because when, as a woman, you come to terms with the fact that you haven't been free to be yourself, and then you risk being yourself, you stand a chance of losing some of your relationships and some of your securities. A lot of women choose their securities instead of really finding themselves.

In what other areas did this growing feminism affect your relationship?

Rob: A lot of what shifted was just the way we related to each other and the maintenance of our everyday life. Ginny stated clearly what she wanted and needed, and I did the same. I think it had implications in all ways—in our sexual relationship, in the way we talked to each other, in the way we listened to each other. I know it had a lot of implications for our relating to other couples, because at that point we were very evangelistic about what we were going through.

I also began to feel pretty lonely as a man, as if I wasn't being a true man. As a man, you're supposed to be part of the male bonding experience, including making sexual comments about women and jokes about your wife. That happens all the time, all day long. And I just refused to go along with it.

At that point Ginny and I spent time with very few couples and hardly any men at all. But even during the loneliness, I had the sense that I was finding out who I really was and who I really am, and that was a good thing.

Ginny: I think it's also important to say that during this whole time we were becoming more political in every area of our lives. We became more active peacemakers. We left the church that we were a part of over the women's issue. We began to eat differently and to refuse to pay military taxes. It was a period of becoming much more concrete in the way we were living out the political ramifications of our faith.

Rob: I think it was feminism that made all the other things real. Feminism was the grid through which we understood racism and classism and nuclear war, by looking at the patriarchy behind them and Ginny's experience as an oppressed person. That was the barometer by which we measured all those things.

Into this experience comes a child. Could you talk about how that affected your situation?

Ginny: We had been married for eight years, and I had been going to school for three years, when we found ourselves with an unplanned pregnancy. I felt really excited at the possibility of having a child. I loved her and felt immediately bonded to her from the moment I knew she was in my womb. But I also felt really devastated by it. I felt a loss of control and had no idea what it was going to mean for my future. Fortunately I was in a situation where I could express those feelings.

Rob: Out of what you experienced and saw around you growing up, I think you viewed motherhood as a kind of black hole you dropped into and maybe didn't get out of. At the same time, I've always been drawn to children, so I was happy about a baby coming.

Did you evolve in your approach to raising Annie, or did you talk before she was born about how your sense of yourselves and feminism were going to affect raising this child?

Rob: It was what I would call a conscious evolution. We were ready to look at parenting in a new way.

Our small community in Bethlehem had broken apart, and we had separated ourselves off and were again taking stock of what it meant to love each other. Annie was born into that experience. She was God's agent of grace to us at the time.

Ginny discovered that motherhood was a different thing than she had expected and feared. It was a very positive, powerful thing. It was such a joyful experience for us both that it wasn't a question of, "Who is going to take care of her?" Instead it was, "We both really want to take care of her. How are we going to do it?"

Ginny: When we first got married, our assumption was that Rob's role was primary and mine was a support role. But over the years our relationship became one in which we wanted to minister to each other and support each other. I went into mothering knowing Rob felt what I did with my life and how I used my gifts were important. And Annie became another factor in that—how to care for this child in a way that's healthy and good for me and for Rob and for her.

It was a very positive experience for me being home with her full-time for the first fourteen months of her life. Nursing was a mystical experience for me; I never in my life had a better prayer life. It was during that time that we moved to Washington, D.C., to join Sojourners Community.

Rob: When Annie was about a year old, I was offered the job of receptionist at *Sojourners* magazine. Ginny and I decided to share the job when Annie was weaned. I stayed home three days a week while Ginny worked at the office, and Ginny stayed home two days while I worked. We did that for about a year and a half. It became obvious that Ginny was much more competent around the office than I was. *Sojourners* needed an assistant to the publisher and offered her the job. It seemed a logical next step for me to stay home full-time with Annie.

It wasn't an accommodation to Ginny, and it wasn't a role reversal. It was something that had evolved over a twelve-year period. This was where the Spirit was leading.

Ginny: It's important to say that we were working through all this in the context of Sojourners Community. People affirmed our commitment to parenting, to feminism, and to each other and helped enable us to do what we really felt we should do.

Rob: When Annie was almost three, she started attending Christian Family Montessori School in the morning, and I started working at the school as an aide, so I was very much part of her life for most of the day.

Ginny: I think that Rob being home with Annie was a good experience. He had to become a primary caretaker for her, which he wasn't trained to do in the same way that I was.

Rob: I learned what it takes to do day-to-day maintenance, and how important it is. It became an opportunity to concretely apply all we had learned. I wanted to do it, but it was still very difficult, and it kicked up conflict in me. It was the last thing I was raised for.

What kind of effects do you see it has had on Annie?

Ginny: She is a child who has an intimate relationship with both of her parents.

Rob: And that is kind of revolutionary in our society. She's going to have a better understanding of her parents—both our faults and our gifts—without any idealization, we hope.

Annie has started me on a very concrete vocational path toward working with young children. The understanding of children and their real worth, what it takes to raise them, to be with them, and love them is a logical extension of Christian feminism.

Ginny: I think Annie's a pretty secure little kid just from being with both of us. I think one of my strengths as a parent is including her in day-to-day activities, such as helping me get supper. One of Rob's strengths has been to put those activities aside and just take her out and play. So she's had the best of both worlds, and they've helped me to see the value of play.

Annie is familiar with Rob's work world, of course, but she also has the sense that I work and that my work is important.

Rob: Children are very welcome at the *Sojourners* office. And the work there is a really wonderful thing for her to know about.

Ginny: She's very aware of the vocational differences between us. She said to me one time, "Rob is very good working with a whole lot of children. But, Mom, you're really only good with one or two children at a time. You're a good mother, but you're never going to be a teacher."

What have been some of the points of struggle for you?

Ginny: A few points of difficulty have come up in the real practical areas of our relationship, having a child and raising that child. Both of our discernments, both of our opinions about a subject come to bear, and we wrestle it through to a decision. I think we share so much common vision and are similar enough in our personalities that we haven't had the real stalemates around decision making that I think can be there for people.

One other point of some tension has been what Rob always calls "working-mother's guilt." I think it is harder for me, at an emotional level, to feel free from the expectations in our culture that I be home with our child full-time.

One of the other points of struggle is dealing with the feminist issue in a community where other justice concerns are weighed so heavily. In the church and culture at large, however, there is a tendency even to trivialize the oppression of women, so many people don't approach feminism as a politically relevant issue. You have to work to convince those people that women are genuinely oppressed and then work to legitimize the issue as something serious for people to deal with.

Would you explain how your theological assumptions and your approach to the Scriptures have changed through your feminist conversion?

Ginny: I think what has changed is that I stopped accepting a particular interpretation of the Scriptures and a particular way of doing theology as the only way of approaching the Bible. Feminist theology approaches the Scriptures with the assumption that women are as valuable as men and both are made by a loving Creator.

It's difficult to come to terms with the whole tradition of male domination and female subordination that's throughout the Bible. But I think that's why Jesus stands out as such a radical departure from what preceded him and then some of what follows with the early church. He seemed to bring such a different sense of the value of women to his relationships and to his interactions with people.

Rob: Our feminist conversion caused both Ginny and me to dig into the Bible more seriously than we ever had before. We've always had a very alive relationship with the Scriptures, and still do. We've been very thankful for the questions that have been raised because of it.

Ginny: I think that God has been very faithful to us in guiding us and giving us what we need.

PEACE PENTECOST:
Moved by the Spirit
Jim Wallis

We have all heard the Pentecost story. It is so familiar that we almost know it by heart. Jesus had been executed by the ruling authorities, and, when the disciples saw what had happened to him, they were afraid they would be next. And so these future leaders of the church, these founders of our movement, remained behind locked doors. They were probably like most of us, lamenting how bad things were, watching the world drift in frightening directions, sunk in their own despair and their own fear.

But the Spirit came upon them and filled their hearts and gave them power. The Holy Spirit set them free of their fears and turned them loose in the streets to proclaim the good news. They preached the gospel, they were sent to jail, and then they returned to their communities. This became a regular rhythm for them—preaching the gospel, going to jail, coming back to community, and I think it is becoming a rhythm for all of us.

In May 1983, on Pentecost Sunday in the Washington Cathedral, we sang until we were hoarse. We sang "We are not afraid, we are not afraid." The next day many of us were arrested in the Rotunda of the U.S. Capitol as we prayed for peace. We spent the night in jail, and while we were being put in wagons the next morning to go to court for arraignment, someone in the back of one of the wagons began to sing, very tenderly, "We're not very afraid, we're not very afraid." Part of the rhythm of arrest is feeling fear and then being set free from fear by the Holy Spirit.

What is the Holy Spirit? I remember once I asked a little child, "What is the Holy Spirit?" And she said, "I don't know, but I think it has feathers." The Scriptures say that we can't see the Spirit; it is like the wind. You can't see it, but you see its results.

Some thought the disciples were drunk, maybe even a little crazy.

Peter says, "No, they are not drunk," and he quotes the prophet Joel: "And in the last days it shall be, God declares, that I will pour out my Spirit upon all flesh, and your sons and daughters shall prophesy. And your young shall see visions and your old shall dream dreams."

That reminds me of the time that some of us moved in with a family threatened with eviction in our inner-city neighborhood. We were arrested and taken to court. We wanted to represent ourselves, but a court-appointed defense lawyer tried to get in on the case. He suggested that we plead insanity. He said that we would have a good case because anybody who tries to fight real estate speculation in Washington, D.C., must be insane.

When we take our prayers for justice, peace, and freedom to the streets, many will believe we are insane, because to pray for justice, peace, and freedom in Washington, D.C., in these days seems to be insane. But, we testify that the Spirit is being poured out on Catholics, evangelicals, Presbyterians, Methodists, Mennonites, Lutherans, Baptists, Quakers, Jews, and all whose faith is coming alive. The Spirit is being poured out, and insane or not we will prophesy.

In June 1984 I was in Cleveland, Ohio, preparing to preach at a citywide Peace Pentecost service. Just as I was about to meet with the Ohio Witness for Peace team, which had visited Nicaragua in April, I received some very bad news in a phone call from the *Sojourners* office in Washington, D.C.

The Maryknoll sisters in Ocotal, Nicaragua, had called to report that their border town was under attack. Six hundred U.S.-backed *contras* had invaded early that morning. The Maryknoll sisters told of many dead and wounded people lying in the streets and said that a U.S.-made mortar shell had exploded in their own backyard. The casualties were mounting and, as usual, most were civilians.

Some victims suffered torture and mutilation, a terrorist tactic frequently practiced by these CIA-supported mercenary soldiers. The *contras* also destroyed grain supplies, power station offices, the lumber mill and processing plant, and the small radio station.

I shared the sad news with the Ohio Witness for Peace volunteers. As I spoke, I could see tears in the eyes of many in the circle. Then I learned that the Ohio delegation had stayed in Ocotal during their visit to Nicaragua.

The people with whom I was sitting had lived with families in Ocotal. They had prayed with the people, played with their children, and shared hospitality, worship, and faith. Real bonds had begun to form. I could see that the concern and pain in their faces was deeply personal, as the Ohio team told stories of the people of Ocotal they had come to know. Finally, someone asked if we could simply pray. We bowed our heads and began to offer intercessions for our brothers and sisters under attack.

Suddenly I realized the extraordinary thing that was happening. I was listening to Ohio Christians pray by name for people in the faraway little town of Ocotal, Nicaragua. I knew at that moment that this was the strength of Witness for Peace. In those tearful prayers, I could feel the ties that had been forged between U.S. citizens and Nicaraguan people against whom our government was sponsoring such violence. Even more deeply we felt the power of Christian bonds, which know no national boundaries and which are finally stronger than the propaganda and violence of political power.

Something has happened to the more than fifteen hundred people who have now gone to Nicaragua with Witness for Peace and have returned to tell their story. It is a deeply personal change that can sometimes only be expressed with tears and prayers. But out of those prayers has emerged a determined resistance to the violence being visited upon the people we now know as our brothers and sisters. The government of the United States dare not underestimate that faithful determination.

As we entered Lafayette Park on May 28, 1985, Timothy McDonald, of the Southern Christian Leadership Conference, led us in verse after verse of *This Little Light of Mine:* "Shine all around the White House, I'm gonna let it shine . . ." The verse was repeated for every place we would be taking our witness that day.

It was Peace Pentecost, and our lights were shining bright and bold. Vincent Harding led the commissioning of those who would march, pray, sing, and engage in nonviolent civil disobedience all over Washington, D.C. In preacher's cadence he named each site where our prayerful protest would be offered and then exclaimed after each, "Tell them we are coming!"

It was a day for the movement of the Spirit, a day when political stereotypes were shattered and ideological labels were swept aside to make room for the new wind of Christian conscience blowing across our land. The selective and inconsistent morality of both the Right and the Left was challenged by a simple message: all life is sacred. "We are here today to love God," said Harding, "and to love all of God's children."

We acted out of the firm conviction that wherever and whenever life is threatened and under attack, Christians must not remain silent but must act to defend God's gift of life. In that spirit we offered our prayers for justice, for freedom, for mercy, and for peace at places where human life is now undergoing such a terrible assault. At each site our civil disobedience was an act of prayer.

We prayed at the White House for the twisted priorities of a nation that reverses biblical wisdom by busily beating plowshares into swords. Our prayer was for an end to the arms race and for a beginning of justice for the poor who are already the victims of our military madness.

We prayed at the State Department for the enormous suffering in Central America. We pleaded that our government stop its promotion of violence and terror in Nicaragua, El Salvador, Guatemala, and Honduras and, instead, join in peaceful resolution of the conflicts in the embattled region.

We lifted our voices and prayers at the Soviet Embassy on behalf of the people of Afghanistan, whose country has been brutally invaded by another arrogant superpower bent on asserting its control over a smaller and weaker nation. We also prayed at the South African Embassy on behalf of freedom and democracy and in protest of our own government's accommodation to apartheid.

At the Supreme Court, we interceded for the victims of crime and for those condemned on death row. There we pleaded for an end to the killing cycle. And at the Department of Health and Human Services, we prayed for the unborn and for an agenda of justice and compassion for women and children that will create alternatives to the desperate, painful choice of abortion.

The many prayers offered at many places became one simple prayer— a prayer for life. To defend, affirm, nurture, and uplift life became our common plea and intercession. What emerged from the day's prayers and protests was a consistent ethic of life that crosses political lines and boundaries. This consistent life theme stood in marked contrast to the kind of politically predictable protests to which Washington, D.C., is very accustomed.

Thus, for many participants, observers, and reporters, Peace Pentecost 1985 became a ground-breaking event and a hopeful sign for the future. The many streams of conscience now flowing in the churches were brought together for a Pentecost weekend of discernment, worship, and action. As we shared, prayed, and acted together, it was increasingly clear that the streams are flowing in the same direction.

After the 248 of us who were arrested for our prayerful actions were released from jail, a lengthy report on UPI radio referred to our movement as the "Christian Conscience Movement in America." Perhaps now the media will stop trying to squeeze us into political categories where we don't belong and, instead, recognize what is truly emerging—a movement of faith and conscience rising up in the heart of the churches in response to an unparalleled historical crisis and to the prompting of the Spirit of God in our lives.

The day has come for Christians to reject the inconsistencies and polarities of the political Right, Left, and center. The political conservatives and liberals each have their favorite causes and victims and ignore the cries of many of God's children. It must not be so with us. We must be those who take our stand on the side of life, especially at the places where life is most threatened in our day.

We must stand with the victims of superpower interventions and violence, both U.S. and Soviet. We must stand with the hungry children of so-called enemy nations who are the targets of our nuclear missiles. We must stand with those who suffer under oppression and racism regardless of whether their governments are communist or anticommunist. We must stand with the unborn at the same time we stand with women in the struggle for justice and equality.

We must defend the dignity of each and every life, whether innocent or guilty, because, while we are all sinners, Christ died for us. Finally, we must choose life, because our God is a God of life.

Against all that we face, we desperately need the Spirit, because without it we will be both helpless and hopeless. When the Spirit moves, it takes the most ordinary and human of people. The early church had some raw material like fishermen, prostitutes, and slaves—those who didn't seem to have the resources of society. But the Spirit came on these outcasts, and the story says that the world was turned upsidedown. And so we pray, "Blow your wind upon us, O Holy Spirit."

On that first Pentecost, Jesus' followers took to the streets and a social revolution began. Peter, who had earlier been so frightened that he denied his Lord, then stood up and boldly proclaimed the gospel. The disciples, who were all somehow lost when Jesus died, came back. The Holy Spirit set them free from their fear. And the crowds, Scripture says, were cut to the heart. Of all the things that have brought us here, we as a crowd of people are together because we have been cut to the heart.

We have heard story after story after story of our brothers and sisters in

Central America who are suffering unimaginable butchery and brutality at the hands of the forces of violence that our government supports, and we have been cut to the heart. We have heard of whole villages destroyed in Afghanistan by the Soviet military, and we have been cut to the heart. We have read and listened until we can't stand to see or hear any more about children and unarmed civilians being shot down in the streets of South Africa, and we have been cut to the heart.

We see a whole generation of black youth simply abandoned in our own neighborhoods, we see children with not enough to eat only a mile from the White House, and we have been cut to the heart. And we have been cut to the heart by our own children asking us, "Mommy, Daddy, how long will it be until there is a nuclear war?"

We have been cut to the heart by women who are denied justice and are pushed to make the desperate choice of abortion. And we are cut to the heart by unborn lives snuffed out before they have a chance to live.

These are not for us matters of politics or theology or political programs; these are for us matters of the heart. But our nation has hardened its heart. Our nation trusts in weapons and wealth and has ignored the cries of its many victims. I believe that we must come to terms more deeply than we have before with the reality of what we are confronting in this country. And on Peace Pentecost, what we are confronting in this country is lawless authority.

Lawless authority defines itself as legal and those who disobey as illegal. However, it is in our best tradition—biblical, religious, and moral—to resist lawless authority in the name of conscience and of law. In so doing we will be deemed illegal, and we will be put in jail. But to love conscience and to respect law is to resist lawless authority. We are going to have to pay the price of those who break the law, and that we must come to terms with politically, morally, emotionally, and spiritually.

More and more of us have heard the voice of God in these days and have been cut to the heart. When the crowds around Peter were cut to the heart, they asked, "What must we do?" Peter said simply, "Repent." And three thousand people repented that day. People were added to the church every day. And in this movement of Christian conscience, people are being added every day. We have felt our unity. We have felt our common witness. We have felt our growing love for one another. And we have come to see more and more clearly that our message is, indeed, choose life, for all life is sacred.

We hope that a single prayer will emerge from the church—a prayer for justice, a prayer for peace, a prayer for freedom, a prayer for life. Our prayer on Peace Pentecost is a prayer of hope in the midst of great danger and great possibility. Pentecost, more than any other time in the church's calendar, is a time for speaking clearly and boldly. It is a time to act. It is time for Christians and those of other religious faiths, those of good will, to speak out, to speak clearly with a unified voice. It is time for the church to see men and women who are unafraid to speak, even at personal risk. It is time for the nation to hear clear words about matters of life and death and to thereby examine its conscience.

It is time for the government to know that it cannot forever continue in official falsehood, violence, and oppression of the poor. It is time the government knows its present policies face a determined opposition—a people rooted in faith and prayer.

Protest is speaking; resistance is acting. Protest is to say that something is wrong; resistance means trying to stop it. To protest is to raise your voice; to resist is to stand up with your body. To protest is to say you disagree; to resist is simply to say no.

To move from protest to resistance is indeed a serious step. But more and more of us believe that our present situation is so serious that such a step is called for.

It is indeed very possible that strong actions entailing risk and sacrifice may prick consciences, change minds, soften hearts, and awaken the public. We have seen that happen before. But deeper issues than political effectiveness are at stake. These are issues of personal faith and personal responsibility.

We don't know if we can win, but we know what the gospel says. We don't know if military madness can be stopped, but we know that Christ calls us to be peacemakers. We don't know if invasions and interventions can be halted, but we know that God cares about the victims and that we must stand in the way of our government's violence against them. We don't know when the poor will see justice, but we know that Jesus stands among the poor and invites us to come and join him there.

A time comes for personal responsibility, and that becomes an even deeper reason for acting than even the hope of success. We must always remember that history has been changed when individuals and small groups of people began to take personal responsibility, usually for reasons of faith and conscience, and thereby opened up new possibilities in their lives and in the lives of others. New breakthroughs sometimes are possible only through a deeper level of commitment. Our prayer of resistance, finally, is a prayer for the grace of God to enable us to make that deeper level of commitment.

PEACE PENTECOST:
"It Won't Be Long Now"
Vicki Kemper

Two days earlier, on Pentecost evening, we had gathered at the National Shrine of the Immaculate Conception in Washington, D.C., to call forth and to celebrate, with great fanfare, the coming of the Spirit. But on this Tuesday morning, this "Day of Christian Resistance," it was the Spirit who called to us.

For three days, during the Peace Pentecost 1985 conference, we had been affirming, claiming, and encouraging "The Rise of Christian Conscience." But on this momentous morning, as more than one thousand of us gathered for a special worship service, the conscience we had validated with countless words rose anew and broke beyond the bounds of our feeble human reasoning. In the vibrant warmth of Washington's Metropolitan A.M.E. Church, this conscience overflowed our hearts and took on the form and life of the Spirit.

Throughout the conference, an ensemble of Sojourners vocalists had been performing songs of hope and life from South Africa. They opened this worship service with the same song they had sung to begin the conference: "Oh, freedom, freedom is coming. Freedom is coming. Oh, yes I know."

On the last note of the song, the audience exploded in a tumultuous burst of spirit and emotion. Within seconds, the entire assembly was on its feet, clapping and cheering. Shouts of "Freedom is coming!" "Jesus is coming," and "Yes!" filled the sanctuary for almost five minutes. We were ready.

We were ready for justice to roll down like waters. We were ready to proclaim freedom for the poor, for the oppressed in Central America, for those held hostage by nuclear weapons, for the suffering blacks in South Africa, for the unborn and for women, for the people of Afghanistan, and for those languishing on death rows.

We were ready to acknowledge the interconnectedness of these issues.

The Rev. Joseph Lowery, president of the Southern Christian Leadership Conference, had reminded us of this in a rousing Pentecost evening sermon based on Ezekiel 37. He exhorted us that the time had come for Christians to breathe life into "dry bones" and to connect "the thigh bone to the hip bone" in a movement that would bring justice and freedom to all of God's children.

And we were ready for freedom within ourselves to seek and proclaim the truth. We were ready, as Henri Nouwen had reminded us on Sunday morning and as Jesus had told Peter two thousand years ago, to so love God and be committed to feeding God's sheep that we would stretch out our hands and let ourselves be dressed and led where we would rather not go.

But it was injustice, oppression, and the systematic disregard for human life that had brought more than one thousand of us to Peace Pentecost 1985, held May 25 to 28 on the campus of Catholic University. We came from across the country and around the world seeking signs of hope and resistance in the churches. And we found them.

The conference was an exciting fusion of the different streams of the movement of Christian conscience. The sanctuary movement, Witness for Peace, the Pledge of Resistance, the overground railroad, the Nuclear Train Campaign, the Free South Africa Movement, the Plowshares actions, the Catholic Worker, and countless other peace groups and advocates for the poor, the hungry, the homeless, the unborn and women, and the convicted on death row were all represented.

During two days of workshops, prayer, Bible study, worship, and nonviolence training, we saw the work of our brothers and sisters across the country, and we turned from despair to hope, from exhaustion to inspiration, from fear to courage. Shelley Douglass, a founder of the Ground Zero Center for Nonviolent Action in Washington state, told about the resistance of the Agape Community to the Department of Energy Nuclear Train. Two attorneys who formerly prosecuted Nuclear Train resisters are now defending people in court for committing the same acts. Don Mosley, cofounder of Jubilee Partners in Comer, Georgia, told how a school bus full of Central American refugees seeking sanctuary made it through a border patrol checkpoint in Texas with the unexpected help of a tornado.

Throughout it all we were reminded that by acting in faith against political, economic, social, and personal forces that oppress and desecrate life, we had found new and more abundant life. We also had found defeat, harassment, failure, and persecution. But, drinking deeply from our spiritual roots, we inspired and encouraged one another to "hold on to the prize."

All this and more brought us to the church that Tuesday morning. There we sang and prayed and worshiped and bathed in the joy of the Spirit. But, as the Rev. Timothy McDonald reminded us, we had not come to stay in church. We had come to take our burden for life to places where life was not upheld. It was time to "stop talking the talk and start walking the walk."

So, with banners and posters and songs, we walked—twice stopping for prayer along the way—from the church to Lafayette Park, which is across the street from the White House. During a commissioning service, Vincent Harding reminded us that we were on a co-mission with many who had struggled for life and justice before us. Those of us planning to commit acts of civil disobedience received stoles, and then all of us, after a final prayer, left the park in six processions to march to the different demonstration sites.

The group with the shortest distance to walk marched around the White House once before stopping in front of it to pray for an end to the arms race and for the poor, its principal victims. When more than seventy Peace Pentecost participants ignored a police warning to move from the sidewalk and continued praying and singing, they were arrested.

A bus full of children who had come to Washington to visit the capital sites pulled up next to a bus loaded with arrested protesters. The children waved to the protesters, many of whom wore clerical collars, and were mystified that they didn't wave back. When one protester stood up, turned around, and showed the children his handcuffs, a police officer told him, "You're setting a bad example for those kids." "No, officer, we're setting a good example," the protester replied.

The spiritual and personal conviction we brought to the actions created its own drama, and, in a paradoxical fashion, the drama moved us to even deeper conviction. A solemn drumbeat accompanied the reading of names of executed prisoners during the march to the Supreme Court. One of the marchers walked in chains, and by the time the group reached the court steps, forty-three names had been read, each followed with the response, "Lord, have mercy." After a short litany, the protester's chains were unlocked, and following a time of prayer the arrests began.

At the Department of Health and Human Services, protesters prayed for a society in which the lives of women and children would be upheld, and in which desperate women would not be driven to having abortions. To show that respect for unborn life also requires respect for women, demonstrators gathered in the formation of the women's symbol.

The group protesting at the Soviet Embassy against the violence in Afghanistan was encouraged by a former Peace Corps volunteer in Afghanistan, who talked of the spirit of the Afghan people. Those being arrested felt reconnected to the other protesters when they heard over a police walkie-talkie that arrests at the State Department had been completed.

The Peace Pentecost action at the South African Embassy was one of hundreds which had already occurred there, yet it too was unique. After the entire group prayed for an end to apartheid, the usual delegation of three persons went to the embassy door and asked to see the ambassador. But when the group received the standard refusal, Timothy McDonald surprised everyone by asking if the demonstrators could use the embassy restrooms.

At the State Department, almost 100 protesters sat in the driveway and sang and prayed for brothers and sisters in Central America who suffer the effects of U.S. policy. In all, 248 people were arrested that day, and with the arrests began a sometimes tense, occasionally moving, always challenging, and often funny experience.

The singing that had begun with "This Little Light of Mine" during the procession to Lafayette Park continued almost nonstop through the rest of the day and the entire jail experience. Both our funniest and most poignant moments came through song. As the police escorted us that first night to a large cellblock reserved for demonstrators, and after the women had already filled one big cell and were starting to fill another, the matron asked one woman if she preferred the "singing or non-singing section."

Later that night we heard the men, who were being held in a cell down the hall from us women, begin singing. Soon we began exchanging songs, singing such classics as "I'm in the Mood for Love," "You Are My Sunshine," and "Take Me Out to the Ball Game." And when the women overheard a male guard remark snidely that he wished we would sing "White Christmas," of course we sang that too.

But it was the Latin song "Ubi Caritas" that became our mainstay, our cry to the Spirit, during times of uncertainty, weakness, and weariness. Even on our last morning in jail, when we were in individual cells, one woman's gentle humming of "Ubi Caritas" awoke us, spread through the jail as we all joined the singing, and reminded us that we were not alone.

Occasionally we got tired of singing the same old songs, but we needed the hope and focus the songs would bring. On the day that we waited to be arraigned and sentenced, we were about to give in to exhaustion and hunger when someone jokingly suggested that we sing the "Hallelujah Chorus." Before we knew it, Ellen Flanders, a fifty-seven-year-old former choir director from Albany, New York, was leading us in a four-part version of the "Hallelujah Chorus." When we finished the song, we almost expected our cell doors to burst open.

We reached the women's cellblock in the D.C. jail at 3 A.M. the next morning and discovered that our reputation as singers had preceded us. If we stopped singing momentarily, the other women inmates would ask us to sing some more. Soon they were asking us to sing their favorite hymns and before long were singing with us. One of the inmates blessed us with her beautiful renditions of "Precious Lord" and "Amazing Grace."

Later in the morning, first a handful, and then several, of the inmates came to the center of our cellblock. They could move about freely, but we were locked in our cells and could only stand at our doors and put our hands through the bars. Black hands clasped white ones, forming a large circle, and we began singing "We Shall Overcome." With each verse, we could feel the hope rising within ourselves and within the inmates. Then, when we thought the song was over, one of the inmates started a new verse: "Moms and kids together . . . ."

We continued to sing and talk with the inmates, and when we left the cellblock, one of the women thanked us for bringing "some peace and unity to this place," but we knew they had given us much more than we had given them. We left as changed people.

We hoped and prayed that we were not the only ones to change. During the arraignment before a District of Columbia commissioner, a cynical and argumentative man, we watched his features soften and his tone become less accusatory as he listened to our statements. He was visibly moved when one man stated, "I prayed for the people who would be arresting and trying me."

"You mean you prayed for me?" the commissioner asked incredulously.

"Yes, and I would have prayed for you by name if I had known it," the convicted protester responded.

Much of the jail experience was a series of "hurry up and wait" times.

To help his fellow prisoners through it, Ed Loring, of the Open Door Community in Atlanta, told the men early on, "It won't be long now." As they waited and waited through endless jail processes, the men reminded one another, "It won't be long now."

What began as a joke became a rallying cry, a sincere belief, and a fervent prayer. As long as we remain faithful, as long as we hold on to the prize, as long as we trust in the God of freedom, we know that it won't be long now until justice rolls down like waters and righteousness like an ever-flowing stream.

GETTING READY FOR THE HERO:
Reflections on Martin Luther King, Jr.— And Us

Vincent Harding

Martin Luther King, Jr. Even saying his name out loud brings a certain kind of feeling—a reverence and a sense of expectancy. For only thirteen years, the nation watched him. All around him was a whirlwind, a whirlwind that blew his country from one era to another. They put him in jail twenty-nine times. Now they have named a national holiday for him.

Martin Luther King, Jr., was a minister whose proclamation of the gospel could not be contained by the churches. He was a theologian and philosopher who made the streets into a classroom, where he taught and tested the greatest ideas of his time. He was a political leader who redefined the meaning and purposes of power.

This Baptist preacher was a man of peace who created more turmoil than anyone else of his generation. He was a brilliant tactician who channeled anger and pent-up frustration into nonviolent direct action and, in so doing, translated the undirected rage of an oppressed people into a disciplined movement of heroic self-sacrifice.

King was a black man who, by speaking the truth in love, became the best friend white men and women ever had, though, by and large, they didn't see it. He made nonviolence militant, truth confrontational, and righteousness a threat to established authority. He became the leader of a race, then of a nation, then of the impulse for justice throughout the world. Martin King was the embodiment of the American revolution and offered to us the best hope yet for its fulfillment.

The best way to remember and celebrate Martin Luther King, Jr., is to measure ourselves by the vision for which he lived and died. Vincent Harding, in a moving tribute to his old friend, helps us do just that.

But we will come to know Martin and honor his memory only by taking his vision as an instrument for creating a new future. The "drum major for justice" would be unhappy with monuments and memorials that enshrined the past. Like another great prophet of God who led his people to freedom, Martin Luther King, Jr., climbed to the mountain top, glimpsed the promised land, but never got there himself. That is left for us. And one senses that Martin's spirit will remain restless until the great journey that he carried so far is one day completed.

—The Editor

he-ro. 1. In mythology and legend, a person, often born of one mortal and one divine parent, who is endowed with great courage and strength, celebrated for bold exploits, and favored by the gods. 2. Anyone noted for feats of courage or nobility of purpose; especially one who has risked or sacrificed his or her life.

Somewhere in the midst of the endless wisdom of the Buddhists this encouraging, disciplining promise stands forth: "When the student is ready, the teacher will appear." For years these simple words and their profound message have been a source of great hope for me, a way to deal with much unreadiness, an opening to many appearings. Then, in late 1985, the promise returned in another form and spoke to me as I wrestled with the possible meanings of the imminent appearance of my friend Martin Luther King, Jr., in the pantheon of our nation's official heroes.

Playing with the ancient wisdom, preparing for January 20, 1986, remembering his public lifetime—thirteen explosive years that became a generation of transformation—two variations on the Buddhist theme emerged: "When the nation is ready, the hero will appear." Or, equally appealing to me: "When the hero is ready, the nation will appear." Taking off from such meandering thoughts, the wondering/wandering began, moving across the serrated surfaces of our wounded, immature, and dangerous nation, probing into the painful, magnificent depths of our broken, beautiful country, Martin's country, a still-being-born country.

It may just be, brother, as the old folks used to sing, "We didn't know who you were." Or did we? And did we also know that we really weren't ready for any hero like you, and so we decided that instead of getting ready, we'd get comfortable?

Of course, some of us tried to get ready for a while, finding a taste of Birmingham and Greenwood and Selma and even a bit of "Black Power, Baby!" to be exciting; but Chicago and Cleveland and Harlem and Detroit and Watts and everywhere North and black and urban, and everywhere poor, unrepresented, exploited, and unemployed, and all the unpronounceable Asian places where women and children and "gooks" were being burned—and all that unromantic, un-American, unglamorous, untelevised, untidy, unsafe, unclear, un-Southern, unpaid-for organizing stuff was just too much for us.

Could it be that some of us did suspect who you were but decided that we first needed to get our piece of the pie, of the rock, of the action—of whatever it is that pieces come off/in?

So it looks like you appeared before we were ready, Brother Martin, and threw us off balance, and we tried to hold on to rocks and pies and sweet, gentle, unchallenging Jesus. Is it too late to get ready? Or should we just smooth you off, and cut you down, and fit you with blinders, and quiet your sound, so that you can crawl into our gilded prison, and be a hero who won't run around with gods—or God?

"When the hero is ready . . ." Were you ready, Martin, to be the hero with a thousand faces for us? Pastor and political leader; seeker and teacher; Moses and Messiah; mystic and mobilizer; husband and lonely traveler; father and world deliverer; child of the black church and satisfier of all the spiritual hunger endemic to white America; adviser to presidents and friend of the unkempt poor; Martin-of-the-March-on-Washington, eloquent, apparently undemanding dreamer, and Martin-after-the-child-killing-bombings, after the Mississippi murders, after the assassination of beautiful Malcolm, after the funerals for Jimmy Jackson, for James Reeb, for Viola Luizzo, after-Harlem-Martin, after Watts, after Chicago, after Detroit, after Newark, after the flames engulfing monks and naked children in Vietnam? After nightmares?

Were you ready, brother, even though you knew it was coming, for the criticism from black folks, from deep in the ancestral community? Were you ready for those of us who didn't want to upset the tantrum-tending president, who didn't want to be uncomfortable just when things were beginning to look good—for us—who didn't want to lose our jobs, who were aching for the rock, the pie, the action, the mainstream? Were you ready for all of us who turned back when you started holding hands with the poor, with the peacemakers, with the Vietnamese "enemies"? Were you ready for all of us who sang the old refrain, "It's bad enough to be black without being Red too"? Dear Martin, dear hero, were you ready for all that pain?

And what about all the other folks "of good will" who were eager to set the white South straight, to use troops if necessary to show those "rednecks" what this country is all about—they said—but who didn't think there were any such problems in their community, Northern and white, and comfortable, and far from all those people whose hands you insisted on holding, and who might just have to get the troops on you if you got out of hand—in the North? Were you ready when they stopped holding and singing and giving and backed away and wondered out loud if you were qualified (meaning ready) to discuss foreign policy and national budgets and militarism and institutional racism and all the things only qualified white experts (and crazy "militant" people) talked about? Does it still hurt in the place where they/we backed off and left you exposed to the coming of the night?

Sometimes I wonder, can you tell us now who was it working in you in those last years, Martin? To get you talking like that and holding hands like that, daring to feel, trying to express the anger, the anguish and the stumbling words of the poor, all the poor, everywhere, standing up to presidents, FBI directors, wealthy donors and death-dealing military and corporate systems like that, calling for new systems and values, acting like you really meant it when you sang the song, "Ain't gonna let NOBODY turn me round, keep on walking, keep on talking, marching up to freedom land." Was it old Dr. DuBois? Luthuli? Lumumba? Gandhi? Claudia Jones? Or just Malcolm sneaking back around and doing it to you, to us? Or could it be that heroes' daddies and mommas do play with gods—or God? If so, then maybe the ashes in Atlanta, and everywhere, are still getting themselves ready for your rising, Martin "Phoenix" King. Are you ready? Are we? Are you getting ready? Are we?

While playing, praying, weeping, and laughing through such clearly un-Buddhist thoughts, I came across a slim volume of poetry titled *Drum Major for a Dream* (ed. Ira G. Zepp and Melvyn D. Palmer, Writers Workshop, InterCulture Associates, Box 277, Thompson, CT 06277; 1977). It consists of a group of poems by black and white North American authors, expressing their responses to the assassination of Martin King—before he was proclaimed hero. The poets ranged in age from schoolchildren to a retired minister, and their work varied much in quality. But almost all were written within the immediate period of King's death and bear an authenticity based on their fundamental honesty and intentionality.

The key that opened them to my wrestling with the National Hero and with his country was found in the words of Gwendolyn Brooks, that magnificent black mother artist, in the last poem in the book. She says of Martin:

> A man went forth with gifts.
> He was a prose poem.
> He was a tragic grace.
> He was a warm music.

He tried to heal the vivid volcanoes.
His ashes are
 reading the world.

  And in her verses on the living prose poem, on the grace, on the music, she opened up to me permission to inhabit the poetry, to dance in the songs, in the grace of the gods, in the amazing grace of God, and allowed me to stand in volcanic ash and sing. She offered—thank you, Sister Gwen—a possible way to see my friend, the hero, and his nation, our nation, again. So I entered this book of poems and let them pierce me and recognized that though they speak of death, none of them is the end of a conversation.

  Indeed, they were my companions on the endless journey to January 20, 1986, and I share my responses to them simply as an invitation to others, many others—black, white, brown, all others—to join the conversation, bring improvisations to the song, song of death, song of life, getting ready.

  Carl Wendell Hines, Jr., was in his late twenties when the bullet came, expected, yet never quite prepared for. And he writes his sorrow in the words:

> Now that he is safely dead
> let us praise him
> build monuments to his glory
> sing hosannas to his name.
> Dead men make
> such convenient heroes; they
>   cannot rise
> to challenge the images
>   we would fashion from their lives.
> And besides,
> it is easier to build monuments
> than to make a better world.
> So, now that he is safely dead
> we, with eased consciences
>   will teach our children
> that he was a great man . . . knowing
>   that the cause for which he lived
> is still a cause
> and the dream for which he died
>   is still a dream,
>   a dead man's dream.

Safely? This man who was called by the FBI "the most dangerous Negro . . . in this nation"? When will he be safely dead? Listen for him in January. Feel the tremors beneath the monuments. Hear the voices from the black past (and future) singing, beyond "Hosannas," singing with Martin, for Martin, "Ain' no grave can hold my body down."

Perhaps the youngest children will hear best, will receive the voices and the songs through ears and hearts not yet filled with the "Top Forty," through eyes that see beyond MTV and other diversions from getting ready. Perhaps they will sense that great men and women do not really die. Perhaps they will ask about his dream, his cause, suspecting that he lives, somewhere nearby. Perhaps we will have the wisdom, the knowledge, and the courage to introduce them to the hero who, by the end of his life, was totally committed to the cause of the poor—in Mississippi, in Chicago, in Appalachia, in Vietnam, in Central America, in South Africa, in Memphis.

Perhaps we will tell them that the older dream, the famous, easier-to-handle dream, the forever-quoted dream of 1963 was no longer sufficient for him. Let them know that at the end, when the bullet finally came, he was dreaming of marching on Washington again, but this time to stay there, not just for speeches and for singing, but for audacious, challenging, divinely obedient action—to engage in a campaign of massive civil disobedience to try to stop the functioning of the national government. Tell them he planned to do this, calling on thousands and hundreds of thousands of lovers of justice until the cause of the poor became the nation's first priority, until all people were guaranteed jobs or honest income, until our nation stopped killing Asians abroad and turned to tend to the desperate needs of its people at home.

Tell them that was the last dream. Then perhaps they will understand the bullet, why it came, from whom it came, and why neither the dream nor the dreamer can die in places where women and men and children give themselves to the building of "a better world" as the best monument to the hero. Wasn't that what our unsafe, lively brother kept saying toward the end: ". . . let us rededicate ourselves to the long and bitter— but beautiful—struggle for a new world." Tell the children. Invite them to walk with the hero, with us, in the cause, in the dream, building, always building.

Facing ourselves, facing the hero, we listen, developing one of the disciplines of those who are getting ready. We listen to Edith Lovejoy Pierce—and more:

Above the shouts and the shots,
The roaring flames and the siren's blare,
Listen for the stilled voice of the man
Who is no longer there.

Above the tramping of the endless line
Of marchers along the street,
Listen for the silent step
Of the dead man's invisible feet.

Lock doors, put troops at the gate,
Guard the legislative halls,
But tremble when the dead man comes,
Whose spirit walks through walls.

Maybe he's still getting ready, too. Maybe that overwhelming sadness in Washington, D.C., in the sodden spring of 1968, that attempt to carry forward Martin's last great, incomplete dream in the face of endless rain and despair and fear and massive disarray, was only the prelude to the coming Poor People's Campaign. In a nation with almost forty million persons existing below the poverty level today (nineteen years later); with thousands of men and women sleeping on the streets of our cities today (trillions of wasted military dollars later); with millions of unemployed and underemployed and no prospects in sight for real humanizing work for an entire generation of young people today (thousands of promises later)—it may be that the rising and the walking of the poor are still to come. It may be that only assassins and their keepers have really heard Martin's words from nineteen years ago: "The dispossessed of this nation—the poor, both white and Negro—live in a cruelly unjust society. They must organize a revolution against that injustice, not against the lives of their fellow citizens, but against the structures through which the society is refusing to lift the load of poverty."

Listen. That was the voice of our hero in the last year of his life. That was his revolutionary spirit on behalf of the poor, on behalf of the nation. Are we ready for him? Can that living spirit really walk through walls? Walk through walls? Walk through walls! Like the barricades of our fears, the insistent shelters of our self-centeredness, the barriers of our great need for respectability, security, and safety?

Such walls! Powerful, surrounding us, devouring us, crushing us, filling us, each, all. Can you walk through, Martin? Are you ready? Am I? Are we? "Oh, sometimes it causes me to tremble . . ."

When the hero appears, will we be ready for the walls to fall?

Sometimes the poet's voice is louder than dear Edith Pierce's measured, church-hymn tones. Another woman, Ruth Howard, coming from another place, shouts from the pages to us (the way Martin could shout, and *almost* get down into his backhome, Baptist, revival preacher thing):

> O nation of greatness
>   And of fools—
> Hearken, hypocrites
> Who mock democracy:
>   You are as guilty
>   As that gutless coward
>   Who held the gun.
> Martin Luther King:
>   Symbol of peace and love,
>   Voice of human rights and justice.
> You could not silence him
> Behind prison walls,
> By obscene threats—
> So you fashioned the bullet.
> Dug the grave—
> The voice is stilled.
>   But you will hear him,
>   For he will live in those
>   Who loved this man—
>   A man whose valour
>   Outshone an army of heroes.

Getting ready is letting the shouts, the accusations, the condemnations cascade over us, enter deep, breaking through the walls, getting under the skin, flaming up the cool. Getting ready, for some of us, is especially hard sometimes, for sometimes it is being black and understanding that poetry is timeless. It is facing the possibility that now, nineteen years later, years of "progress" and "equal opportunity" and getting our piece, and swimming in the main one, and sitting paralyzed in front of television for hours at a stretch every impressionable childhood day— that now the screaming, revival-time words might be not just for white folks, but also for us, *for us*, to warn us of how fearful we are now, today (nineteen years after the Memphis balcony). How terrified, how guarded we have become against all that Martin King was called then in his last, beleaguered years: "Agitator," "Troublemaker," "Radical," "Communist Sympathizer," "Fanatic," "Unpatriotic," "Un-American," "Naive," "Dangerous" to the status quo.

Do we dare fantasize about what we would do now, if he came back to our black-administered city, to challenge our leaders; if he tried to question our values, and our bank accounts, and our political machine; if he dared to undermine the morale and question the Christian faith of our soldiers, of our officers, of our chaplains—as they landed in Grenada, as they poise themselves on the borders of Nicaragua, as they enjoy equality of opportunity to press the buttons of nuclear destruction, as they prepare for possible duty fighting "the communists" on behalf of the government of South Africa?

Are we, too, now frightened by people who organize unkempt and unrespectable folks to struggle for peace and justice here and abroad, who now take risks to do for escaping Central Americans what the Underground Railroad did for us—while we stand back, as far back as possible? Are we, too, now frightened in our respectable blackness by all the strange folks who, with King, really believe the way of love is more faithful to Jesus of Nazareth than the well-paid "defense" occupations of war-making, war-thinking, war-threatening, and death? Do we, too, mock democracy each time we back away, each time we fail to participate actively in the struggles for the transformation of our institutions and of this nation, in the defense of the poor, in the protection of the environment, in the questioning of our political leaders, in the teaching of ourselves and our children who the hero really was—and who he, and we, may yet become?

Can we still hear him? "Beautiful voice," we said. But did we hear what he was saying as the bullet smashed its way to our heart? Listening is getting ready. Has he penetrated beyond the messages of the mainstream, into our piece of the rock, to let us know that he was killed because he loved us, because he wanted us to discover our greatness, wanted us to see the task of working for human rights and justice as more crucial than our private agendas of "making it"?

If we listen, we may well hear him. Right at the beginning, back in Montgomery time he dreamed us a great dream when he said to us, "If you will protest courageously, and with dignity and Christian love, when the history books are written in future generations, the historians will have to pause and say, 'There lived a great people—a black people—who injected new meaning and dignity into the veins of civilization.' This is our challenge and our overwhelming responsibility.''

He was twenty-six years old when he saw that, said that, at the very first meeting of the Montgomery bus boycott. What a vision for that child/man! Seeing black folks, the stones the builders had rejected, seeing us, not floating contentedly in the mainstream, but challenging, standing, speaking, acting in such a way that new life, new meaning, new dignity are brought to an entire civilization? Oh Martin, did you mean it? Did you really love us so?

Are we ready? What will it mean to become our best selves, his best dream, "an army of heroes" for peace, for healing, for justice, for the poor, for life giving rather than life taking? Does it begin to feel good yet?

When the people are ready . . . Did we think being black meant automatically being ready for the hero? Did we forget that we now know how to build and maintain prisons, to fashion bullets and missiles and bombs and dig the graves of the human race? Lord, what would Sojourner and Harriet think about such equal opportunity for death? Maybe, just maybe, they'll help their young brother Martin walk through our walls. Help him, sisters. Help us.

> Getting ready, getting ready
>   for the King's walk through.
> Sometimes,
> Sometimes,
>   It causes me to tremble.
>   What about you?

And who knows how much time we have to deal with the trembling walls—white walls, black walls, brown walls, fear walls, respectability walls, personal and national security walls, "my-country-right-or-wrong" walls. Who knows? Poet Frank Carmody said:

> We have too little time to mourn the dead
> Bandage black around our hearts and arms
> Less time yet to build a dream
> Of what the living might become.

No matter what the time, we take it, use it, and see the dream. It was grand, it was magnificent, constantly expanding, enlarging his heart and mind, encompassing more than most of us could bear, this dream "of what the living might become."

This was the dream that haunted, besieged, exalted him, that would not let him go. He dreamed a world where all were free to serve their sisters and brothers in compassion and hope, where fear had no dominion, where the resources of the nation were redistributed to meet the needs of the overwhelming majority of its people, where no one had to fear old age, or sickness, or being left alone.

Oh yes, he saw the rest, the other. Couldn't you tell it in his eyes? Didn't we feel the pain of what he saw, this brother from another planet? At all the funerals of his adopted children, sisters, brothers, mommas and daddies, in all the jails, at every confrontation with dogs and guns and frightened, narrowed, brutal men, he had seen us humans, plumbed the depths of our terror, our cruelty, and our fear, he had seen our selfishness and our blind ambition. But he never stopped looking there.

Always the dream pressed him on, inward, outward, deeper. In the depths of our eyes, roaming even then beyond the walls, he had found the fugitive hope, crouching in corners; he had seen the compassion, gnarled and unused, felt the love, unnamed, unrecognized, unclaimed; he had grasped the oneness, denied and bombed to shreds.

Something in this man saw the sister, brother, momma, fearful child in all the strangest places, faces, and he sang to us of what we might become, beyond walls. He sang in the night, sang the old Negro songs, sang the strong black songs, sang the African-sun-soaked songs, and beckoned us, red, white, brown, black, toward ourselves, told us, like Langston—dear brother Langston Hughes—told us, "America is a dream." And we of every hue and cry, we are the dreamers, creating, dreaming with him, singing with him, dancing with him, to Native American songs, Mexican songs, Scotch-Irish songs, German songs, African songs, Vietnamese songs, Puerto Rican songs, Appalachian songs.

Organizing, marching, singing the songs, standing unflinching before the blows, going to jail, challenging all the killers of the dreams, he called us to sing, dream and sing and build—and stand our ground, creating a new reality, a new nation, a new world, ready for the hero. He saw us dancing before we knew we could move. He recognized what we had not seen and was ready to live and die for it, for us.

Early in his movement toward us, back in the fifties, he was sensing what he saw, saying, "I still believe that standing up for the truth of God is the greatest thing in the world . . . come what may." And for those of us who are getting ready, what truth of God could be greater than the truth of our rich, unexplored human possibilities, our fundamental oneness, our essential union with all life, and our responsibility to live out that truth, politically, economically, socially, spiritually, ecologically, culturally—come what may—against all the systems of separation, dehumanization, and exploitation that deny "what the living may become."

Are we ready to be what we may become? Oh nation of greatness, do we know who we are, really are, getting ready for our hero, and ourselves?

Long before the bullet struck, Martin was getting ready, moving toward our rendezvous. In the little book of poetry, John Dixon catches a glimpse of the hero becoming and shares his insight with us:

In an age when courage is measured by destruction, his courage was the courage of love. In an age when men are commodities with a price, he believed in the reality of persons. In an age afraid to believe, his faith was as innocent as a child's. In an age when subtlety of intelligence serves profit or power, his mind sought the liberations of peace.

What embarrassing words: courage, faith, love, liberation, peace. Haven't they been outlawed yet? Lock doors, put troops at the gate, guard the legislative halls against courage and faith, against liberation, love, and peace! But here comes the dead man, living, walking, still becoming. He comes piercing our walls, planting courage, planting faith, planting love and peace toward the center of our hearts, reminding us that "intelligence" was not meant to be another word for espionage, spying, and dirty tricks, that doctorates do not have to be sold to the highest bidders, that there is another way, a liberating way, to be shared, as he used to say "by no D's and PhD's." Are we ready? Is this implacable lover really our hero? Hero of a nation not yet born, but borning. God, are those the pangs we feel?

The poet continues:

He was never perfect in wisdom nor ever pretended to be. He was never perfect in conduct, nor free from temptations nor ever pretended to be. But holiness is not perfection; it is transparency to the grace of God. This great, good man has shattered the pride, the selfishness of millions of men and women. If we now have the courage to begin anew, to remake what his life exposed, then he will be one of those chosen of God to be an instrument of grace.

My flawed and wounded brother-hero, who knew grace better than you? Battered, tossed, and sometimes possessed by your own powerful weaknesses, how did you go on, how did you stand, how did you begin again and again your struggle toward getting ready?

The poet says grace, amazing grace—how sweet, so sweet the sound—lost/found brother-hero, the poet says grace. Depending on it, immersed in it, forever opened to it, by it, you now walk through our walls of guilt and fear and take our battered hands and broken lives and hold us, gently strong, as we rise, again, and again. For we, like you, are chosen to choose, to become what we might be—means of grace, sacraments of life for each other, rainbow warriors, peacemaking defenders of the earth, creators of a new world. Is that you, Brother Martin, singing, shouting:

"Rise, shine, give God the glory!"
Getting ready for the hero,
Rise, shine, our light is come.

Are you getting ready, Charlotte Nuby, you and your children? Who are you? Where are you now? The note in the book says only, "Charlotte Nuby was a ninth grade student at Haynes Junior High School, Nashville, Tennessee, when she wrote her poem on King's dream."

Growing up around Freedom Rides, sit-ins, wade-ins, kneel-ins, watching marchers wind through Nashville's streets, singing freedom songs in reverberating churches, hearing folks testify about jail and dogs and hoses and billy clubs and Jesus and grace and the beloved community beyond race, you must have known something. Coming of age near Jim Lawson and Diane Nash, near Jim Bevel and Jim Zwerg, listening to Kelly Miller Smith and John Lewis and all the hosts of Nashville's valiant, crucial army of freedom fighters, your child heart had its own understanding of liberation heroes. So when the word from Memphis erupted within us all, you were already becoming woman, writing:

> There was a man who loved this land.
> But hated discrimination
> And took his stand. . . .
> He was shunned and criticized by some;
> But he always said
> "We Shall Overcome."
> He fought for all to see the light
> And in their hearts they knew he was right.

He fought for equality; he fought for peace
And knew that someday
All prejudice would cease.
He fought against war; he fought against strife
Until a sniper's bullet took his life.
And when we say our prayers of silence
Remember he died for nonviolence.

Some things are very clear in the ninth grade, aren't they, Charlotte? Our hero loved us, loved this land, kept seeing beyond our walls, kept tugging at our consciences and our hearts, kept urging us toward what we might become. And took his stand, yes, sometimes against the gates of hell, took his stand. Fought hard, didn't he, Charlotte, fought hard for those he loved. Fought against our mistreatment of black folks, na-palmed folks, missile-targeted folks. Took his stand, Charlotte.

Tell it to your children. (Do you have some? What are their names?) Tell it to your nieces and nephews, tell it to your Sunday school children, tell it to your public school children, tell it to your Afrikan Free School children, tell it to your many-manicured-acres-private-school children, tell it to your welfare children, Charlotte.

This was no "nice Christian minister," only; no "great orator," primarily; no "civil rights leader," alone; this was more than a dreamer of black and white children holding hands. Tell them, Sister Charlotte, wherever you are, that he fought for the poor, that he fought against greed, that he was against war, that he was ready to give his life for the way of nonviolence in the struggle for truth and justice.

When you were in the seventh grade, my young sister, and Brother Martin was hemmed up against the wall by all the understandable fires of rage exploding in black communities across the nation, he declared again and again, "I still believe in nonviolence, and no one is going to turn me around on that. If every Negro in the United States turns to violence, I am going to stand up and be the only voice to say that it is wrong."

When he said it, Charlotte, he made it clear that he meant it for Vietnam as well as Chicago, for poor people and for generals. Then he spent the rest of his life, a brief life, trying to fashion creative, audacious modes of nonviolent resistance, trying to transform the values and structures of this nation toward compassionate, radical commitment to the poor, toward a new vision of democratic participation and decision making for us all, moving toward what we might become.

Remind the children that this man with a doctorate died in the midst of a struggle for garbage workers. Tell them, Charlotte, that he was calling black and white young people to refuse to serve in a U.S. military force that is so readily used to suppress poor people and their revolutions. Let them hear Brother Martin calling for another service, a more constructive, creative way of standing up for this land that he loved.

When you say your silent prayers, Charlotte, pray for the children—yours, mine, all—for the courage, the wisdom, and the strength they need to take their heroic stand in the midst of a land that romanticizes violence everywhere. When you enter the silence, dear sister, pray for us older ones—you, me, all—that we may remember who our hero really was, and how he loved us, and what he was calling us to do, to be, to become. Find someone, Charlotte, wherever you are, and hold hands with them, and work with them, and take your stand together.

It's easier when you're holding hands, Charlotte. Martin, though often surrounded by crowds, too often walked alone, with no covenanted community of sharing, seeking, bonded folks. Find what he didn't have, daughter. Get ready. Take your stand, Charlotte Nuby, wherever you've gone from Haynes Junior High. Take your stand. There's a hero waiting. Teach the children. There's a new nation to be born. Getting ready.

To teach the children is to get ready. To rescue them from the slick appeals of militarism, materialism, hedonism, and social irresponsibility is to get ready. For without such nurturing care we allow the poet N. Ellsworth Bunce no space for his vision:

> Where one dies thousands rise
> For Martyrs are made to
> multiply
> The stars catch the sound
> The wind carries the word. . . .
> In the silence
> Where he once stood
> The children grow
> The poor gather
> And those now mourning know
> They shall be comforted
> —Comforted—and fulfilled.

Poets and sweepers, mothers and teachers, deacons and barbers, cashiers and fathers, pastors and nurses, teach the children, everyone, for they are the thousands (and we are the thousands) who must rise to meet the hero. They are the catchers of the falling stars, the riders on the rising wind. Teach the children, let them grow, knowing the hero as a strong man, hearing his voice, seeing his face as lover of this nation, as implacable foe of injustice and exploitation, as courageous speaker of the truth to senators and streetboys, as dreamer of a land where the weak, the sick, the old, the poor, and the tender young become the center of our attention, the focus of our "defense," the apple of our eye.

Gather with others to teach the children, by word and by deed. Conspire, band together in communities of resistance, healing, and hope. Wean them and us from the terrible thought that they become men—or women—by becoming uniformed killers of people and dreams. There is a better way. The brother hero was on pilgrimage toward that way, searching for that way, creating that way. He was obsessed by a voice that would not let him go, drawing him, pressing him on the way, saying, "Blessed are the peacemakers . . ."

Is it too late to teach the children? Can the churches, with whom he carried on so fierce a lovers' quarrel, still get ready, committing themselves to explore alternative ways for the children to become women and men by working with the poor, gathering with the Native Americans in their struggles for survival and renewal, building armies of heroes in the inner cities, developing new links of compassionate solidarity overseas?

Is it too late for us, any, all, to walk through the official hero walls around King and enter into the last years of his life, dance imaginatively into his dream process, open beyond it to the dreams of saints and lovers over generations of struggle and create new realities, take our stand, teaching the children, with and without words, that there is another way, a better way than the way of weapons and war, to be all they can be?

Too late to get ready? Can't be. Late, but not too late, for we are here in this now, and it is ours. And the poor are gathering, and there is much mourning, and the thousands and the tens of thousands (are the faces familiar, hero faces, our faces?) are being called to comfort and fulfill.

ful-fill. To bring into actuality.

On April 6, 1968, two days after the bullet of fear and greed, of racism and militarism, and of ignorance and blindness had finally caught up with her husband, Coretta Scott King offered her own prose poem to the world:

He knew that at any moment his physical life could be cut short, and we faced this possibility squarely and honestly . . . without bitterness or hatred. . . . He gave his life for the poor of the world—the garbage workers of Memphis and the peasants of Vietnam. Nothing hurt him more than that humankind could find no way to solve problems except through violence. He gave his life in search of a more excellent way, a creative rather than a destructive way. We intend to go on in search of that way, and I hope that you who loved and admired him would join us in fulfilling his dream.

The invitation remains. Clear, precise, direct: fulfill the dream, fulfill the dreamer, fulfill the people, fulfill the nation. Bring it into actuality. Let it be born. Let us be born.

Calling all friends, lovers, and admirers. The invitation is here, still here. R.S.V.P. Now. It's getting late, and Charlotte is waiting with her children, to stand and walk and struggle and fly with all who will go with the hero, continuing the search, life-long search, soul-deep struggle, for the "more excellent way."

R.S.V.P. Get ready, if you please.

Returning to the source, the last half of Gwendolyn Brooks' poem closes the small book and opens the great path:

> His Dream still wishes to anoint
>   the barricades of faith and of control.
> His word still burns the center of the sun,
>   above the thousands and the
>   hundred thousands.
> The word was Justice. It was spoken.
> So it shall be spoken.
> So it shall be done.

Getting ready. The balm in Gilead flows, and we are anointed, sanctified, rescued from the mainstream, delivered to the ancient river. And the dream expands, explodes around, within, like a burning, rising sun filling every crevice of our trembling, yearning hearts. Justice. Compassion. Peace. Liberation. Love. Let them be spoken, let them be done, in us, in me. Getting ready.

Martin, Fannie Lou, Dorothy, Amzie, Bapu, A.J., Mickey, Sojourner, Clarence—all of you, we're getting ready. Charlotte's getting ready. The children are getting ready, to catch stars, to ride winds, to do the word, to fulfill the dream. Don't know about the nation, Martin, but some justice-loving, people-serving, peacemaking folks of every color and condition are getting ready. I see them, feel them, carry them in my bones. Rainbow warriors, anointed, burning bright, getting ready.

Walk through our walls. It's an invitation. R.S.V.P. Soon. 'Cause it's late, and we've found ourselves: we too are the heroes, singing, dancing, unrelenting heroes. And ain' no grave can hold our body down. Are you ready?

PART TWO

Roots of Conscience

COUNTING THE COST:
A Sermon on Discipleship
Jim Wallis

Now great multitudes accompanied him; and he turned and said to them, "If any one comes to me and does not hate their own father and mother and husband and wife and children and brothers and sisters, yes, and even their own life, they cannot be my disciple. Whoever does not bear their own cross and come after me, cannot be my disciple. For which of you, desiring to build a tower, does not first sit down and count the cost, whether you have enough to complete it? Otherwise, when you have laid a foundation, and are not able to finish, all who see it begin to mock you, saying, 'This one began to build, and was not able to finish.' Or what king, going to encounter another king in war, will not sit down first and take counsel whether he is able with ten thousand to meet those who come against him with twenty thousand? And if not, while the other is yet a great way off, he sends an embassy and asks terms of peace. So therefore, whoever of you does not renounce all that you have cannot be my disciple."

LUKE 14:25–33

T his very familiar scripture is about the cost of discipleship, the true meaning of following Jesus. Most of us grew up in churches in which texts like this were never preached about. But during the birth process of Sojourners Community, it became an important message for us.

At the evangelical seminary where the community began, it was one of the first ideas that we took hold of, and it sparked a renewal among us. People began to refer to what we were doing as "radical discipleship"; the movement that began to grow among younger evangelicals in the early 1970s was first called the "radical discipleship movement." Dietrich Bonhoeffer's classic book *The Cost of Discipleship* became an early text for us and Bonhoeffer an early teacher.

The rediscovery of discipleship as the basic call of Jesus was the foundation upon which Sojourners was built. It has been the beginning point, not only for us but for many others. But now that message comes back to us in a new situation with a new and deeper meaning. We are more aware now than before of what discipleship might mean.

In Luke 14:25, Luke reports that great multitudes accompanied Jesus. He was becoming very popular and successful as people responded to his teaching, healing, and power. Everywhere Jesus went the crowds followed.

The disciples must have been quite excited by all this success and perhaps thought to themselves that they might have a mass movement on their hands. But just as the crowds began to swell and press in on every side, just when it looked as though Jesus had sparked a popular response, he would always begin to say things like he says in this passage. And slowly the crowds would fall away, and only the disciples would be left.

Texts like this one record what are often called the "hard sayings" of Jesus, and indeed they are. When Jesus spoke in this way, his disciples became quite confused and disappointed. Self-doubt crept in. "What about us?" became their question.

What is the meaning of this passage for us today? Again, we see growing multitudes attracted to the gospel message. We see the beginnings of conversion in the churches. A tremendous response is developing to the biblical vision of justice and peace. Signs of new awareness and evidence of change exist in many sectors of the church's life. Both at the grass roots and at the level of church leadership, people are speaking out and acting in new ways. The media is taking notice, and the government is increasingly worried about the influence of the church. All of this brings us great hope.

The historical crises that have sparked this renewal of faith are the nuclear arms race, the situations in Central America and South Africa, and the desperate plight of the poor not only around the world but in our own cities and neighborhoods. We see many signs of a revival brewing and a movement spreading. As I travel around the country speaking and preaching, I find larger and larger crowds of concerned people— ordinary Christian people from churches across the entire spectrum of evangelical, Catholic, and all the Protestant denominations.

Peace Pentecost and so many other actions for peace around the country show that we have entered a new phase of escalated Christian opposition to the spiraling arms race. One can sense a growing network of people, groups, communities, and congregations all over the country slowly being knit together.

With all the signs of hope and change, movement and conversion, I sometimes feel like the disciples must have felt at the sight of the great crowds and their tremendous response to Jesus. I too find myself running to Jesus to say, "Look at what is happening throughout the churches all across the country. It's tremendous. I see so much hope."

But Jesus says, "If any one comes to me and does not hate their own father and mother and husband and wife and children and brothers and sisters, yes, even their own life, they cannot be my disciple."

Hate. What can Jesus mean by using the word "hate"? It means that our love must be so great for Jesus that in comparison everything else seems like hate. Our closest relationships must pale in significance compared to our relationship with Jesus.

This scripture cuts right at the heart of some of our flimsiest excuses. We would live among the poor, change our lives, give up our securities, risk going to jail, and put ourselves on the track of downward mobility, except for our families. "What about my spouse? What about my children? I would be willing to take the risk, but my husband, my wife, my kids—what about them?"

Jesus also says we must "hate even our own life." That means even our plans, career, vocation, security, success, fulfillment in life. We must hate even our own life. Indeed, these are hard words.

After hearing this my enthusiastic report to Jesus is stopped short and becomes more subdued, but Jesus goes on. "Whoever does not bear their own cross and come after me, cannot be my disciple." In the New Testament, the cross symbolizes suffering and the willingness to suffer. Jesus says that whoever is not willing to suffer for the gospel, for his sake, cannot be his disciple.

I remember a day with Allan Boesak, the South African leader, and his wife Dorothy Boesak. They were in Washington, D.C., for the August 1983 March on Washington. Dorothy spoke with great concern about her fears for their four children, for her husband's life, for the security of her family. She said, "We have had more death threats in the last week than in all the previous three months."

I was struck by what lies behind that kind of statement. What does it mean to live under the threat of death as a way of life? The reality behind Dorothy's statement is so different from most of our experience.

Dorothy went on to say that during their time here she spent some time with Coretta Scott King, which proved to be very meaningful and comforting. Coretta said that she and Martin always knew he would be killed. The only question was when. Coretta said they received every day as a gift of the grace of God. Each day was one more day to be together.

Several weeks later I spent a few days in St. Louis with Catholic women religious from many orders at their National Formation Conference. While I was there, an article came out in one of the local papers reporting that thirty-five Catholic women religious have been killed in Central America during the last five years. Women religious are beginning to understand something about suffering and the cost of discipleship.

But for most of us, suffering is still very foreign. Even though our own economic and political system stands behind the threats against people like the Boesaks and the Kings and supports governments that murder women religious in Central America, suffering is still alien to most of us in the North American churches.

A few weeks later, a friend of mine was in town for a visit. I was sharing with him the vision of a growing number of Christians in the United States of establishing a presence of North American Christians on the Nicaragua-Honduras border. The desire was to make a nonviolent witness for peace, to put ourselves in a situation of risk. We want to obstruct with our bodies the U.S.-sponsored war that is causing such destruction and taking so many innocent lives in Nicaragua.

My friend was playing the devil's advocate. While I was speaking of the grass-roots movement in the churches—how much it is growing and how strong it is becoming—he asked, "But how deep does it go? Are people even willing to go to jail for more than a few days, or at all, let alone risk their lives for the sake of justice, for the sake of peace, for the sake of another, for the sake of poor people threatened by policies of our government?"

A few weeks earlier, another friend and I talked about the Witness for Peace. We spoke of the possibility of a "nonviolent army" being formed. We talked of Christian people rooted in prayer and the Bible, ready to intervene nonviolently in situations of conflict, especially where the U.S. government and its policies are a great source of human suffering. We both became very excited as we talked. But when I raised the issue of not paying war taxes, he responded as many of my friends have by saying, "But if I don't pay my war taxes, I could lose my house."

Discipline. Sacrifice. Suffering. We must be willing to risk our safety and security and to put ourselves in real danger. This is the Achilles' heel of the North American middle class. The avoidance of pain and the fear of suffering are our leading characteristics.

Mohandas Gandhi led a movement for independence in India. Martin Luther King, Jr., led a movement for freedom in the United States. In each case the army of the movement was poor people—people who were used to suffering because of their daily experience. When they suffered in the streets, in jail, or on the back roads of Mississippi, it was not a new experience for them. They were ready for it. They had learned freedom would have its cost, and they were willing to pay it.

The great uncertainty of our movement, the great uncertainty for ourselves is, are we ready and willing to suffer? Suffering is foreign and feared. When (not if) the time comes, will we be prepared to suffer for justice, peace, the lives of other people, and for those who are threatened by the policies of our government?

To a great extent, the peace movement is still based on self-interest, fear, and desire for survival. I remember a comment made in our neighborhood by an old black man at the beginning of the nuclear freeze campaign. He said, "You know, white people have always gotten organized when their survival was at stake. When will they ever get organized for the sake of our survival?"

The peace movement is still not based on a willingness to risk and suffer. My friend playing the devil's advocate made another telling point. He said, "Ultimately disarmament will take risk and will require more than simple, rational persuasion. It's not honest to tell people that disarmament will come without any threat to their security, without any changes in their lifestyle, that there are no chances to take, that it's simply a matter of convincing people to be more reasonable."

It is true that disarmament will entail risk. Those in the peace movement who say there is no risk in disarmament are simply not being honest. And even more than being aware of the risks, people will need to be ready and willing to take them.

"For which of you," Jesus says, "desiring to build a tower, does not first sit down and count the cost, whether you have enough to complete it?"

"But Jesus," I say, "these people are really interested, they're really concerned." Jesus always replies, "But have they counted the cost?"

An undeniable shift is taking place in the North American churches. We have moved from being almost totally unaware of the gospel's meaning to a new place where we are genuinely interested in renewal.

We are excited about discipleship. We are beginning down the path of the kingdom. We are part of a growing multitude following after Jesus and hanging around the gospel.

Many people these days are wanting to hang around the gospel, hang around the places, people, actions, and communities where the gospel is being rediscovered. But when the hard word of Jesus is spoken, the crowds trickle away again, and only a few remain.

Are you interested? Count the cost. Are you excited? Count the cost. Do you think you are ready to follow Jesus? Count the cost. This is the clear message of the passage. It is as if Jesus says, "Don't be like those who start a building, lay a foundation, but never finish it. People will mock you and your faith."

The cynics will rise up to say, "Great movement, eh? Christian opposition? Radical discipleship? Political resistance? Constructing alternatives? Where? Show us. We don't see it. You never finished." Instead, we will have left only half-completed works, projects, actions, communities, and it will all be in ruins, memorials to a movement that did not count the cost.

Jesus points out that those who make war always count the cost. They are realistic, and they prepare. To make war, soldiers accept discipline and sacrifice and are ready to suffer. The cost does not take them by surprise. But what about those who would make peace, who would seek justice? Are we ready? Are we prepared? Will we be surprised by the cost and then turn away?

If we are not ready, we had better go to our adversaries—the rulers, the governments, the powerful, the warmaking institutions, the systems, the large corporations—to make our peace, negotiate, and compromise before we get routed in battle. This is what Jesus is saying. We had better count the cost.

Finally, Jesus gives us as hard and stark a word as exists in the New Testament. He says, "So therefore, whoever of you does not renounce all your possessions cannot be my disciple." In other translations it is often rendered, "So therefore, whoever of you who does not renounce all that you have cannot be my disciple."

Anything we cannot give up will certainly get in our way, hold us back, slow us down, be a heavy burden, and be used against us. That is a fundamental principle of the gospel. Those who have many possessions are not free. North Americans are not free.

Perhaps the reason we speak of freedom so much in this country is because we have so little of it. Freedom is not a license to accumulate, as some think. Rather, freedom is measured by how much we can give away, how much we can give up. We are not free in the United States because we are slaves to our wealth and security. Yet Jesus is asking if we are free enough to follow him.

Jesus also says, "Come to me, all who labor and are heavy-laden, and I will give you rest. For my yoke is easy, and my burden is light" (Matt. 11:28, 30). But to follow him, Jesus asks us to love him more than any other, even more than our own life. He asks us to take up the cross, to bear it as he did, and to be willing to suffer for his sake.

Jesus asks us to count the cost. We cannot know everything that lies ahead, but we need to be ready to do what he asks of us. He expects that if we start with him, we will be prepared to finish with him also. He asks us to give up everything else so we will be free enough to follow him, not by standing still, not by trudging and plodding, or even by just walking, but by running after him—unfettered, unencumbered, and untired.

When Jesus gave his disciples the great commission, he also gave them an extraordinary promise. He asked them to give up everything else, but he promised to give them the most important thing of all. That promise stands for us as well. Jesus says, "Go therefore and make disciples of all nations, . . . teaching them to observe all that I have commanded you" (Matt. 28:19–20).

And then he promises us the best gift of all, "Lo, I am with you always, even to the close of the age."

SPIRITUALITY AND COMMUNITY:
Reflections on Evil and Grace
Gordon Cosby

Gordon Cosby is the founder and pastor of Church of the Saviour in Washington, D.C. Through involvement with various inner-city ministries, including Jubilee Housing and Columbia Road Health Services, Cosby and the Church of the Saviour have pioneered a model of Christian spirituality, church renewal, and ministry that works to balance the inward, personal journey with the outward, activist journey. Christians in congregations across the country have benefited from their witness and experiences.

The following two-part interview with Gordon Cosby was conducted by Jim Wallis in Washington, D.C., in the spring of 1986 and covers issues related to spirituality and community.

—The Editor

Taking Evil Seriously

Jim Wallis: Your ministry and the Church of the Saviour are often associated with spirituality—the spirituality of ministry and the spirituality of community. But the word "spirituality" is sometimes difficult to understand. I think there is a tremendous hunger for and at the same time a lot of confusion about spirituality. Based on your life and your experience with the Church of the Saviour, what do you mean by spirituality?

Gordon Cosby: I think the image of spirituality that's best is one of intimacy in a relationship with Jesus. Jesus talked about his abiding in the Father and the Father abiding in him; he didn't do anything his Father/Mother didn't tell him to do or say anything God didn't tell him to say.

It appears to me that Jesus promises us the same sort of intimate relationship with him that he himself enjoyed with God. His own life was based on that intimacy, and he promises that the basis of our life can also be that intimacy. The relationship he has promised us—and the freedom that results from it—are, to me, the heart of spirituality.

How does prayer relate to spirituality and intimacy with God?

Prayer *is* this intimacy. Prayer is the sharing, the dialogue, the openness to God.

People often think of prayer in terms of techniques or how much time is given to prayer. But the goal of prayer is not just to develop a life of prayer but to develop the intimacy, the freedom, the authenticity, and the power that come from prayer.

They said of Jesus that he spoke with authority, not as the scribes and the Pharisees. It seems to me that his authority was the authority of intimacy. He was in touch with God's truth and reality, and when he spoke he was speaking out of the depths of that truth. So it is that intimacy, authenticity, and freedom that we long for.

We long to be true. We long to speak with authority. We long to be free so that all that we potentially can be will extend, unfold, and come into being, and we can be faithful to what we were intended to be. To me, all of this flows out of that intimacy.

It seems as if the creative and exciting ministries spawned by the Church of the Saviour in the low-income Adams-Morgan neighborhood of Washington, D.C., continue to proliferate. Yet, in the middle of a conversation one day, you said to me, "Despite our best efforts and intentions, all the work and sweat, and our prayers and faith, the neighborhood has gotten worse; things continue to deteriorate."

You also said those of us who are working for justice underestimate the power of the demonic. That raises very painful issues of effectiveness, success, and faithfulness, and finally the question of what we mean by the cross. What do you mean when you say the demonic is always underestimated?

It seems to me that the whole business of effectiveness and success is so deeply ingrained within us that we often think of our efforts solely in terms of successes, which can be very superficial. The real issue is our faithfulness to discovering our own personal call and our corporate call. And that call is always a call to connect with the pain somewhere in God's world.

In our case, Adams-Morgan is where we connect with pain. We are opened up to the capacity to enter into solidarity with people who enlarge us. And we also learn that whatever we are doing against the increasing need there seems laughable.

Therefore, somehow, we have to learn to get our satisfaction and our joy in faithfulness and in our intimate relationship with Christ. Then the question of effectiveness and success, in the usual sense of those terms, is not the issue. We can transcend that and get energized and nourished by faithfulness, knowing we are doing what we must do to live—not what we must do to change the neighborhood. The constant struggle is the deepening of faith that enables us to really trust that somehow the whole show is going to come off right in God's timing.

The assumption many of us make in the early stages is: "I'm going to be faithful. God's going to bless my faithfulness. I'm going to give it the best I've got. I've got this amazing vision of what can happen." The cross is the fact that all those amazing visions and all those dreams and all those things that are going to happen don't work.

In the early days I believed that if I were faithful, if I could just bring adequate faith to the task, God would honor my faithfulness and amazing results would occur. Well, I'm sure that those amazing results are occurring somewhere and they are going to be all added up in the final score. But they are not added up in ways I can see.

So I have to do some dying to what I feel I can do through my own efforts and my own capacity. Somehow it's a matter of becoming aware that evil and the demonic are much tougher and much more resistant than I thought they would be. It takes a deepened faith for me to keep hope when there appears to be a deterioration of the political climate and the neighborhood where we are struggling.

I can talk for a long time and very excitedly about what I feel are the manifestations of God's power in the neighborhood and in the lives of the people we are working with. But if one is looking at it from the standpoint of whether we're seeing a real flow toward love and sharing and unselfishness, and the blacks and the Hispanics and the whites and the rich and the poor coming together to the feast of the kingdom, and children not being abused and the elderly having the essential minimums for human beings in my neighborhood—that is just not happening.

What does it mean then to take the demonic as seriously as we ought to, and how does that change the way we respond, whether to the arms race or a neighborhood or any situation we're in?

We tend to think in terms of projects—housing projects, job programs, and so on. For instance, we've got 258 units of housing, and we're planning now to buy another building. We placed about eight hundred people in jobs through our Jubilee Jobs program last year. And we've got The Family Place, where we are working with parenting needs. But there's something important that is beyond those programs: it's what happens to the people in those buildings; it's getting access to the deepest levels of their lives.

But to get access to the deepest dimensions of the lives of people is something we cannot humanly do. That is where Christ is the evangelist. That is where the Holy Spirit has access to a person's inner life and produces a conversion. And we, through our programs, are getting very few conversions.

No matter how hard I try and no matter how well I plan and no matter how many gifted people I gather around for one of our programs, the real change is a change that takes place at a level of human life that I don't have access to. And I don't think it comes about through our programs. All the configurations of life keep changing, and if the poor get power you change the players but you're not getting a change in hearts and lives.

So part of what I'm talking about is evangelism, and not just with service efforts. How do we present the things of Christ? How do we pastor these lives? How do we let them pastor us so that fundamental change takes place?

Part of the secret of it, it seems to me, is really believing that we are not the ones doing it. As Scripture tells us, unless the Lord builds our house, those who build it labor in vain; unless the Lord watches over the city, the watchman stays awake in vain. And how then do we tangle with the powers of darkness? How do we "go down to Jerusalem" and expose those powers? We need to trust God that we are the instruments of another level of change taking place.

I see the social justice programs as a sort of "stage setting." But I see a tendency to stop there: "Here is our program. Isn't this wonderful!" Sure it's wonderful, and we are grateful for it; but all you have is the stage. How to get the kind of conversion that drives me and drives the community into a deeper level of our own inner conversion is the question.

Part of the power of the demonic is evident in how hard it is for me to be converted. It's not just in the poor and the situation out there that I see the demonic working; look at how it works in me. Look at how it works in our communities, in how we set the limits as to how much we are going to give of ourselves, or in how our own darkness is triggered and can use our energy up in working through crises that come up again and again. It's that darkness, the power of death, in me and in our communities, that I'm more aware of; and then I see it working out there in the inner-city environment.

I'm now part of our church's Evangelism and Pastoral Care Group. Our task is to assume responsibility for developing a spiritual relationship with two people in the neighborhood and working with them until the time comes that we can present the claims of Christ to them. If they are already in the faith in some sense, then we will pastor them and serve as spiritual guides to them. This is the hardest thing; all of the programs are easy compared to that.

It's the right direction, but it's hard to make that shift in mission to building the sort of relationship that will help a person to meet God, to meet Christ, and to be pastored. That's a new revelation—that it would be that hard. In developing those relationships we cross cultures and racial boundaries. Presumably we are there because Christ is in this thing, because Christ has called us to this, where we can begin to be in a spiritual relationship with the people we work with in our programs.

This has come about from sensing the inadequacy of the service programs by themselves. But you're not disparaging the programs; you're not about to disband them, are you?

No, I think they ought to be deepened and expanded, and we will do so. But unless we can put primary effort and energy into the work of conversion, I don't think the real, radical, fundamental change that we all long for is going to take place.

So without conversion, the social programs you've engaged in end up not changing very much?

I think they are a very important contribution, because it's important that we have the minimal essentials of housing for 260 families, rather than leave them on the street. I think it's important that over the years we've been responsible for putting fifteen hundred to two thousand people to work. I think that feeds into their dignity, their self-image. I think that's right and so to belittle that would not be fair.

If we are not willing to pay that price, then it seems to me that the work of conversion is cheap. To talk to people about Jesus without demonstrating that we care about the essentials of their lives is shallow and has little meaning. All I'm saying is that social justice work alone is only the stage setting.

Jesus fed the five thousand. Great! But he also said, "You shall not live by bread alone." He fed them. But he knew there was a deeper dimension and that bread alone was not the whole answer. That's the paradox I'm trying to describe.

We've got to be willing to be with people at the point of their physical hunger, their need for housing, their need for health care, and all of these things. If we have anything of the love of Christ in us and concern for the pain and the suffering of the world, then we must be concerned with those issues. But we can't stop at the point of those concerns. It must not be assumed that conversion will somehow happen on its own.

The concerns of social justice are a necessary foundation of evangelism. But to assume that because we're doing projects people will be converted, will touch the gospel, will come to know God is a wrong assumption. Therefore, on this foundation we must learn ways of relating, of sharing the gospel, and a new depth of intercessory prayer, so that this yearning, this hunger will be so heightened in people that they will cry, "What must I do to be saved?" In these programs people would find a community that can then be the midwife to get them into the kingdom.

When Sojourners Community first came to Washington, D.C., we met a young teenage boy who has been our friend now for a long time. He lived with one of our families for several years. Then he went back home for a while.

He became involved with a fundamentalist, evangelistic group that works in the city. When he came back to us and the family he had lived with, he said, "I learned so much from you about the meaning of following Jesus. But I never was clearly told what I needed to do to be saved."

The fundamentalist group had told him that, and he was converted. Although he had trouble with its politics and legalistic attitudes, something happened for him in terms of conversion. It was a clear word about conversion that in our early years in the neighborhood I don't think we were giving.

This is my point, you see, and I think this is happening all around the nation with the groups that are working with the various neighborhood responsibilities. It's very, very hard to bring together both the work of justice and the work of conversion.

Wasn't that indeed the experience of the early church—a church that in some cities would feed five thousand people a day and that was so known for meeting the needs of the people that it was profoundly evangelistic? In that sense it was not like most of the evangelical churches today, on the one hand, or most of the more liberal churches, on the other hand.

Bringing these seeming polarities together in that sort of integration gets back to the question of spirituality. It is an expression of spirituality to get social justice programs under way. It is an expression of spirituality to share the gospel in a more explicit way. Both of them are expressions of it.

And this integration has also been the only adequate response to the power and pervasiveness of the demonic.

This is where we started our conversation, you see. We must work with our social programs; but they are not going to stop the flow of the demonic. They're pathetic against the flow of the demonic.

We've got to deepen our capacity for Christ's whole life and being to penetrate us at a deeper level. And we've got to know that as we are working with all of these other efforts, our task is to help open up people for Christ to break into their hearts.

If we leave it at the level of just providing minimal necessities, that does not necessarily open the human spirit. Some of us have our basic needs met, but that doesn't mean we are open for Christ to penetrate our lives. By our actions we have not arrested a fundamental selfishness. And that's what I'm talking about—the darkness is a fundamental selfishness.

Now what's going to break that fundamental selfishness? That's the power of the gospel; that's the power of Christ breaking in.

It seems that you're saying there is also another problem: it's a lot easier to give and minister, to conceive and carry out projects and programs, to have meetings and make sure you have all your resources and your personnel. It's a lot easier to do that than to enter into your own conversion. Good, well-meaning people can do those things without ever facing what their own conversion might mean.

Unless there is a continuing inner journey, it's much more painful to get the plank out of our own eye and open ourselves to our own continuing conversion than it is to see the problems out there and then develop the programs to address those problems.

The witness of lifestyle is being made to the poor, even while we're serving the poor. Here's a guy who never had anything, and he's being witnessed to about the gospel by Christians, who are also witnessing by their lifestyle regardless of what they're saying. It seems to me that you can sometimes say exactly what Jesus said in Matthew 23 about the scribes and Pharisees—" . . . you traverse sea and land to make a single proselyte, and when that person becomes a proselyte, you make them twice as much a child of hell as yourselves."

What Jesus is saying is that you can bring people into your religious system and your scale of values, all of which is done in the name of God. They will accept your religious system and your value system, but they are worse off. We've had some success in helping people break out of the poverty cycle, and that's good. But some have adopted our upward mobility kicks. They will have a harder time having the kingdom break into their lives than before.

In some ways it's not only a problem of the social programs finally not getting to the heart of the issue, but also those administering the programs don't get to the heart of the issue in their own lives.

That's right. If we are not being changed and energized by our programs and projects, then the first mission isn't taking place. And if we are not being converted, then we are only satisfying a certain need to do good or to be generous. Without the inner change taking place within us, our good deeds can "protect" us from the deeper plan of the gospel, rather than serve the purpose of nurture.

There is no protective antidote to the demonic. It's ridiculous to be up against the demonic without spiritual armor. Everybody knows it's a tragic world that we're living in, but somehow you can know that and not carry a serious view of the demonic. When you're aware of it, you've got to put on this spiritual armor.

Just as you were talking, my mind went immediately to Paul's words in Ephesians 6. What does that passage on the spiritual armor, which begins with verse 10, mean to you?

"Finally then, find your strength in the Lord, in God's mighty power." What that means to me is to work as faithfully as I can with all of these things but to know that what matters is what God chooses to do through

162 / ROOTS OF CONSCIENCE

what I am doing. The tendency is to feel that I'm doing it, that I'm going to use my best thinking and my best organizational powers in whatever it is.

"Put on all the armor which God provides, so that you may be able to stand firm against the devices of the devil. For our fight is not against human foes." The fight is against the cosmic powers, the powers and potentates of this dark world, and against the superhuman forces of evil in the heavens. I need to be aware that as these forces are superhuman, they're beyond what I can handle, or what a committed community can really do anything about. They are *beyond* me.

I think this is the reason that many of us are exhausted. We have been up against these superhuman forces, and we have been trying to do it on our strength. As a result, we haven't taken up the whole armor. ". . . Then you will be able to stand your ground when things are at their worst, to complete every task and still to stand."

"For coat of mail put on integrity." Integrity, it seems to me, would be the embodiment of the truth. As we really are rooted in that which is eternal, then we are rooted in Christ and this intimacy. The truth is that love is available to me in Christ and that I can have an intimate sort of relationship with Jesus. Integrity is for that to be integrated within me, not compartmentalized.

Integrity is bringing the whole of your life into the situation and not living a different lifestyle while taking on this ministry.

That's right.

"Let the shoes on your feet be the gospel of peace, to give you firm footing; . . . take up the great shield of faith . . . to quench all the flaming arrows of the evil one. . . . Take salvation for a helmet." What does salvation mean then?

It may mean the conversion that you're talking about. The shield of faith protects us from the flaming arrows of the evil one or the assaults that seem to be coming at us constantly. I don't think we're conscious very often that we need a shield, the shield of faith, to protect us against those assaults.

If we don't have that shield, then all of the assaults register at an inner level; we have to deal with them, and they are exhausting to us. A shield would keep those darts away from the human body. One of the ways I would interpret that would be as detachment: I can take what comes and act detached from it and not bury it within myself, because I know that there are protections around me and around my loved ones.

"For sword, take that which the Spirit gives you—the words that come from God." That ties in, it seems to me, with the temptations that Jesus had. That phrase, "the words that come from God," is almost the same expression as "You cannot live on bread alone, but on every word that God utters."

And so we hear once again that word of intimacy. That's the word that has the power to change, to do what needs to be done. It has the power to penetrate, to go where human words cannot go.

And this ties in with whether we are offering the Word of God in our programs and our work. Is the Word of God being offered, or simply affordable and safe housing?

That's exactly right. You can't offer that Word of God except out of intimacy with God.

"Give yourselves wholly to prayer and entreaty; pray on every occasion in the power of the Spirit. To this end keep watch and persevere, always interceding for all God's people; and pray for me, that I may be granted the right words when I open my mouth and may boldly and freely make known his hidden purpose, for which I am an ambassador in chains. Pray that I may speak of it boldly, as it is my duty to speak."

This refers back to community and its members' obligation to pray for one another, so that each of us may be able to speak those words boldly every day. Then they are words that are going to have penetrating power.

Not long ago President Reagan appeared on television to pressure the Congress to give aid to the Nicaraguan contras. I was impressed with the power of evil to mask itself in light. He lied, and it sounded like the truth. Then the Democratic Party opposition came on, and they basically said, "We think he's right about everything he said, but we think there's a better way to do this." But no one tells the truth.

And so you despair. You look at your own resources and your own power, and you wonder how in the world you can counteract all of that. You envision educational campaigns, but you know that what Reagan is appealing to finally is the same values and assumptions in the American public that need to be changed. He's saying, "We don't want to lose what we have, and we're going to do whatever it takes to keep it."

The Bible doesn't say that the armor of God is, say, an hour of TV time to respond. How do we respond and keep ourselves from being over-whelmed?

Well, I feel all of the things that you are saying very, very deeply, and it is the most unmatched face of evil that I've seen in my life. We have the American public believing the lies or knowing that they're being told lies and not minding, which may be worse.

I would look at what happened during the Nazi regime in Germany. It feels to me like that is the kind of thing that is taking place. And I don't want to just go belly up on it, I want to put on that armor of God.

I think we have to do what we can do, get whatever television time we can get, and so forth. But it won't be enough unless something is happening at a deeper level with the people of God in this nation, and around the world, and unless God is hearing the people who are crying out in their pain and their suffering. Because God hears those cries, God is raising up Moseses here and there to respond and help bring the deliverance. And we need more of these Moseses.

We've got to recognize the flaming darts of the wicked one and try to protect our own inner integrity and the inner integrity of our communities. We've got to hold on to the faith, no matter whether death comes to us personally, corporately, or as a nation. As this stuff swirls around us, we witness to the fact that life is one long storm. I think we are reduced right now to thinking in terms of whether we can retain our own hearts in purity and in faith.

The power of evil becomes so strong that simply battling it on its own terms cannot suffice. All we can hope for, cry out for, is a deeper and deeper awakening of the power of God in our lives and in the community of faith. And that conversion, finally, is the only response that is spiritually sufficient to counter what I saw on television that night—not getting an Op-Ed piece in the New York Times *the next day saying it isn't true.*

That's what I feel about our neighborhood, you see, and the same thing is occurring within the nation. You can feel the power of the demonic. It's unbelievable. And therefore fighting it on its own terms is a joke.

And yet it's interesting that one can see the power of evil and not be depressed by it. I'm much less depressed by all this than I used to be, but I think I care more.

I'm much more impressed with the necessity of that cross—for me or for anybody. God's getting into this situation was not just something that was peripheral. Jesus' living, dying, and being raised again is absolutely essential for any of us to make it.

The response to the power of the demonic, whether it be in the neighborhood or in the nation, is the traditional affirmation: "Christ has died, Christ is risen, Christ will come again." Finally that's all that we can say, and it's the only thing that is sufficient to respond to the power of evil.

That's right. And it's the only thing that's got a prayer of a chance in this universe.

Depending on God's Grace

We have talked about conversion and faith. Now I'd like to hear your thoughts about community. How is community an expression of faith, and how does community nurture faith?

The conversion experience brings one into a conscious relationship with Jesus, but at the same time it brings one into a conscious relationship with other people. When the conversion experience is a whole conversion experience, one is brought into a corporate reality and therefore, in some genuine, authentic sense, into community. If conversion to the gospel begins with individual praying, it becomes a matter of the person moving from that individualism into being part of a corporate entity. It's a long journey from individualism to being a "corporate" person, but a necessary one.

So you're saying that part of the call of the gospel itself is a call to a new community as well as to Christ.

That's right. You can't have one without the other. All of the images in the Scriptures having to do with the church are corporate images—the people of God, the body of Christ. The person who says, "I want to belong to Jesus, but I don't want to belong to community," is saying something that is impossible from a biblical understanding of the church.

How is the community a crucible of conversion? How does continuing conversion occur in the context of community?

It seems to me that individualism is so strong in each one of us that we have to be converted step by step to get to the place where we really are corporate people. A community has to have different stages for that continuing conversion to occur. So you have exploratory steps, such as intern or novice membership.

Becoming a corporate person has to happen step by step because community is very, very frightening and extremely difficult. It is much more difficult than that new person realizes. Community is hell for many, many people—or an experience to be tolerated.

Why is that so?

I think that's because we are so individualistic. We have our own ego needs, and every new step of community is a threat to the false self. We hope that the false self will die and the true self will come into its fullness and completion. That is the self that is the corporate self and that is concerned with the common good, not only within the life of the community but for the larger common good. But the process of that false self dying so that the true self may be actualized is a very, very painful process. We resist that death even though community insists on it.

The dying of the false self is not a conceptual death. It's an actual death in the context of other selves that each of us comes up against in community—and they are wounded, fractured, and broken individuals, just as we are fractured and broken and wounded. With all that woundedness rubbing up against the woundedness of one another, it's a difficult phase. But that's the context for the movement away from the false self, the inauthentic self, to begin.

I'm intrigued by your description of this movement from being a person who is individualistically preoccupied to one who has a corporate sense of self and vision. How would you describe those two kinds of people? What happens to people as they enter community as "individual" persons and become more and more corporate persons?

I think most persons who come into a Christian community want support for their lives, but feel that they must make fundamental decisions themselves. They want to be associated with community for comfort's sake, for a sense of support with other people. They want to be associated with a group of people that is doing significant things and is on the right side of the issues. But they are not at all ready to surrender any part of their sovereignty to a larger call.

What I'm talking about is the sort of thing that happens between two individuals in marriage. You can have two individuals who have a very close, wonderful friendship with one another. They are associated with one another, and they give one another support. But that's different from a union in which those two give up some sovereignty and the two become one.

I think that's something like the process that happens when a person genuinely enters into community. We are not only associated with one another and giving one another support. Something happens, and we begin to conceive of ourselves as part of a larger entity, as members of a body, not existing except as members of that body. Our deep, authentic existence is drawn from a body to which we belong and from playing a part in its life.

I think this movement is a gradual process. Some people, even after having been in community for quite a long time, will still be making basic individual decisions and then may announce to the community that they have decided to leave it. They will have done it on their own, not as a part of a process. They haven't considered that they really were a part of the body, nor said, "I need your discernment, I need your help on this."

It's very important for me to play my part as a member of a body and not just work for my individual fulfillment. And the same principle applies to how we belong to the totality of the body of Christ, so that we transcend the local community of which we are a part.

I'm struck by how you differentiate association from union. A lot of people think they want community, but what they really want is an association with others that will enhance their own individual capacities and fulfillment. They are not really seeking union with other people that entails, as you say, a surrender of sovereignty.

I think this is the heartbeat of the issue. For a community to be maintained and its life deepened over a period of time, there must be a "critical mass" of people who understand just what the community is about. It is this critical mass of people that is seriously in union with the community and is not seeking personal enhancement in and through the community or making demands of ego on the community.

Dietrich Bonhoeffer called these personal ego demands "wish-dreams." Bonhoeffer said they are imposed on the community, which then tends to destroy the community. But if you've got that critical mass who really understands the community, then it can deal with the people who come in expecting the community to enhance their egos and their own fulfillment. In one sense, it is very desirable that certain of their dimensions be enhanced; but the death process has to take place so that what has been enhanced is now serving the community, rather than enhancing and serving the ego needs of the person.

Every community has to be aware of and see whether it has that critical mass. And it needs to sustain that critical mass and not give itself in so many different types of outreach or mission that it doesn't nurture this inner core of its life. It's not an easy thing to see. You can't say, well this person has really made this transition and this person over here has not. It's very subtle. But if I know that it is going on, I've got a better chance of being aware of what the community needs and how to nurture it.

A few months ago, when you were sharing an evening with Sojourners Community, we learned about the breakup of a community that has been very close to us for a decade. You instinctively responded about the fragility of community and how forces, particularly the forces of evil around us, want to break up community. Can you say more about what nurtures and sustains a community for the long haul?

First of all, I think that it's very right for some communities to go out of existence. It's not always a tragedy, because the Spirit can call people together for a period of time. Sometimes it's appropriate for that time to end and for the Spirit then to call those people, and other people, to new combinations of life. That's important to recognize, because sometimes we assume that anything that is good ought to go on forever, and I just don't believe that.

So if there's that sort of call into being and out of being, I rejoice in it. But I think a lot of communities are not really called out of being, but instead they are destroyed by the forces of our society and the demonic working through the forces of our society. I think that's what you were talking about, and we need to be aware of it.

Then how do we sustain it? One of the important things is the process through which people come into membership in any community. That is where the battle is lost for most of us. We don't have people who are discerning enough to be able to detect some of the inauthentic motivations and deal with them ahead of time.

Now the minute a new person comes into membership, that person has ultimate power to determine the direction and the destiny of the community. That's really what membership means. But all of the members of a community are not members on the same basis and understanding of Christian community.

If a community is going to have a life that is an alternative life to the dominant culture and the dominant consciousness, then it must clearly define what its corporate life is and is not about. It must clearly prepare people who want to explore that life and who are making the transition from noncommunity to community life. A fundamental difference exists between what the new person has lived through within the dominant society and what they aspire to in this alternative community which is the church. It's in that initial period of spiritual formation that the person really enters into the community. That is where I feel we can lose the battle.

Sometimes it comes to be a power struggle between the people who see community at a deeper level and the people who were attracted to the excitement and the vitality and the works of the Holy Spirit in the community. This latter group finds that the price is too high for them to pay; they do not really want this death and resurrection, and the next death and resurrection, and the next death and resurrection. Then you've got a battle going on within the membership.

A community that was at one time called into being can move into a period when the Spirit departs and it does not have that critical mass. This is what I mean by the fragility of community. Without people who have the gift of discernment, you may not know until several years have gone by that the Spirit has really been lost. The community can start operating on its natural power, on the basis of sound, rational planning and efficiency—all of the things that the world operates on. And people who are gifted can do a lot of good things even when the community has shifted. It may have shifted slowly and without members discerning it.

Another reason why community is fragile is that sometimes a community is held together not only by a certain combination of persons but by one person who is crucial to that combination, and when that one person is lost, the community is gone. Nobody can pull it back, because this is the person who had the spiritual authority within the life of the community to keep reminding the community or bringing it back to where it should be.

What are the temptations that threaten a community after it has been formed and existed for several years, after it has become more or less successful?

Any community in good, strong shape is existing by God's grace. Yet, the stronger and more powerful it is, the more vulnerable a community is, because it has to deal with power and success. It has to deal with its fame and with the way other people and the society perceive it. It has all of the temptations that Jesus had in the wilderness. The community, therefore, faces new temptations because of its effectiveness.

Another way to describe this is through what is called the "monastic cycle." The cycle is that devotion produces discipline, discipline produces abundance, and abundance destroys discipline. The cycle happens both individually and corporately. Through the devotion that comes in knowing Christ, meeting Christ, and being overcome by the grace we have been given, our sins are forgiven. We then want to be open to the disciplines whereby the grace can be enhanced in our lives. The disciplines are an opening to grace that can fill our lives. So we do that, and grace pours into us individually; it pours into us as a community. In terms of the gospel image, we are faithful with one city, with its human intensities, opportunities, and responsibilities, and so we are asked to be faithful with ten cities or a hundred cities.

But at this point the temptation, it seems to me, always is to believe that we have done the work rather than accepting that we were the channels, or instruments, of God. It's almost impossible for those things not to slip in at that point, because we think we've got the key to this thing, we know how to go about it, and we've gotten sophisticated enough to make our way around the world. People ask us how to deal with things, and they treat us as authorities.

The critical question then becomes: can a community stand the pressures of abundance? It takes a deeper level of faith for a community to rejoice in its abundance and to know that abundance is the result of grace rather than its own capabilities and maturity. So it's an issue of whether or not the community can sufficiently deepen its faith.

In the early days, all of us had to depend upon grace, through whatever resources came to us, to survive a week. Now, most of us have a financial basis that can survive a longer time. So we're not as dependent. At the same time, we declare that we are depending upon God's grace. We don't have to depend on it in the way we did earlier, so it's important to learn how we can be dependent in our own hearts and spirits for the Spirit to be with us every day now, as when we were literally dependent on it each day. I just think it takes more faith to do that.

Are there essential elements of community? Are there secrets, perfect models, key structures, or unchanging institutions that make community work? Are there other elements, in addition to a critical mass, that really need to be present for the core community to begin, to endure, and to sustain itself?

I think you've got to have one or two people who somehow have been so touched by God, Jesus, the Holy Spirit, that they can call the community into being.

Do you mean a founder or founders?

I mean a founder who soon has founders, but I think it usually starts with a founder. You may have a couple of other people who are exploring and saying we need to do something. Often, out of that group, you have one person who says, "I am going to do it." Then some of those other people who are exploring say, "Well, I'd like to go with you." But often it's that one person who simply starts trying to create community, without having done much of this intellectual work regarding models. I think it usually starts at a deeper level.

Those who gather around that leader have to work with what they perceive to be the fundamental dimensions of the community that they are bringing into being. They have to get down to very clear specifics of what are the marks of community for them. Everybody's got to get down to the hard work of saying that my call is a call to be a part, to bring into being, to be evolving with the community, and these are the necessary minimums to make it worthwhile for me to lay down my life.

These minimums vary, because mine will be different from yours. But if certain things that are fundamental for me no longer exist here, then I'm going to start over agin. While they are not to be absolutized, the minimums have to be made specific, because otherwise the community is lost very, very quickly.

Can you give some examples of what some of those specifics might be, even though they may vary from place to place?

I think that the people who come in to the community must be committed to the deepening of the inner life, which means moving toward the death of the inauthentic self, whether you call it the "inward journey" or another name. Then you have to work with the structures whereby that takes place so you don't separate the concept from the structures through which it will happen.

The second thing is that commitment to community must issue in some relief of the suffering of humankind—locally or around the world—since God is calling us to connect with that suffering. At some point we've got to suffer to relieve it, to bring about liberation and to bring about freedom. That will become very specific for every community.

The community also will have to decide the frequency of its gathering together and celebrating common life in worship. I feel that for the deepening of the inner life, some clear, personal discipline of prayer and working with the Scriptures is essential, in addition to the work that goes on corporately. If a person coming in says they are not going to have time for that, or they can't get into that dimension, then you simply say they have to wait a little while, because this is essential to community for us.

I think one of the most important disciplines for anybody coming in is a discipline of money. Money, and what it represents, is an idol for almost all of us, and, therefore, to think that one is going to have genuine community without giving up money is an illusion. Oftentimes that's been a more healthy discipline for us than prayer, because you can fudge on prayer and make everybody think you are doing it. If you have a money discipline, it's clear whether you are or are not following it. We've had more people who have not come into the community because they couldn't deal with the money discipline than because of any other discipline.

One very basic element of community has to do with the authority and obedience issue, which centers around gift evoking. Whatever the gifts within the life of the community, the person who exercises a gift must exercise authority when offering the gift; and the people who are responding to that gift are thereby being obedient to it. So the issue of authority and obedience comes into play around identified gifts, or functions, within the life of the community. This means a community is not operating as a democracy. A community operates around the gifts of the Holy Spirit, which have been identified and which are being exercised. And where you exercise a gift, there is authority.

You say community is not a democracy but operates by the exercise of the gifts of the Spirit. How does this relate to the difficult questions about consensus versus hierarchical forms of decision making and leadership?

Normally, the way we think about organizations is that we all have an equal vote and that the majority rules and will make a decision about the issues before that group. But the church functions under the guidance and power of the Holy Spirit, which transcends human power. I don't feel there is a prayer of a chance in the world of any of our missions being effective unless they use the pentecostal power, the power of the Holy Spirit, which is formed through us.

It seems to me that the whole book of Acts has to do not with majority rule in the first days of the church but with the gifts of the Spirit. In Acts 8 Philip goes up to Samaria under the guidance of the Holy Spirit. There he gets the guidance to go down to the Gaza road. Down at the Gaza road, he gets the guidance to join the chariot and talk to the Ethiopian official who is reading Isaiah 53 and wondering what it is about. Philip says, "I can help you with your problem." And so the gospel gets to Ethiopia, without a committee and without a budget.

In Acts 16 Paul is wandering around, not allowed to go into Bithynia or Asia. The scripture says that the Spirit of Jesus did not allow it. He goes to Troas and gets a vision: "Come over to Macedonia and help us." Now, that's guidance, that's the Spirit, and so the gospel begins to travel west.

That sort of movement of the Spirit within the life of our communities is what we've got to depend on. Who are the ones who have the call and the gift that have been identified and have emerged from within the life of the community? Whatever your gift within the life of the community, which the community has identified, it has to be trusted in those areas. Whatever the gifts of the other people in the community—the gift of pastoring, or the gift of publishing, or the gift of administration—they must be recognized and respected as gifts of the Spirit through those people.

This doesn't mean that the judgment of those persons is never questioned. To have all of these gifts functioning in concert under the orchestration of the Spirit is the way the community is to operate, rather than to say these are the things we need to work with and devise some strategy. It is not that we don't have to do that, but that's not the primary emphasis.

If we can function under call and under gifts, then people can support, encourage, and be a part of us as we are faithful to that call and the gifts that are evoked in the service of that call. But that is an entirely different way of functioning than saying we've all got an equal voice in this thing, and we are going to work for the majority vote. It is a process that is constantly working itself out if we are committed to it.

GOD'S GIFT OF DISPLACEMENT:
Learning Our Place in Creation
Elizabeth McAlister

When you were young, you fastened your belt and walked where you chose; but when you are old you will stretch out your hands and a stranger will bind you and lead you where you have no wish to go.

JOHN 21:18

These words from the last chapter of John's Gospel reduced Peter to silence for perhaps the first time in the Gospels. Well they might. In them Jesus painted a vivid image of what Peter's fate would be as a witness to him. In dramatic relinquishment of control over his own life, Peter became a prisoner and was crucified for his Lord.

This is the kind of image that, at worst, fills our hearts with terror and, at best, causes us to falter or flee, especially when the cross of Christ passes its shadow over our lives. With diffident hearts we want to calculate with our God: "This much, Lord, okay? Just don't let 'such and such' happen to me. Don't touch this part of my life!" We project horrors and tragedies beyond our strength to endure.

I know moments when I go into a cold sweat about the future. A familiar interior monologue goes something like this: "God has asked this sacrifice of me. It is livable—not so bad, if the truth be known. . . . It's painful—unbearably so at times (or so it seems), but if I let God think *this* is okay, what will God exact next? So I'd better pretend it's harder than it is or that I'm weaker than I am."

The monologue is foolish in the extreme. I emerge from it laughing at myself and trusting that God laughs too, because God knows what I perceive but dimly—that the sacrifice, the pain, the strength, and the joy are all God's gift and that there can be no pretense before God.

Part of that gift is the ability to look over my shoulder and understand that the moments of deepest pain have been those in which I was most alive, most in tune with the sufferings of others, and, by a strange paradox, most joyful. I emerge from the fear and sweat only with an act of faith, with gratitude for all God's gifts, with laughter, and with a renewed commitment to live in the present moment, the only time and place in which I can live or praise God.

Still, it is hard to surrender to God's future. Something in me seems to need to believe that there is something other than love in God.

These are prison musings. They flow from the experience of having stretched out my arms and having "a stranger bind me and lead me where I had no wish to go." They confess the pain that surrounds me in this place as well as my own grief at being separated from those I love passionately. And maybe they are the kind of musings that equip me to say something about the relinquishment or displacement to which we are summoned as Christians.

Displacement is moving from one's "ordinary" or "proper" place in this culture or society. Usually it's a place we have chosen for ourselves, one to which we have aspired and struggled. Usually it implies that we have come of age, have "made it," or at least that we are on the way to "making it."

Displacement is moving into a life of solidarity with the countless millions who live disrupted lives. We have all seen them: in Africa, fleeing famine in their emaciated bodies; in Central America, fleeing war and torture at the hands of tyrants; in Mexico, seeking refuge from a city split apart by earthquakes; in Colombia, displaced or killed by volcanic eruptions; and in this country, left homeless by floods or poverty.

These are but a few of the current, visible images of displacement, reminders of the fragility of all our settled places. We cannot refuse to see the sufferings of others—not anymore. The news is an endless litany of human pain. And, as if against a coming storm, we try to establish shelters, insurance policies, and nest eggs and become settled in an artificial comfort that denies our shared humanity and vulnerability.

I would like to hold up an image for our consideration. Imagine the refugee woman as the figure who replaces the hero in our consciousness. She is the archetype of our vulnerability fleshed out in the hostage, the homeless, the poor, the prisoner, the victim of human-made and natural disasters. Her image calls us to acknowledge that we are all vulnerable. No one is secure. It tells us that the more we cling to our securities, the more we become playthings of illusion.

If we know anything about the forces at work in our world, we are—all of us—adrift without bearings, out of our depths. The threat of annihilation is over us and our children, and our special accounts and insurance policies are useless. The "self-reliant" do not fare better than the "dependent." The passengers aboard the Achille Lauro or the Korean Flight 007 were not homeless refugees. Their faces may be more like us than those referred to earlier.

To deny our vulnerability is to stand against life, to join forces with those who would destroy all of life rather than accept the displacement to which we are summoned. In this context the options before us become clear, as does the meaning of our nuclear arsenals and the religion or antifaith they have become. Let us look, for a few moments, at these images and try to feel them as two poles, each seeking to lure us to itself and press us to its service.

At the one pole, we are, most of us, citizens of a country with imperial claims and policies and weapons. We are enticed into absolutizing the state. Our nation-state has created weapons (idols) that its people, in the name of loyalty and patriotism, are told to trust in (worship)—trust in the security they offer us and our way of life.

With insatiable appetites our presidents, military, arms manufacturers, and media incessantly cry for more and more of the resources of our country and its people to serve the research, development, and deployment of these weapons. They appeal to our fear of enemies, our selfish clinging to what is ours, to the threat we instinctively feel as we see the "refugee"—the poor of the world—reaching, stretching, straining for the basic necessities of life.

Allowing ourselves to be drawn to this pole means accepting the irrationality of the whole stance of our civilization—threatened with annihilation, waiting for it to happen, using much of its resources toward making it happen and virtually none toward preventing it; accepting the injustice through which we claim so much of the world's resources as our right; and accepting the none-too-gradual erosion of our freedoms in the name of national security.

The other pole calls to our hearts, to our shared humanity, to our dependency on and interdependency with the earth, air, water, fire. It speaks in whispers to what is best in us, not as citizens of one country over against all that threatens us, but as people who are part of one world. At times accusingly, at times with gentle coaxing, this pole speaks of the image of the refugee woman and all that she stands for, calling us to go where it hurts, to enter those places where pain is part of life, to share her brokenness and anguish and fear. To become vulnerable.

Standing with the world in this way means: learning to listen in compassion and to exchange competition with service to one another; learning reverence for the mystery of life and the intricate network of nature that serves life; learning that real strength is created through standing with one another in corporate vulnerability; and learning that suffering is not an end or goal but the occasion for healing, for birthing, for growth.

These two poles are the dramatic choices before us in this age and season. We cannot wait long to choose. Even as we wonder and weigh the choice, we are inducted. The imperial state requires little more than our silence and our monies to serve its purposes. Until we determine to withdraw them, we remain in complicity with it. That is to remain hopeless and faithless. And that is a hopelessness that doubts the power of God at work in our world. It is a faithlessness that fails to live in covenant with God and with life. In our waffling we choose to make covenant with other "gods" and so abort the promise of God before it can come to birth.

The atmosphere in nuclear nations must challenge us as Christians. Our God is a jealous God. God will not take a "rightful" place beside country, occupation, or family. Our God has made it clear that to know and worship God means to be just with one another—especially to be just toward those who are most needy. Our God calls us to that displacement which is only a matter of learning our place in creation.

We can choose displacements, or they can be imposed. The issue is to make them voluntary, to will them by acceptance if we are unwilling or unable to choose them. So we can choose to uproot our lives to serve the refugee, the prisoner, the poor one, or we can accept it with a willing spirit, if we are made such through some disaster or decision of conscience.

While there is no woman in this prison by choice, the way each chooses to live here radically affects the lives of us all. Whether chosen or accepted, poverty can be voluntary. As such it has a healing quality that finds its antithesis in the grasping, hoarding spirit.

If we cannot choose freely, we can choose to be chosen. If we cannot, in grace, come down to where we ought to be, perhaps we can confess, in the words of the poet Wendell Berry in his poem "We Who Prayed and Wept":

> Those who will not learn in plenty
> to keep their place

must learn it in their need,
when they have had their way and
the field has spurned their seed.
We have failed thy grace.
Lord, I flinch and pray:
"Send thy necessity."

LET US BELIEVE:
Jesus' Presence in a Prison Cell
Allan Boesak

The following sermon was preached by Rev. Allan Boesak in his own church in Bellville, South Africa, on Sunday, September 22, 1985. This was the first Sunday after his release on bail from Pretoria Central Prison, where he had been detained for nearly four weeks on charges of sedition. The sermon is based on Mark 9:14–27.

—The Editor

> And Jesus said to him, "If you can! All things are possible to him who believes."
>
> MARK 9:23

I came upon the text for today exactly a week ago, while I was in my cell in Pretoria Central Prison, after one of the most difficult weekends in all my life. The first two weeks of imprisonment I could bear, even the silence, even not being able to speak with anyone, not being able to open my heart, not being able to share my feelings, my fears, my anxieties, or my longings. I could bear not being able to tell anyone how much I missed my wife and my children, my family, my congregation. It was only in those days that I discovered how much I love this congregation in Bellville and how much all of you have become part of my heart and my life and why it is that God, through very difficult days, has kept me in this congregation for nine years now.

But the third week became almost too much for me. By 3:00 in the afternoon they bring your supper. By 3:30 they lock up and slam the grill in your cell and double-lock it. Then they slam the steel door and double-lock that, too, and finally the two grills in the passage. That Friday afternoon of the third week was no different. As I sat silently in my cell, the noises of the wardens leaving the prison building faded away, and on the floor above me I could hear the other prisoners talking with one another, reading the newspapers of the day, discussing this or that, sometimes laughing—and I had no one to share this with, no one to talk to.

I had been on my knees almost constantly for three weeks, praying to God to lead me out of that darkness and out of that pain and out of that suffering. And nothing happened. Then the moment came when I fell on my knees and I cried as I never cried before, maybe for the first time since I was a little boy. I then said to God, "I do not understand this. Why have you brought me here? It's been three weeks now, God, and I have prayed every day and I have tried to believe that you in your power will take me out of this place of imprisonment and bring me out into the world again, to the community of the living again." When you are locked up like that you sometimes feel as good as dead.

For three weeks I believed that somehow God would work through the international community to put pressure on the South African government to let me out. After three weeks, that did not happen. All my life I have tried to hold on to my faith. I have preached the gospel as honestly as I could, because I believe that Jesus has called me to do that. I said to God: "Why, if I am your servant, if I have tried to do what is right in this world, have you done this to me? I have said it all. You know God, what happened to me in this year, in 1985. Wasn't that enough? Why must I now sit here in this prison, not understanding, not seeing any way out of this?"

I wrestled with God. I fought with God. I said, "I was a fool! If I were a little cleverer, I would have accepted one of those positions offered me in America, to become a professor of theology at some university or other. I could have pursued the nomination to become the general secretary of the World Council of Churches. I could at least have asked my supporters, yes, please lobby for me. Instead, I wrote to the search committee and said no, I do not want this position because I believe that my place, at this time in history, is in South Africa. If I were wise, I could have taken my wife and my children and left South Africa because I know what happens to people in this land who try to struggle for justice and for peace. If I had done this," I said to God, "my wife and my children would have been with me. If I had done this, I would have been safe now. If I had done this, I would not have been in this place now."

I said to God: "You made me believe that the struggle for justice and human dignity, the struggle for peace and humanity in South Africa is also *your* struggle. You made me believe, from the very beginning, that my opposition to the South African government was never my own. It was an opposition that was based always upon my faith in Jesus Christ. And upon the certain knowledge that apartheid is a heresy and that it cannot be defended on the basis of the gospel. I believed that my involvement in the political struggle for the sake of the weak and the poor and the needy is an integral part of my discipleship, is the heart of my discipleship in this country. This is what you, God, have called me to do. Why have you made me believe this and yet brought me to this place?"

I do not mind telling you this morning, my brothers and sisters, that this was the most difficult moment of my life. As I knelt there, the words couldn't come anymore, and there were no more tears to cry. Friday night went by and Saturday morning dawned, and there was still no answer. Saturday night came, and I wrestled through the night and still I found no answer. My difficulty with this God whom we cannot see, whom we have to believe in although he will not break through the prison walls and make his voice plain to me so that I could hear another voice apart from my own to reassure me—this difficulty became unbearable.

I thought to myself: I have always preached from this pulpit (and you are my witnesses!) that I believe in the power of God, that Jesus Christ is Lord and King, and that therefore no government on earth can detain the power of God. But as I sat there in that jail, and as the days and the nights crawled by and that weekend dawned upon me and I still could see only darkness, I said to myself, "Am I to believe that the power of P.W. Botha and Louis le Grange [South African minister of justice] is greater than the power of this almighty God?"

But on Sunday morning, I opened my Bible to read. I am not one of those who believe that you just open the Bible and mysteriously God will show you a passage. But I opened my Bible to find a word of consolation, a word of light, a word of inspiration, a word of truth that would take away from me my uncertainty, my fear, my anxiety—a word that I could hold on to. And without my having looked for it, my Bible fell open at Mark 9, and like the blast of a trumpet the words of Jesus fell on my ears: "If you believe, all things are possible to those who believe." And then I knew. That night, Sunday, September 15, I sat down, and I wrote a letter to my wife and said to her, "I have wrestled with God and it is over. I now know that I will be with you before the weekend."

In this passage I saw my own dilemma as I came to understand the dilemma of this father who brought his sick child to Jesus. The dilemma of this father begins with the fact that his child was ill. Today we would say that this child was an epileptic. All the symptoms are there. But in those days, they did not know this. They only saw something they did not understand, that threatened their existence, their lives, and the meaning and worth of their lives. And when they experienced something that threatened the good order of God as God meant it to be, the only way they could express their feelings of fear was to say: "This is an evil spirit."

They understood their struggle as not so much against the illness, but as a struggle against the spirit of evil that had seized this boy, that had this boy in its grip, that would not let go, and that would kill this boy. "Sometimes," the father said to Jesus, "the spirit would grab him and throw him in the water and sometimes in the fire." He might burn to death any moment; he might drown any moment. What was he to do?

The issue here is not merely their inadequate understanding or our knowledge of illness based on modern scientific methods and research. Neither is it a question of our superiority, since we no longer speak of "evil spirits" when someone is ill. There is something more to this.

We like to believe that through our scientific know-how we have conquered all. We make believe that we can control everything— including life and death. We have conquered the world, and we have enslaved nature. We colonize the heavens, and we plant our silly little flags and nationalistic symbols on the planets and the stars. We take giant steps for humankind, or so we claim, and we wait for God to crawl back into the corner and leave the world to be run by those who through their knowledge and power can do it—namely, us.

But we cannot face the reality of evil either in our world or in ourselves. Yes, we conquer space and we win battles against killer germs. Yet at the same time, we are destroying the world and we create killer germs and nuclear arms, enough to destroy not only this world but also worlds yet undiscovered. We want to create life while we still have not learned to respect life. The same governments that claim to be the protectors of the unborn child dish out medals of honor to the soldier who kills more efficiently than the "enemy." But we ignore or deny these contradictions because we do not want to face the reality of evil.

The gospel wants to tell us very clearly that evil is real. Let us make no mistake. Evil in this world is real, it is tangible; you can see it, you can taste it, you can feel it, you can experience it. For anything, anything at all, that goes against the will of God, anything that threatens our human existence, anything that destroys humanity, anything that is violent or destructive or inhuman is evil, and that evil is real. That is something we so-called modern people have lost sight of. So we have no reason to say, "Oh, in those times they were primitive and they did not understand as we understand it; it is out of ignorance that they spoke of evil spirits."

No, people of God, even today we must understand that evil is real. And evil spirits in this world are real.

Let me say again: anything that goes against the will of God for this world, that tries to destroy the vision God has for this world of peace and justice, of human dignity and wholeness, of life and love and of the community, that is evil and it is real. That is why it makes sense that the apostle Paul writes: "For we are not contending against flesh and blood, but against the principalities, against the powers, against the world rulers of this present darkness, against the spiritual hosts of wickedness in the heavenly places" (Eph. 6:12).

This is true. When we confront the utter callousness of people who will do anything at all, destroy anyone at all, simply to hold on to power, then we must understand that evil is real. We are facing a government that will allow children to die of hunger, that will allow people to be shot on the street as if their lives do not matter. When this happens, you must know that evil is real. And when lawlessness dresses up as law and when inhumanity and brutality pose as law and order, when injustice claims to be justice and when the heresy of apartheid is defended as Christian, evil is real.

Christian churches send telegrams when we plan a peaceful protest against this government, because our resistance threatens their vested interests. But when we are thrown in jail under a law that should not even have existed, a law that is a travesty of justice and a denial of every basic human right, then they keep quiet. When our people are terrorized, when the police and the army make war against our defenseless children, when pregnant women and our old people are beaten with shamboks and brutally assaulted in their own homes, they are quiet. When our young people are shot to death for daring to resist, they do not speak or send telegrams of protest. No, they are as quiet as the graves our children lie in. When this happens, evil is real. And let us not say that evil spirits existed only in the times of Jesus when people were "primitive." No, my brothers and sisters, evil exists in this country, even now.

Evil dresses itself up in black ties and black suits and top hats and sits in parliament and makes the laws that will undermine the dignity of the people of South Africa. Evil sits in parliament and defends the cold-blooded murder of our leaders. Evil stands on the pulpit and justifies the oppression and ongoing violence of apartheid. Evil sits in padded chairs in air-conditioned boardrooms, continues the financing of apartheid, and self-righteously claims it is protecting the poor. And in the meantime, the prophets of God are silenced, not because we want to kill, or destroy, or hate, but because we preach a message of peace, love, and justice. We are thrown in jail because that message of truth is too much to bear for those who live on untruths.

Let me make it clear to you. Even today I have not given up my conviction for our nonviolent struggle for justice in this country. If it is God's will, it is God's struggle, and I will continue to do that for as long as God gives me breath in my body. I want to say to you, my sisters and brothers: do not give up this struggle. We must not turn to violence, because violence will destroy us as much as it has destroyed the people who are using it against us. Violence will destroy our soul even as their violence has destroyed their souls. They have no wisdom left, they have no understanding, they have no insight. They have no God left except the god of their guns, their casspirs, their tanks, and their weapons of destruction. Let them pray to that god. Our God is the living God—the God of justice and freedom. To this God we will pray. To his service we will dedicate ourselves.

And so, people of God, understand that our struggle is against the evil spirits of this world. Let us remain with Jesus. Let us remain with the Spirit of God in our hearts. Let us depend on his power, not on the power of guns or destruction of life. That will be my message to you always. Let us seek the peace that only God himself will give us in this country, although they who rule so harshly may not understand it. Even today I do not hate them. I will not hate them, but I will resist them until the very end, because I love this country and I love them, and I love my people too much to allow the oppressors to destroy us. This we must know.

In our gospel story, the father of the sick boy came to Jesus and explained his dilemma. At the same time, his dilemma became the dilemma of Jesus' disciples, because they could not heal the boy. It was painful. After all, they knew Jesus best, walked with him, heard his voice, understood him better than anyone else. They heard his teachings. And yet they were not able to heal the boy. That was *their* dilemma, a dilemma that became an embarrassment not only before the father, but especially also before the scribes and Pharisees.

As our story begins, there was an argument between the scribes and Pharisees and the disciples of Jesus, because the disciples could not heal the boy. They seemed helpless. They had heard Jesus say that if you have faith, you will tell this mountain to move itself from here into the sea. Why couldn't they do it now? They had heard Jesus say that if you have faith even like a mustard seed, you will tell this tree to uproot itself and remove itself to another place. Why couldn't they do that? This was their dilemma.

But as Jesus arrives, the real nature of the dilemma is revealed. Jesus comes and tells them, "Oh faithless people, how long shall I be with you?" And that, in essence, is the real dilemma of the father or the disciples—their faithlessness, their inability to believe. Jesus says, "All things are possible for those who believe."

I smiled a little cynically when I read that the first time. I thought: "God, if this were true, why am I still in this prison? If this were true, why is this government still in power? If this were true, why can they roam our streets and shoot our people while there is nothing we can do about it? If this were true, how is it possible that the church of Jesus Christ cannot stand together? That even in the church we are still divided? Why is it that some in the church are willing to sell our brothers and sisters for the sake of position or out of fear or for love of money? Why? How can I believe that if we only believe, *all things* are possible, even the removal of this evil government?" That is possible, if you believe, Jesus says.

But the problem lies not with Jesus, or with God, or with the promises of God. The problem lies with *us*, with you and me. We are the problem. And in this respect the problem is not even the government of this country with all its power, because God can remove them as I can remove this little piece of paper. And they know it—that's why I was in jail. But the promises of God are clear. We must learn not to be intimidated by the so-called realities of our world.

Right through the Bible the promises of God are there. "Abraham," said God, "you will have a son. Even though you are so old, you will have a son." And Abraham and Sarah did have a son, for the promises of God endure. Joseph dreams. God promises him in that dream: "I will lift you up, even though you do not count amongst your brothers, and I will make you one to whom even they will look for help." Joseph is sold by his brothers as a slave. Joseph is thrown in jail by Potiphar and it seems that all is lost. Yet somehow the promises of God remain true, and Joseph is raised up to become the symbol of God's providence not only for Egypt but for the whole world.

Mary hears the promise of God that the Messiah will be born and God's new day will dawn. The high and the mighty will be thrown from their thrones. The rich will be sent away empty, and the poor will be lifted up from the dust of the earth. The humble will be lifted up and placed in high places by God, and the hungry will be filled with good things.

This is the promise of God. I heard and I believed. I learned to depend, not on Allan Boesak, who thinks he can talk and argue his way out of anything, but on the promises of God alone. I was humbled before God for almost four weeks. Twenty-five days of solitary confinement, spent in prayer, sometimes fasting, have taught me to depend on the Spirit of God alone and that the word of God is true.

And as this word from the gospel came to me then, I said to God: "You will lead me out of here, you will change my situation, you will change this land, you will bring our people our freedom, you will give our people back our dignity, you will give our people vision, you will give our people your love, you will give our people their land, you will give our people the strength to stand, and to believe and to fight, *if I believe*. If I believe, all things are possible."

Today I am here, back in this pulpit, not because of *my* faith but because the God of heaven and earth is alive. And I say to you, my people, my own congregation, we have gone through so many difficult times this year, but God has brought us closer together. Keep that love in your hearts. Keep each other in love and in communion of spirit and in communion of commitment.

Let the congregation of Bellville become a light and a symbol of love and of commitment to Jesus Christ, of love and commitment to the world. Let this church become a symbol of how Christians in this country must participate in this struggle for the sake of Jesus Christ, but also for the sake of justice and peace. Be an example to the N.G. Sendingkerk, even to your Moderatuur. Be an example to every single church. Be an example to every organization.

Let the light of Jesus become alive in this congregation, not for our own sakes but for the sake of him who died for us and for the sake of the truth, for the sake of justice, for the sake of peace. Let us challenge the tensions within ourselves. Let us not become cynical. Let us not become hopeless. Let us believe in a committed, faithful, peaceful community. Let us see visions of love and peace and harmony and dignity and liberation for our country, for *all* the people. And all things are possible for those who believe.

To believe is to stand up and be counted for Jesus and for justice. To believe is to stand up and to work for justice. To believe is to be willing to take the risks knowing that God is on your side.

I can tell you this now with more conviction than ever before. He who believes, she who believes and works for justice and for peace will never be alone. You will never be alone because Jesus promised that whatever happens, he will never leave us alone. Even in the darkness of a cell in solitary confinement.

So, let us believe and not despair. Let us believe and work for justice. Let us believe and seek peace. Let us believe and challenge evil in this world. Let us believe and build together a community of love and joy and power and liberation.

There is one last word. If you believe, you can make this your own. Dietrich Bonhoeffer, that courageous German theologian who has had so much influence on my life—as much as Martin Luther King, Jr.—was killed by the Nazis because of his resistance to their evil. A few weeks before Germany was freed by the Allied forces, they hanged him. He was only thirty-nine years old. I love that man, and I love his testimony and praise God for him. In January 1935 Bonhoeffer wrote to his brother and said: "There are things in this world that are worth fighting for without any compromise whatsoever. And it seems to me that peace and social justice, which is really Jesus Christ, is such a cause."

That is my belief. My people, believe in Jesus Christ and make this your conviction. That is what I told the major in prison when I had read that piece. I told him that again on Thursday when I was told I would be released. I say this to you this morning and to those of the security police who are monitoring this sermon this morning. There are things in this world which are worth standing up for and fighting for without compromise: peace and justice, which is really Jesus Christ.

I believe in Jesus. I believe in justice. I believe in peace. I believe in liberation. I believe in God's vision for this country.

I believe, also, that it will come true, for Jesus is saying it again to me and to you. Don't worry about my detention or my bail conditions. Don't worry about my trial. God will take care of all of us. I do not worry. I sleep well at night. My life is in the hands of God. God will take care of us. You, you must commit yourselves anew.

Believe in Jesus. Believe in Jesus and fight for what is right. God bless you all. Amen.

Reprinted from *The Reformed Journal*, November 1985.

IDOLS CLOSER TO HOME:
Christian Substitutes for Grace

Jim Wallis

For by grace you have been saved through faith; and this not your own doing, it is the gift of God—not because of works, lest anyone should boast.

EPHESIANS 2:8, 9

Grace is the logic of a loving God. There is nothing we can do to earn it, win it, or deserve it. Grace is simply a gift, not a reward. We can receive it only by faith, not through good works.

As familiar as that is to us, we have great difficulty coming to terms with the meaning and reality of grace. We seem to find innumerable ways to deny the grace that is the free gift of God's love to us. Either we abuse it and make grace self-serving, or we dismiss its reality altogether by acting to establish our own righteousness. In twisting God's purposes to suit our own or in striving to justify ourselves through our own efforts, we have, in fact, denied the grace of God. In so doing, we have denied ourselves the ability to simply rest in that grace, to be changed and used by God's love.

Perhaps the greatest denial of grace in our time lies in its abuse. Dietrich Bonhoeffer named it "cheap grace." The grace of God is cheapened and distorted when used to cover over our sin rather than to cleanse it. The language of grace is impoverished and exploited when employed to justify our disobedience and lukewarm attitude.

True grace convicts of sin, softens the heart, and prompts repentance. Cheap grace overlooks sin, hardens the heart, and breeds complacency. True grace accepts and redeems the sinner. Cheap grace accommodates to and justifies the sin.

As Bonhoeffer reminds us, grace that comes at such a heavy cost to God cannot be used cheaply. Grace is not meant to obscure the path of discipleship and obedience. On the contrary, grace opens that path to us.

Cheap grace proclaims salvation without repentance. The evangelism of cheap grace has no real power to challenge either our personal status or the political status quo.

But there is another denial of grace among us. It often rears up in reaction to the cheap grace most prevalent in our churches.

The reaction to cheap grace can be so strong, the emphasis on radical discipleship and obedience so firm, that eventually there is little room left for any grace in our lives. The response to cheap grace can wrongly lead us to the loss of grace altogether. Its replacement with new forms of works righteousness is a great danger to those who call themselves "radical" Christians. This danger is my chief concern here.

Radical Christians face the tendency to seek justification in our lifestyle, our work, our protest, our causes, our movements, our actions, our prophetic identity, and our radical self-image. It becomes an easy temptation to place our security in the things we stand for and in the things we do, instead of in what God has done. It is a temptation to depend on things other than God's grace.

In our reaction against cheap grace, we are always in danger of producing radical alternatives to grace. In our desire to be obedient to the gospel and to prove our faithfulness, we could lose the freedom and the power that come from resting and fully trusting in God's grace as sufficient for our lives and for the world.

In the language of the passage from Ephesians, radical Christians have things they tend to "boast of." These are the things that can most easily become idols for us. They are not the idolatries of the established society and the comfortable church. We have identified those and confronted them so often that they have become familiar and easily recognizable. Therefore their power over us has been diminished.

But there are idols closer to home. We are less able to recognize them and can, therefore, more easily fall into their grasp. In very subtle ways, they are the idolatries that have the most power over us.

Idolatry must be identified and unmasked if it is to lose its power. Illusion is, in fact, the source of an idol's power. We place our trust in that which is not trustworthy but appears to be. We are deceived by the image of the idol which replaces that which is worthy of our trust.

Not to fully trust God's grace is to engage in illusion. It is to underestimate the power of sin and death and to overestimate our ability to overcome it. Not to rely on the work of Christ is to rely on our own work to save ourselves and the world. When we don't trust grace, we take ourselves too seriously, while not taking sin seriously enough.

What are those things in which we are tempted to place a false trust, things that threaten to become idols for us, things that can become substitutes for grace?

Our lifestyle can become an idol. To live simply is a biblical virtue, especially in a society choking on its own consumption and waste. Economic simplicity clears away the material obstacles that block dependence on God. Living with less also helps open our eyes to the suffering of the poor. It enables us to participate more easily in their struggle for justice, instead of in their oppression. The motive for living simply is that we might love both God and the poor more freely.

But it is not a simple lifestyle that justifies us. It is, rather, God's grace that enables us to live more simply. Displaying our style of life as if it were a badge of righteousness contradicts the whole spiritual foundation of economic simplicity. We live simply not out of obligation and guilt but to be less hindered in serving God and the poor. It should not be a duty, but a joy. Our lifestyle must not be used to judge others, but to invite them to share in the freedom and the grace we have found.

It was the worst tendency of the Pharisees to seek justification before God through their scrupulous lifestyle. May we never be like the Pharisee who stood beside the tax collector (read: the wealthy corporation executive) and thanked God that he wasn't such a sinner. Complex legalisms employed in the name of simple living could well rob us of the freedom and joy that are the intended fruits of such a lifestyle.

Our identification with the poor can become an idol. That the God of the Bible is on the side of the poor and the oppressed is beyond dispute. Christ's presence among the lowly and the afflicted is a doctrine drawn from the very heart of the gospels. But taking up the cause of the poor can have its own pitfalls.

There is a tendency among concerned people to romanticize the poor and their poverty. Poverty is ugly and bitter, and the poor suffer from the same sinful human condition as the rest of us. It is insensitive to represent the poor and the brutal circumstances of their lives as uniquely noble and virtuous. That may serve the fantasies of people experiencing downward mobility, but it will not serve the needs of poor people.

The suffering of the exploited is too easily exploitable. The misery of the poor advertises well to serve the personal, ideological, religious, and financial interests of others, and new forms of colonial exploitation replace old ones. The poor become the objects of public rhetoric, the targets of charity projects, and the pawns of political ambition. To use the poor for the sake of Christian ministry or leftist ideology is again to make capital out of their suffering. We have seen too much of religious and political radicals building their personal careers on the oppression of the poor.

Poor people are best served by those who desire to be their friends. We identify with the poor not to save ourselves, but so that we might better identify with Christ. He is already among the suffering and forgotten ones and invites us to join him there. He has taught us to love and serve him by sharing his special passion for those who are loved the least.

Our actions of protest can become an idol. The Scriptures tell us that love and truth show themselves in action and not merely in words. Direct action in the public arena has become a central means for bearing faithful witness, for making peace, and for seeking social justice. Those actions bring to light what is dangerous and wrong and point to a better way.

However, there is an inherent danger in public protest. Critical tests of any public action or campaign are: what or whom is being made known and visible? Is the truth being made more clear? Or is a person, a group, an institution, or a movement being made more prominent?

All our public actions must be rooted in the power of love and truth. We act for the purpose of making that power known, not for the purpose of making ourselves known. Our motivation must be to open people's eyes to the truth, not to show ourselves as right and them as wrong.

Whenever our protest becomes an effort to "prove ourselves," we are in serious danger. Our best actions are those that admit our complicity in the evil we protest and are marked by a spirit of genuine repentance and humility. Our worst actions are those that seek to demonstrate our own righteousness, our purity, our freedom from complicity. When our pride overtakes our protest, we may simply be repeating, in political form, the self-righteous judgment of the fundamentalists—"I'm saved, and you're not."

A Christian friend recently wrote, "I have seen so much of the 'heresy of good works' in the religious Left, a belief that is based on the arrogance that *we* have to save the world, and a very real denial (if not in words, then in actions) that the world has *already* been saved. And believe me, it is very tiresome to go around feeling like the fate of the world rests on your words and on your deeds. . . . Sometimes I think that numbers of arrests have replaced indulgences in the 'new church,' and that is *not* spiritual progress.''

Our actions do not have the power to save us. Instead, they can have the power to make the truth known. Although the actions we undertake will never substitute for grace, they can indeed be witnesses of God's grace. Since they lack the capacity to justify us, a better purpose for our actions would be communication.

Because communication is so basic to public action, the nature of what we say and do becomes very important. Actions that mostly communicate a threatening and desperate spirit should be carefully questioned. Free and open evaluation of all public action is necessary to protect the health and character of our protest. The quality and integrity of what we communicate will be its most crucial element.

Action done in public will always carry with it the great danger of presumption. We ought to act with the awareness of how risky it is to claim to be making the truth known. The ever-present threat is to identify the truth with ourselves, instead of the other way around. Because of the inherent presumption of public protest, it should always reflect a spirit of confession, humility, and invitation.

Judgment, arrogance, and exclusiveness are signs of spiritual immaturity. Protest characterized by such things will have the effect of hardening hearts, confirming people's fears, and convincing them of their present opinions. Public action has sometimes done more harm than good. It can drive people away from the very things we are trying to say. It can perpetuate, as well as dispel, public blindness.

Our principle of nonviolence can become an idol. Never has the absolute need for nonviolence been greater than in a world living under the nuclear shadow. But even our position on nonviolence can be self-serving and hide deeper motives.

Nonviolence aims for truth and not for power. Its chief weapon is the application of spiritual force, not the use of coercion. A very serious problem in nonviolent movements is the hidden aggression, the manipulation, the assertive ego, and the desire for provocation that can lurk beneath the surface of repetitive platitudes about the commitment to nonviolence. The rhetorical cloak of nonviolence can be used to hide the will to power, which is the very foundation of violence. The desire to win over others, to defeat one's enemies, and to humiliate the opposition are all characteristics of violence and are too painfully evident in much of what is called nonviolent action.

The infighting, media grabbing, and intense competition of the radical movement is hardly an evidence that the will to power has been overcome. Some of the worst tyrannies have been hidden behind anarchist principles and the myth of leaderless groups and communities.

We should know by now that all violence is of a piece. If that is true, then the violence of dissent is directly linked to the violence of the established order. It is, in fact, a mirror reflection of it. Therefore, the violence present in the peace movement can be said to be part of the violence that fuels the nuclear arms race. We can no longer justify the "excesses" of the peace movement by appealing to the greater violence of the system. The urgency of the nuclear situation calls for more, not less, care in the actions we undertake.

Nonviolence does not try to overcome the adversary by defeating him, but by convincing him. It turns an adversary into a friend, not by winning over her, but by winning her over. Knowing that today's enemy may become tomorrow's friend should cause us to examine our treatment of opponents more closely. It is interesting how military and business leaders who "defect" to the peace movement are transformed from demons into saints overnight.

Patience is central to nonviolence. Nonviolence is based on the kind of love the Bible speaks of as "enduring all things." Thomas Merton taught us that the root of war is fear. If that is true, we must become much more understanding of the fears people have. The most effective peace-makers are those who have experienced the healing of their own fears and can now help lead others out of theirs. There is still too much fear in the peace movement to heal the fears of a nation. How can we be peacemakers when we are still afraid of one another? Our hope is in the deepening of our experience of the "perfect love that casts out fear."

Our prophetic identity can become an idol. The prophetic vocation is deeply biblical and highly dangerous. It is a calling most necessary for our time, but one that requires the most intense scrutiny.

Prophets have always challenged idolatry. The people of God forget who they are and to whom they belong. Before long, their forgetfulness causes them to fall into the false worship of idols. Prophets are then raised up to name the idolatries, to speak the word of the Lord, to lead the people out of their false worship, and to bring them back to God.

The need in our day is for clear words of God's judgment and mercy. The prophetic vocation is to faithfully communicate that judgment and mercy in a way people can hear and understand. A genuinely prophetic message will never show selectivity, partiality, or parochial interest. A prophet in the biblical tradition will not challenge some idols and leave others untouched. He or she will not rage against injustice and violence in some places and be strangely silent about oppression elsewhere.

It is painfully apparent that radical Christians have not always been true to the whole counsel of God's judgment. An ideological selectivity intrudes, a political bias that undermines the credibility and power of prophetic witness. The idolatries of the establishment are attacked while the idols of the antiestablishment receive less critical treatment. The evils of the majority culture are assailed but the sins of the counterculture are often passed over. The political prisoners of right-wing dictatorships seem to generate more interest than those languishing in the jails of leftist regimes.

A long-time Christian pacifist recently wrote to me on this subject:

A child dead from a revolutionary rocket we tend to see quite differently than one dead from an "imperialist" rocket. The revolutionary sponsors are guarded by the sanctuary of holy words that make certain allowances for dead children. The death is a tragedy rather than a crime against humanity. Actually, the other side is finally to blame for it. And so forth.

Someone tortured in Chile, we find, is far more needful of response and protest than someone tortured in the Soviet Union. A priest arrested in Argentina is a more pressing matter than a monk arrested in Vietnam. Indeed, the latter need hardly be noticed. The heavy-handed methods of the shah of Iran are a different kettle of fish than those of the Chinese or the Cubans. For the latter are merely breaking eggs in order to make an omelet, as it has often been put to me.

Political orthodoxy is anathema to prophetic integrity. The maintenance of the party line describes propaganda, not prophecy. Prophecy is, in fact, profoundly anti-ideological.

Karl Barth once wrote these words:

The Christian Church must be guided by the Word of God and by it alone. It must not forget for an instant that all political systems, right and left alike, are the work of [people]. It must hold itself free to carry out its own mission and to work out a possibly quite new form of obedience or resistance. It must not sell this birthright for any conservative or revolutionary mess of pottage.

Politicized theology is no substitute for prophetic witness. Radical proof-texting is no better than fundamentalist proof-texting. We are keenly aware of the conservative, militarist, patriotic, racist, and sexist distortions of the Bible. Likewise, there can be neither a leftist agenda in reading the Scriptures, nor anarchist, nor pacifist, nor communitarian, nor any other bias, for that matter. The Word of God is intended to judge all our priorities, to overturn all our biases, to correct all our perceptions.

If the prophetic vocation is to bring the judgment of God to bear, then the prophet must be the first to be placed under that judgment. The prophetic calling must be, by definition, an extremely troubling one. It must be as troubling to ourselves as it is to those who bear the brunt of our prophetic pronouncements—or more so.

Smugness and complacency are the prophet's worst enemies. The hardest words of judgment must always be reserved for our own group. God's word must be allowed to confront the idolatries closest to us before it will destroy those furthest away. Pride, alienation, and bitterness are the worst sources of prophetic zeal and will corrupt and distort our witness.

The biblical prophet loved the people, was a part of the people, and claimed them as his own. Therefore the disobedience and sin of the people hurt the prophet, and his first response to their faithlessness was grief, not indignation. The prophet was the one who spoke the hard words. But he spoke with a broken heart.

The prophets would not conform to the people, but they never lost their relationship to them. Jesus, in the tradition of the prophets, showed just such a capacity to love the people without conforming to their sinful ways. In our desire not to be conformed to the sins of the nation, we could lose the capacity to identify with the people that is so basic to the prophetic calling.

Those who would avow a prophetic vocation to the church must ask themselves a question: do you love the church? Or do you hate it? God will not entrust us with a prophetic ministry merely to cloak our own rage and judgment. But if we love the church, if we love the people, if our hearts ache when we see their folly, then God may trust us to be vehicles of divine rage and judgment, to express God's purposes for the people.

The most basic question for the prophet is to whom he or she is accountable. Prophets not accountable to anyone but themselves are a dangerous and destructive lot. The worst things in history have been done out of prophetic zeal.

Grace saves the prophetic vocation. The knowledge and experience of grace can ease the seriousness with which we tend to take ourselves. Grace can restore our humility, our sense of humor, and our ability to laugh at ourselves. All are regularly needed by prophets. Only sinners make good prophets.

Our biggest idol is ourselves. Radical Christians, like all creatures, tend to boast most of all of themselves. To trust in our lifestyle, our commitment to the poor, our actions, our nonviolence, or our prophetic identity is, in the end, to trust in ourselves. It is to trust in our work, our principles, our causes, and our self-images.

Idolatry is the worship of anything other than God. And an idol is simply an image. When we worship an idol, we are worshiping an image. How important our images are to us! Our lives can so easily become exercises in image building.

We reject the prestige society offers only to find prestige through our radical status. We eschew success in the world, then pursue it through "alternative" channels. We snicker at the system's professionals while establishing a career in the movement. We leave worldly fame behind but enjoy the special status this society grants to its radicals and prophets. We rail against the power structure and build a power base of our own.

As the Bible says, "There is none righteous, no, not one." Grace can overcome the greatest temptation of radical Christians: to believe that we are better than those who need convincing and converting. Grace imparts to us the capacity to forgive because we know that we have been forgiven. The marks of grace are gentleness, hope, and faith. The most dependable sign of its presence is joy.

To trust grace is to know that the world has already been saved by Jesus Christ. It is to know that we cannot save the world any more than we can save ourselves. All our work is done only in response to Christ's work. To receive the gift of grace is to let go of self-sufficiency and to act out of a spirit of gratitude.

We must seek not a successful strategy but a deeper faith. Only then will we have the assurance of salvation, not because of what we have accomplished, but because we have allowed God's grace and mercy to flow through our lives.

PART THREE

Disciplines of Conscience: Nonviolence

FIGHTING FIRE WITH WATER:
A Call for Assertive Nonviolent Resistance
Richard K. Taylor and Ronald J. Sider

We are in the midst of a very rapid and large shift in human consciousness regarding questions of war and peace. In 1980, one of the main preoccupations of the peace movement was how to inform and arouse the public about the dangers of nuclear war. Given the current front-page stories on the nuclear issue, it is hard to remember that the 1970s saw very little public discussion of the nuclear peril. Very few church bodies or religious leaders were speaking out. No mass movement was addressing itself to stopping the arms race.

Now the concern is so widespread that one commentator estimates that the peace and antinuclear movements have involved a greater number of people from a wider variety of backgrounds in more countries than any other issue of our century. In the United States more than eleven million citizens voted in favor of a nuclear freeze. And the largest demonstration in U.S. history addressed itself to disarmament on June 12, 1982, in New York City.

Hundreds of thousands of Europeans have demonstrated for the same cause. Millions of people around the world are deeply concerned and are becoming active in disarmament advocacy. Religious leaders have come out so strongly that *U.S. News and World Report* describes them as "the key force behind the American antiwar crusade."

These millions of newly involved peace advocates are looking for practical answers as to how the world can back away from the nuclear abyss. If they find meaningful answers and creative ways to act, they will stay involved and will draw in others. Their involvement in the nuclear freeze movement showed the power of a creative idea to involve people in meaningful, large-scale peace action.

But what are the next steps? What are the long-range steps that will move humanity away from self-obliteration and toward real peace?

At times our no to nuclear weapons has been loud and clear. We have condemned reliance on nuclear arms as idolatrous and suicidal. We have called the production, possession, and willingness to use nuclear weapons one of the chief manifestations of human sinfulness and rebellion against God in our age.

But this no is only half a message, half an answer. It tells people what to be against, but not what to be for. It says that defense through nuclear weapons must be rejected as immoral, but it does not tell us whether defense through some other means is viable. It condemns deterrence through nuclear terror, but it does not say whether there are alternative, acceptable ways to deter aggression.

At a peace retreat sponsored by Sojourners several years ago, a participant said, "I hear you saying, 'Put your security in God, not the bomb.' That's great. But it doesn't really tell me what to do. What does the God-truster do when Russia invades Afghanistan?"

This comment expresses the dilemma felt by many sincere people who have become involved in antinuclear activities. On the one hand, they agree that nuclear weapons are an abomination and must be abolished. On the other hand, they worry about how the peace movement would cope with aggression. What if some hostile, totalitarian power threatened to invade the United States or some other country? What would peace advocates do? It is not enough of an answer to say, "Trust in God, not the bomb," since this does not tell the questioners how they are to express that trust in the concrete situation of invasion or occupation.

The Pentagon and other military establishments have a clear answer: "We must defend ourselves through military means." As long as the peace movement does not have its own answer that is an alternative to the military's answer, people will continue to trust military means, even if they have moral qualms about them; their support for disarmament will be weak and vacillating.

Nor can people's concerns about aggression be brushed aside as naive or based solely on government propaganda. Whatever we may think of the "Soviet threat," it is true that powerful nations regularly try to impose their will on others through military force. As Christians we know that "wars and rumors of wars" will persist and that "nation will rise up against nation" until Christ returns (Matt. 24:6–7).

Political science and biblical faith both attest to the world's conflicts and power struggles. History gives countless examples (including current ones) of one state attempting to extend its influence by threatening or invading another. Tyranny and despotism are far from dead. It is not inconceivable that a totalitarian government—a new Hitler perhaps—might try to impose its will on the world.

Just as the commitment to justice carries Christians into struggles to defend the rights of the poor and the oppressed, so our commitment to justice should express itself in strong resistance to aggression, invasion, or occupation. We are under a biblical mandate, not only to be peacemakers, but also to "seek justice, correct oppression, defend the fatherless, plead for the widow" (Isa. 1:17).

Christians are called to be reconcilers, but also to actively resist injustice, evil, and oppression. The oppression that Isaiah calls us to correct certainly includes the oppression that an invading totalitarian regime would try to impose on the people of an invaded country. The parentless we are called to defend certainly includes all those vulnerable people that an expanding despotism would try to crush.

But how can Christians engage in this resistance while living in obedient faith to the one who commands us to love our enemies?

A provocative answer comes to us from those who were closest to Jesus—the Christians of the early church. We often forget that Christianity grew up in a region occupied by a foreign invader that used fierce military power to enforce its rule. It was in territory that had been conquered and placed under the brutal heel of imperial Rome in 63 B.C. that Jesus instructed his disciples to love their enemies and turn the other cheek.

During the centuries of persecution, Christians were crucified, torn to pieces by dogs, set afire to illuminate Nero's ghastly circuses. Imprisonment, torture, and execution were common measures used by the Caesars in their attempts to bring Christianity to heel. Early Christians, therefore, had to respond to the tyranny and oppression of totalitarian rulers.

These Christians engaged in active resistance and struggle against what they saw as evil. When Rome passed decrees that violated Christian conscience, church members responded with protest and noncooperation. Cecil John Cadoux writes in his book *The Early Church and the World:*

One Christian tore down the first edict of persecution posted up by Diocletianus; another fearlessly seized the governor's hand as he was in the act of sacrificing and exhorted him to abandon his error; another strode forward in open court and rebuked the judge for his ruthless sentences. A Christian woman, dragged to the altar and commanded to sacrifice upon it, kicked it over.

Though early Christian leaders would be considered pacifists, they were far from passive in their response to persecution. They poured forth a torrent of protest, defiance, and censure against the persecutors and their decrees. But unlike those who choose a military response to oppression, they acted without violence and with a willingness to endure suffering for their faith. St. Chrysostom, a church leader of the fourth century, summarizes the balance between resistance and nonviolent suffering when he says:

What, then, ought we not to resist an evil? Indeed we ought; but not by retaliation. Christ hath commanded us to give up ourselves to suffering wrongfully, for thus we shall prevail over evil. For one fire is not quenched by another fire, but fire by water.

The early Christians did not simply refuse to kill their enemies. As Justinus said, "We pray for our enemies and try to persuade those who hate us unjustly." And as St. Cyprian said to his persecutors, "It is not lawful for us to hate, and so we please God more when we render no requital for injury. . . . We repay your hatred with kindness."

This total commitment to the way of Christ, combined with the gospel message, had enormous power. Christianity began as the faith of a tiny minority whose founder was executed by a repressive state. Yet in time it not only overcame its persecutors but also won the professed allegiance of much of the empire's population.

As with the early church, our commitment to justice should make us speak and act clearly against tyranny's injustices. But our commitment to the love of Christ invites us to find concrete ways to love our enemies and to reach them with the powerful, saving message of the gospel.

Throughout history can be found many cases of groups—and even several instances of whole nations—that confronted and overcame ruthless tyranny by nonviolent means similar to those of the early church. Christians often played a key role in the resistance.

One of the most interesting cases is Hungary's battle against Austrian rule in the mid-1800s. After crushing a Hungarian military uprising in 1849, Austria put Hungary under martial law, divided it into military districts, suppressed its parliament, and repealed its constitution. Militarily defeated, Hungary seemed to have no alternative but to submit to foreign rule.

Both political and religious leaders, however, united in a nonmilitary strategy of absolute resistance. Hungarian citizens refused to recognize

Austrian rule. They treated Austrian officials as "illegal persons." They would not follow Austrian decrees and instead continued to abide by their own constitution and laws. Ferencz Deak, a Hungarian jurist and leader of the resistance, said: "We can hold our own against armed force. If suffering be necessary, suffer with dignity."

The Protestant church spearheaded the resistance. When Austrians tried to prevent church councils from meeting, the councils met in full force. When the Austrians demanded that a decree be read from every pulpit, every minister refused. Many were arrested as a result. Police broke up church meetings only to find that huge crowds would gather wherever a church leader spoke in defiance of Austrian rule. To show solidarity with arrested church leaders, students dressed in black held silent demonstrations. Those ministers not arrested carried on with church affairs as if Austrian decrees did not exist.

Austria finally was forced to reopen the Hungarian parliament and restore its constitution. Hungary won complete internal independence and equal partnership with Austria and prevented all of Austria's attempts to destroy the autonomy of its churches.

It is often asked whether such nonviolent tactics would work against the brutal and demonic policies of one such as Adolf Hitler. Whether something "works," of course, is not the basic criterion of Christian action. A Christian's first concern must be to be obedient to the Lord, even if this leads to suffering, death, and apparent failure. However, an assertive nonviolent stance was often effective even in the face of schemes as satanic as Hitler's.

In Bulgaria in the early 1940s, for example, Bishop Kiril told authorities that if they attempted to deport Bulgarian Jews to concentration camps, he would lead a campaign of civil disobedience, including personally lying down on the railroad tracks in front of the deportation trains.

Thousands of Jews and non-Jews resisted all collaboration with Nazi decrees. They marched in mass street demonstrations and sent floods of letters and telegrams to authorities protesting all anti-Jewish measures. Bulgarian clergy hid Jews and accepted large numbers of Jewish "converts," making clear that this was a trick to escape the Nazis, and that they would not consider these vows binding. These and other nonmilitary measures saved all of Bulgaria's Jewish citizens from the Nazi death camps.

Similar nonviolent resistance in Norway prevented Vidkun Quisling,

Hitler's representative, from imposing a fascist "corporative state" on the country. The Norwegian Evangelical Church, a state church that embraced 97 percent of the population, was overwhelmingly committed to the resistance to fascism. Its bishops published a declaration saying:

As the time came for Luther, so it has come for us to follow our convictions and to uphold the righteousness of the Church as opposed to the injustice of the State. . . . God himself stands opposed to tyranny through the power of His Word and His Spirit. Woe to us if we here do not obey God rather than man.

When Roman Catholic bishop Mangers issued a supporting statement, he was summoned to Gestapo headquarters, threatened, and ordered to withdraw his signature. "You can take my head, but not my signature," was his firm reply. Norwegians did not give in, even when resisters were imprisoned, tortured, and sent to death camps.

In the face of this staunch resistance from almost every sector of Norwegian society, Hitler himself finally ordered Quisling to give up the whole plan for a corporative state.

Although always a minority movement, similar nonviolent resistance to Hitler took place in many parts of Europe, with Christians often being key actors. Danes, led by their deeply Christian king, saved 93 percent of their Jewish population in a dramatic nonviolent rescue action. Adolf Eichmann, head of the Nazi office for extermination of Jews, admitted that "the action against the Jews of Denmark has been a failure." Finland saved all but four of its Jewish citizens from the Nazi death camps. Finland's foreign minister told Heinrich Himmler, chief of Hitler's dreaded SS security police: "Finland is a decent nation. We would rather perish together with the Jews. We will not surrender the Jews."

In the Netherlands, clergy issued strong pastoral letters against the Nazis. Citizens gathered in large protest demonstrations and went on strikes. In France, Pastor André Trocmé, a strong pacifist, made his whole town of Le Chambon a center for hiding Jews and smuggling them to Switzerland. Students at Trocmé's school handed a fascist official a letter saying:

We have learned that in Paris Jews are herded into the stadium and then deported. After that, all trace of them is lost. This, in our Christian eyes, is unbearable. Even though such may be the law in northern France, we will not obey it if applied here in southern France. No matter what the government does, we will hide Jews.

Most non-Jews in Europe failed to speak or act against Hitler's genocide. Those who did resist paid a heavy price in imprisonment, torture, and death. Yet their actions saved tens of thousands of Jewish lives. They did not submit to Nazi rule, yet they fought nonviolently. They refute the notion that only military means are effective in defending people and their values against the very worst form of outside tyranny.

During World War II, forty million people died on battlefields using military weapons against Nazism. What if forty million people had been willing to give their lives in a nonviolent struggle, using the defiant but nonmilitary methods of Bishop Kiril?

A literature of nonviolent resistance to tyranny is growing that catalogs and analyzes nonmilitary campaigns in many parts of the world and in many periods of history. These include Germany's nonmilitary resistance to invasion by France and Belgium in 1923, successful Latin American campaigns to overthrow dictatorships by nonviolent means, and the Indian independence movement against British occupation led by Mohandas Gandhi.

These historical examples point to a power to resist evil and oppression that does not rely on the ability to kill and injure. They suggest that it may be possible to defend cherished values in a way consistent with both the prophets' call to justice and Christ's call to love our enemies.

Today millions of newly involved peace advocates are asking: how can we get rid of nuclear weapons while defending precious values against tyranny's onslaught? How can we disarm militarily, but also stand up against the evil, injustice, and oppression that an invading totalitarian power would bring?

Our answer might be: yes, we must resist tyranny, but only with the means taught by Jesus and exemplified in his life, death, and resurrection. Yes, we must stand up against evil and oppression, but with the self-sacrifice of a Bishop Kiril, who was willing to lay down on the railroad tracks to prevent Nazi deportation of Jews, and with the love for enemies of St. Cyprian, who said that because we are Christians it is not lawful for us to hate.

Those who are attracted to this approach can begin to work for it concretely. We can talk to people about it. We can encourage research into the largely neglected history of nonviolent resistance. We can form groups that use nonviolent means to attack existing social injustices and participate in nonviolent demonstrations to oppose specific military programs, while educating the public about an alternative means of defending precious values.

If a nonviolent approach to aggression were ever adopted on a large scale, its participants would certainly experience suffering and sacrifice. But such are also the requirements of military means, as any battlefield will attest. And "defense" through nuclear weapons has the potential to make us mass murderers, extinguishers of all life, and ravagers of God's precious creation.

Perhaps the main question for Christians looking at any system of defense is not: will it work with 100 percent certainty? The questions are rather: does it offer a realistic possibility of success? And, if defeat comes, can it be a "defeat" such as the one Jesus suffered on the cross?

Defense through nuclear weapons cannot give an affirmative answer. Defense through assertive nonviolent resistance can. And nonviolent resistance knows that even defeat, if it is the defeat of the cross, is the dynamic out of which resurrection comes.

WELCOMING THE ENEMY:
A Missionary Fights Violence with Love
Sarah Corson

It was midnight. Before retiring I walked out on the screened porch where my fifteen-year-old son was sleeping. I was leading a team of seventeen young people, including two of my own children, on a three-month work assignment in a jungle area two hundred miles from the nearest city in a South American country. Four years before, my husband and I with our four children had first come to this area at the request of the village people to help them start a church, build a fish hatchery, and develop other forms of appropriate technology to meet basic human needs. After the church and appropriate technology center had been established, we moved to work in another country. This summer the village had asked us to return to experiment with a vegetable protein project.

When we received the invitation, my husband was already committed to a project in Haiti for the summer. We decided to divide up for three months in order to work in both projects. My husband took our fourteen-year-old Karen with him to Haiti while our fifteen-year-old Tommy and sixteen-year-old Kathy went with me, leaving our nineteen-year-old Chris to take care of things at our headquarters in Alabama.

The air on the porch was chilly, so I laid a blanket across Tommy's cot, then stood a moment looking out across the fishponds that were bringing hope for more food to the village. The light from the moon made a rippling path of white across the water.

Suddenly I heard a crash. Turning quickly I could see in the moonlight that a soldier had slid into our water barrel. I was paralyzed with shock as I looked out over the clearing that separated our temporary home from the jungle. About thirty soldiers were rushing our house.

Our host country had just held elections, not the usual custom, and the military did not agree with the results. It had taken over one week before, exiling the newly elected president and repressing any resistance, real or imagined. Since we were in such a remote frontier village, I had not expected the fighting to reach us.

While I stood there, frozen in fear, watching the soldiers surround our house, the message a neighbor woman had brought me that day flashed through my mind.

"Sister, keep your team in the house," she had urged. "I just came from the market over near the military camp. I overheard two soldiers saying the Americans were to blame for the resistance to their takeover. They said they would not rest until they had exterminated every American in this zone."

Since we had not been involved in political activities in their country, I thought that she had misunderstood. I did not think that we would be suspected of participating in such resistance, but now what the neighbor woman had warned me about was taking place before my eyes. Evidently, the soldiers were intent on carrying out their threat. If they wanted to kill us, there was no way to stop them.

My heart was beating so fast, I thought my blood vessels would burst. It felt as if I was about to have a stroke. I knew I had a responsibility for the team members inside the house, but I could not even call out to them. I was paralyzed with fear.

I had only a split second to pray before the soldiers found me: "God, if I have to die, take care of my family. And God, please take away this fear. I don't want to die afraid. Please help me to die trusting you." I was suddenly aware of the presence of God.

We do not always feel God. Usually we trust God by faith. However, at that moment God's presence was very real, seemingly touchable. I still thought I was going to die, but I knew God had things under control. I remember thinking that maybe our deaths would accomplish things that we had not been able to accomplish with our lives.

I found myself stepping up to the closest soldier and speaking words I could never have thought to say. "Welcome, brother," I called out. "Come in. You do not need guns to visit us."

At that the soldier jumped, dropped the bullet he was putting in his gun, and shouted, "Not me. I'm not the one. I'm just following orders. There's the commander over there, he's the one."

I raised my voice and repeated, "You're all welcome. Everyone is welcome in our home."

At that the commander ran up to me, shoved the muzzle of his rifle against my stomach, and pushed me through the door into the house. Thirty soldiers rushed into the house and began pulling everything off the shelves and out of drawers, looking for guns. They herded the team members into the kitchen where they sat quietly by the glow of the two candles we used for light.

The soldier who led the attack turned his gun on me and demanded angrily, "What are you Americans doing down here trying to stop our revolution? Seventeen Americans would not be living in this poverty if they did not have political motivation."

"Sir," I responded truthfully, "We have had nothing to do with your revolution. We are here for two reasons. We are teaching self-help projects to the hungry and we are teaching the Bible."

"That tells me nothing," he responded. "I have never read the Bible in my life. Maybe it is a communist book for all I know."

"You have never read the Bible in your life? Oh, sir, I am so sorry for you. You have missed the best part of your life. Please let me tell you what it says."

He made no objection. He had to stand there with his gun on us while the other soldiers ransacked the house looking for the guns we did not have.

I picked up a Spanish Bible and turned to the Sermon on the Mount. "We teach about Jesus Christ," I said, "God's son who came into this world to save us. He also taught us a better way than fighting. He taught us the way of love. Because of him I can tell you that even though you kill me, I will die loving you because God loves you. To follow him, I have to love you too."

In that particular Bible there were paragraph captions. He glanced at them and read plainly, "Jesus teaches love your enemies," and "Return good for evil."

"That's humanly impossible!" he burst out.

"That's true, sir," I answered. "It isn't humanly possible, but with God's help it is possible."

"I don't believe it."

"You can prove it, sir. I know you came here to kill us. So just kill me slowly, if you want to prove it. Cut me to pieces little by little, and you will see you cannot make me hate you. I will die praying for you because God loves you, and we love you too."

The soldier lowered his gun and stepped back. Clearing his throat, he said, "You almost convince me you are innocent—but I have orders to take everyone in the house and the ham radio. I will let you get some warm clothes and a blanket; you will be sleeping on the ground."

They marched us two by two at gunpoint down a trail to where a truck was waiting on the one little road that came into our village. We saw that others in our town had been taken prisoner also. The district superintendent of the church, the leader of the youth group, and other leaders were lined up at gunpoint, ready to be loaded on the trucks with us.

Suddenly the soldier changed his mind: "Halt!" he commanded. "Take only the men. The women will come with me."

He led us back to our home, saying, "I don't know why I am doing this. I was about to take you into a jungle camp of more than a thousand soldiers. I know what they do to women prisoners. You would be abused many times. I cannot take you.

"In our army no one breaks an order," he continued sternly. "I have never broken an order before, but for the first time tonight I am refusing to obey an order. If my superior officer finds out that you were in this house when I raided it, and that I did not take you, I will pay for it with my life." He strode to the door, stopped, and looked back again.

"I could have fought any amount of guns you might have had," he said, "but there is something here I cannot understand. I cannot fight it."

Then the hard part began—waiting to hear what had happened to the men of our team and the leaders of the village. The waiting, the uncertainty, seemed endless. If a twig snapped outside our window everyone jumped, thinking the soldiers were back again. The people of our village were as distressed as we were. They stood around in our house all day—some weeping, others coming to offer their sympathy. No one knew what would happen next.

The local people insisted we could not have a service in the church on Sunday because the soldiers considered any meeting held to be for the purpose of political agitation. "Soldiers will be there if you have a service. They will take more prisoners," they told me. We all agreed to pray at home on Sunday.

But on Saturday night a messenger came to our door. "I bring a message from the man who commanded the attack on your village Thursday night," he said. "He says he will be at your service Sunday. However, he has no vehicle on Sundays so you are to bring the church's jeep and get him. He said to tell you that if you don't come he will be there anyway, even if he has to walk the ten miles." It sounded like a threat.

I sent a message to everyone in the town that night. "We will have the service after all," I told them, "but you are not obligated to come. In fact you may lose your life by coming. No one knows what this soldier will do. Do not come when the church bell rings unless you are sure God wants you to come." I knew that the villagers feared the military and stayed out of sight when soldiers were around. I did not expect any of them to come.

The next morning I took the jeep and went to get the commander. He came with a bodyguard. The two of them marched coldly into the church and sat down, still holding their rifles. The women on our team came in, the bell was rung, and we began to sing. The church was packed before the first hymn was over. The people came pale and trembling, but they came. They had felt that their faith was at stake, and they were determined to attend, even if it meant imprisonment.

Since the leaders of the church had been taken by the military, I led the service. I tried to do just what I would have done had the soldiers not been there. It was church custom to welcome visitors by inviting them to the platform, singing a welcome song, and waving to them. Everyone would then line up to shake the visitors' hands, hug them, and say some personal words of greeting.

How could I ask these people to hug the very man who had taken their husband, son, or brother prisoner? That was asking too much. I decided that I would ask them to sing a welcome song but that I would stop there and leave out the hugging.

The soldiers were surprised when I asked them to come to the platform to let us welcome them. "Welcome us?" they asked in amazement. "Well, all right," they shrugged. They came forward and stood very formally with their guns across their backs.

The people stood, singing weakly and waving their hands timidly. I expected them to sit back down, but no. The first man on the front seat came forward and put out his hand. As he bent over to hug the soldier I heard him say, "Brother, we don't like what you did to our village, but this is the house of God, and God loves you, so you are welcome here."

Everyone in the church followed his example, even the women whose eyes were red from weeping for their loved ones whom this man had taken prisoner. They too said words of welcome. The looks on the soldiers' faces became ones of surprise, then incredulity.

When the last person finished greeting them, the head soldier marched to the pulpit and said in a very stern voice, "Now I will have a few words. Never have I ever dreamed that I could raid a town, come back, and have that town welcome me as a brother. I can hardly believe what I have seen and heard this morning. That sister told me Thursday night that

Christians love their enemies, but I did not believe her then. You have proven it to me this morning," he said to the congregation.

"This is the first church service I have ever been to," he continued. "I never believed there was a God before, but what I have just felt is so strong that I will never doubt the existence of God again as long as I live."

He turned from one side of the congregation to the other. "Do all of you know God?" he asked. "If you know God, hang on to him. It must be the greatest thing in this world to know God." As he spoke in an urgent voice he motioned with his hand, clenching it as though to hold on to something, while in his other hand he held a gun.

"I don't know God," he confessed in a low voice, "but I hope some day I shall, and that some day we can once again greet each other as brothers and sisters, as we have done this morning."

He came home with us for lunch. The men caught fish from the ponds to cook for his meal. The women helped me cook, even those who had lost a loved one. While we prepared lunch, the men took him around to see the brick project for dry housing, the chicken and vegetable protein project, and the clean water project. At last he said, "I have taken innocent people, but I did not know it when I did it. Now it is too late. If any of you need anything since you do not have your men, please tell me, and I will pay for it out of my pocket." He left, planning a return visit that was never to transpire.

Seven days later the bishop of our church sent a message for all Americans to come immediately to the capital city. He urged us to return to the United States as soon as possible, since he feared that our lives would be endangered by a possible countercoup.

Once in the capital, we learned that the American men who had been taken from our house at midnight had been taken by dump truck to a military camp ten miles from our village. There they had been loaded on a plane with many other prisoners from the local area and flown to the capital, where they were held in a basement cell.

Three days later the U.S. Embassy was successful in negotiating the release of the Americans and helping them leave the country. The local men, however, were not released for two weeks. Some, particularly the religious leaders, were tortured.

Often I think of the soldier and his thirty men who stormed out of the jungle ready to kill us. Within fifteen minutes he had changed his mind and risked his life to save us. I thank God for putting divine love in my heart for a person I could not love on my own.

I cannot forget the last thing the soldier said to us as he left: "I have fought many battles and killed many people. It was nothing to me. It was just my job to exterminate them. But I never knew them personally. This is the first time I ever knew my enemy face to face, and I believe that if we knew each other, our guns would not be necessary."

THE HOSPITALITY OF GOD:
Christian Sanctuary as Nonviolence
Bill Kellermann

In 1982, a United Methodist congregation in Detroit made public declaration that its sanctuary would serve as a refuge for resisters of draft registration. It set out the spiritual welcome mat and later commended the practice to sister and brother congregations. In the debate that ensued there was animated discussion about war, civil disobedience, and the portent of a draft. Lacking in the debate was the most forthright suggestion that the whole proposal simply acknowledged the proper theological and historical implication of a Christian sanctuary. The church had merely recommended that sanctuaries be sanctuaries.

The ancient notion that altars, holy sites, and temples be regarded, by their very nature, as places of refuge is not uniquely biblical or Christian. Sanctuary was a more or less formalized practice, for example, in ancient Egypt, Syria, Greece, and Rome. Political fugitives, criminals, debtors, and slaves on the run all passed beyond the pale of revenge and justice by making it into the precincts of a recognized shrine.

A specifically rich history and theology of the practice, however, exists within biblical tradition. Psalm 27 appears to be a sweet song of trust in God elaborated from the refuge and security of the altar:

> The Lord is the refuge of my life;
> of whom shall I be afraid?
>
> When evildoers assail me,
> uttering slanders against me,
> my adversaries and foes,
> they shall stumble and fall.
>
> Though a host encamp against me,
> my heart shall not fear. . . .
>
> One thing I have asked of the Lord,
> that will I seek after;

that I may dwell in the house of the Lord
all the days of my life,
to behold the beauty of the Lord,
and to inquire in the temple.

For God will hide me in shelter
in the day of trouble;
and conceal me under cover
of the Lord's tent
setting me high upon a rock. . . .

The main incidents of the claiming of sanctuary in the history of Israel occurred when Adonijah and later Joab sought protection from Solomon by laying hold the horns of the altar (1 Kings 1 and 2). But the most clearly spelled-out tradition of sanctuary is found in the Torah passages concerning the "cities of refuge" (Exod. 21:13–14; Num. 35:6–28; Deut. 4:41–43; 19:4–13).

The six levitical cities named in Deuteronomy apparently reflect the historical fact that the right of asylum was commonplace at the local altars of Yahweh. When worship was centralized under the deuteronomic reforms, the local shrines continued to function as places of refuge, and the cities were afforded a special vocation in that respect. The residents of these towns were charged with a rigorous task of protection, "lest innocent blood be shed" (Deut. 19:10).

The asylum of the refuge cities was specifically for those accused of manslaughter—killing without intent. By the law and tradition of bloodguilt, the accused were subject to the private justice of vengeance (an eye for an eye . . .). The sanctuary, in the interest of justice, provided a break in the cycle of vengeance. At the city gate, a limit to the violence of pursuit was established. The killing stopped there.

Perhaps the most ancient instance of sanctuary was that granted to Cain. He did, admittedly, commit a premeditated murder. The earth cried out for blood vengeance—and his curse was to be forever a fugitive and wanderer. Nevertheless, in response to Cain's plea God granted mercy and marked a limit to violence. The notorious mark of Cain was not really the public stigma of shame so often represented. It was a mark of protection. He carried upon his very person the refuge of God. He was a walking sanctuary, as it were.

Sanctuary is quite literally a sign and space of nonviolence: check your weapons at the door. Indeed, in the early church, it was the ministry of protection and mediation that by far preceded any public or civil acknowledgment of Christian sanctuary. "The early Christian Church," one historian notes in *Sanctuaries and Sanctuary Seekers,* "was strongly opposed to the shedding of blood, and ready to do all in its power to prevent violence which might result in bloodshed. Thus, the clergy speedily became intermediaries between criminals and those who desired vengeance, and acted as ambassadors of mercy before the throne of justice." Fugitives were protected, slaves interceded for (think of Paul's Letter to Philemon on behalf of Onesimus), and debtors sheltered until a bargain could be made or forgiveness given. In particular the growing recognition of the office of bishop as intercessor paved the road to the sanctuary door.

Certain illustrations of sanctuary incidents in medieval England portray the fugitives at the door or near the altar with daggers in their hands. The historians and scholars are quick to point out, however, that this is a "blemish" on their accuracy, for "everyone in England knew full well that the Church never suffered any sanctuary seekers to approach who bore in their hands or on their persons any kind of weapon."

In one of these paintings, the sanctuary seeker at Hexham is sitting on the *frith stool,* or peace stool, a stone seat often placed near the altar, especially in the designated sanctuaries of England. In the foreground of the picture, with a firm gesture of rebuke, a member of the clergy blocks the way of intruders who have violated the gates, perhaps with weapons of their own.

From the levitical cities of refuge to the heyday of sanctuaries in England, sanctuary nonviolence has not been passive or sedentary, despite being grounded in the altar.

Another notable epoch of active sanctuary nonviolence occurred during the Peace of God movement in eleventh-century France, a time of social and political chaos. Petty principalities squabbled over turf, private armies defended and devoured property, the judicial system was all but worthless, and debtors were hounded with a vengeance. The movement preached and prayed and negotiated and compacted peace. And the common reverence for sanctuary often bought time and played a role in these ministrations and restraints.

Sanctuary seeds its nonviolence in history and implies resistance, beginning at the altar. A United Methodist congregation recently set upon its front lawn a large sign bearing the international symbol for a nuclear-free zone, a region where nuclear weapons are neither built, nor based, nor permitted traverse, nor relied upon for military security.

For a church to declare its building a nuclear-free zone is either redundant or lucid: the weapons are perforce excluded, in fact and in spirit. A geography, very nearly a realm, of nonviolence is suggested and represented: not a bomb shelter, but a sanctuary circle of refusal and rebuke. On this end of our bloody history, the church might yet declare itself the limit of nuclear violence: the arms race stops here.

The sanctuary as sanctuary celebrates the sovereignty of God in history and our lives, marking the limit of civil authority. The long arm of the law stops and knocks at the front door. Because the foundation of every state or political authority has recourse to (more or less) "legitimate" violence, and because they more or less pretend to the sovereignty of God, these issues are not entirely separable.

Although the function, practice, and theology of sanctuary is not to be circumscribed by civil acknowledgment, in the history of the church Christian sanctuary has enjoyed various seasons of legal recognition. It is provoking to reflect that Constantine was probably the first to sanction it early in the fourth century (though initially as a simple delay of pursuit while clergy made intercession). Whatever might be impugned cynically about the depth or reality of Constantine's conversion, whatever might be said (and much ought) about the seduction of the church by the emperor, here was symbol and acknowledgment by the emperor of limit to his own authority.

For all the politics, there's something intriguing in the picture of him leaving his guard outside the door and seating himself (with the permission of the council) on a stool to listen in on the theological debate at Nicea. Not many years prior, under the political rituals of the imperial cult, any statue of the emperor had been the seat of legal sanctuary— even clinging to his picture had been sufficient to afford protection from pursuit and suspension of civil law.

The period and place, however, of greatest exercise of sanctuary privilege was in medieval England, where for several centuries at any given time there were more than a thousand people under protection of the church's peace. The ecclesiastical turf was carefully set forth and elaborate procedures for the sanctuary seeker obtained.

One of the most interesting corollaries of English sanctuary law was a provision for "abjuration of the realm," whereby a person accused of a felony and admitted to the church might forswear the right of all protection under the king's law and be permitted a strictly limited time to travel on foot to the nearest port and quit the kingdom, never to return except by the king's leave. It was as though every church door stood at the very boundary of the nation-state.

Until recently the notion of sanctuary had fallen into widespread disuse. In the United States particularly the practical theology of sanctuary has been subject to confusion and neglect. The intrusion of civil religion is a prime candidate for cause on this score. Picture the altar of your own local congregation. Is there a flag in the sanctuary? I know of certain young and impetuous pastors who have attempted with great ceremony and as a sort of dramatic sermon illustration to remove the flag from their chancel. The whole affair ends badly in something of an unresolved wrestling match with disgruntled parishioners. The confusion is deeply and emotionally held.

Perhaps in another context the dangerous idolatry, the political implications of our theological confusion might be more plainly evident. Eberhart Bethge reports that after Hitler seized power in January 1933, the altar of Magdeburg Cathedral, like many other churches in Germany, was surrounded with swastika flags. From the pulpit, the dean of the cathedral explained:

In short, it has come to be the symbol of German hope. Whoever reviles this symbol of ours is reviling our Germany. The swastika flags 'round the altar radiate hope—hope that the day is at last about to dawn.

It was an invasion—the precursor of many to come.

But not every sanctuary door and altar was so easily accessible to the spirit of power. On perhaps the same Sunday morning Dietrich Bonhoeffer preached a different word:

The Church has only one altar, the altar of the Almighty . . . before which all creatures must kneel. . . . He who seeks anything other than this must keep away; he cannot join us in the house of God.

In France, the village of Le Chambon became a city of refuge for Jews fleeing the Nazi persecution. Its central figure was André Pascal Trocmé, the town's Protestant minister. He pastored the little village into a community of compassion—a refuge where genuine hospitality was resistance.

Le Chambon was the very incarnation of sanctuary. Its residents took risks and suffered loss, and some of them died—all as a matter of course, as though it were simply in the nature of things and part of what it meant to be human.

The suggestion that sanctuary is not finally a place or a building made with hands but is embodied in a person or a people is not new. In fact it is recognizably biblical. In John's Gospel when Jesus drives the money changers out of the Temple, he engages in the following remarkable exchange with the authorities (2:18–21):

"What sign have you to show us for doing this?"
"Destroy this temple [*naos*—sanctuary or dwelling place—all the same in Greek] and in three days I will raise it up."
"It has taken forty-six years to build this temple and you're going to raise it up in three days?"
But he spoke of the temple of his body.

It is said that at the crucifixion of Jesus the curtain of the Temple was torn in two from top to bottom. Our comprehension of that sign may now be altered.

In the New Jerusalem envisioned in Revelation 21, where the sovereignty of God is finally vindicated in the whole of creation, it is made explicitly clear that there is no temple as such, for the temple is the Lamb.

Paul more than once admonishes the congregation at Corinth to remember that they are the temple of the Lord. And to the Ephesians (2:19–22) he writes:

So then you are no longer strangers and sojourners, but you are fellow citizens with the saints and members of the household of God, built upon the foundation of the apostles and prophets, Christ Jesus himself being the chief cornerstone, in whom the whole structure is joined together and grows into a holy temple in the Lord; in whom you also are built into it for a dwelling place for God in the Spirit.

In certain churchly circles these passages about the bodily temple are read in conjunction with whether you smoke cigarettes or drink or have sex or even eat too much. That's not an entirely fatuous reading, but it misses the bulk of the point. It is about community and has wide political implications with respect to the sovereignty of God and the limits of violence and civil authority.

Sanctuary is not a question of fortress mentality, of thick walls and heavy oak doors that power may lock tight. It is a matter of truth and faithfulness. The deepest meaning of sanctuary is revealed in Jesus' death and resurrection. Even in death Jesus takes his refuge only in faithfulness and truth, revealing both radical nonviolence and the sovereignty of God, and becoming our refuge.

As it happens, there is currently a growing sanctuary movement in the United States wherein Christians and congregations are comprehending

politics and the truth of their lives. Christians are opening their hearts
and church doors to fugitives from Central America.

An increasingly organized "underground railroad" connects places
of hospitality for these "illegal aliens," and that network is being linked
with emerging self-declared sanctuaries. This public disobedience is a
risk for the refugees as well as for the congregations—in fact more so.
Most are from El Salvador and Guatemala and have fled at great risk from
the greater risks of disappearance, torture, and political murder. If
caught, they face deportation and likely death in their homelands.

In Revelation 6 is an image and a question. The image is of the
martyrs, the souls of the faithful dead, crouching under the altar. They
seem to be granted sanctuary in death. And they appear to be granted
also a clearer view of history from that vantage point.

A question is upon their lips, and it has been suggested that the
question is a form of their faith. What they ask is more plaintive than the
sweet song of trust composed in Psalm 27, but not surely to be uttered
apart from it. They pray: "O Sovereign Lord, holy and true, how long
before thou wilt judge and vindicate our blood upon the earth?"

How long indeed?

WHERE EAST MEETS WEST:
Breaking the Power of the Cold War
Danny Collum

In the last ten years, a truly remarkable thing has happened in our country and in most of the world. The widespread alarm of ordinary citizens at the prospect of nuclear war has become a major factor in domestic politics and international diplomacy. Humanity's silence in the face of a precarious balance of terror has been decisively broken. From town councils and church committees to houses of parliament and superpower summits, the question of nuclear war is finally at, or near the top of, the public agenda.

That great awakening didn't just happen. It was in large part the result of hard work and difficult struggle on the part of thousands of dedicated activists. And churches and Christian communities played a key role in that process. Because of those efforts, combined with the tides of history and providence, we now live in a world where masses of people in almost every nation are awakened and mobilized against the nuclear threat.

We called for a freeze on the production, testing, and deployment of new nuclear systems. And that call was ratified by an overwhelming majority of the American people. We called for one of the superpowers to break the deadly cycle with a bold, unilateral initiative for peace. And with the Soviet testing moratorium, that has come to pass. Even our fondest and often unspoken dream—the complete elimination of nuclear weapons as instruments of national security—is now discussed with apparent seriousness by world leaders. We can look back over the last decade and, paraphrasing the hack politician's dying words in *The Last Hurrah,* say to ourselves, "We've done great things—among others."

Yes, "among others." "Among others" because, despite the great distance we've traveled, in many ways we've gone nowhere at all. The first-strike weapons we railed against so dramatically are now mostly in place, or well on the way. The historic Soviet test ban initiative was greeted by our government with a stone wall of silence backed by a strangling web of disinformation. At the Reykjavik summit, the superpower arms control agenda seemed to take a quantum leap from the medieval days of nosecone counting. But Reagan's slick intransigence has, at least for now, turned aside the threat of peace. And, speaking of lost history, the United States recently deployed its latest load of airborne cruise missiles, shattering for all time the feeble constraints of the SALT II agreement.

How did it happen? How did so much exhilarating promise turn into so many squandered opportunities? One quick and easy answer to those questions is "Ronald Reagan." Only a president can make a disarmament treaty and we happen to have one who is ideologically incapable of it. And he happens, through a quirky combination of history and personality, to be our most popular president in at least twenty-five years.

The other quick and easy answer is actually just an elaboration of the first: "Star Wars." The fantasy of a technological shield in space may never deflect any missiles, but in the hands of the Great Communicator it has worked quite well in deflecting Soviet disarmament proposals and American public opinion.

Those are the quick and easy answers, and they are true as far as they go. Ronald Reagan and his Star Wars dream are the great obstacles in the way of a safer future. But those answers in themselves aren't good enough. If we look deeper and are honest with ourselves, we must also recognize that even Star Wars is itself partly a symptom of one of the peace movement's failings.

By now it is a truism among us that the Star Wars scheme is a misguided technological solution to the political problem of the superpower arms race. It is that. But, to the extent that it has succeeded, it is partly because we in the opposition have too often attacked the arms race as a technological problem and failed to address its political roots. We educated masses of people about the scientific and medical effects of nuclear weapons and created a widespread public consciousness that a nuclear war would be an unthinkable disaster. We sounded the alarm about the new first-strike weapons and convinced a large segment of the public that if the present course continued, that disaster was a very real and present danger.

What we did not do so well was address the question of why the nuclear arsenals on both sides exist and why the arms race continues. We tended to treat the weapons as some mutant aberration in human history and to explain the arms race with reference to the blind momentum of technology and public complacency. Our proposals were often framed with the underlying assumption that if public complacency could be broken and the nuclear mutation amputated, then geopolitical business could proceed more or less as usual.

We failed to sufficiently address the fact that nuclear weapons, insane as they may be, are also practical instruments of the permanent state of conflict between the United States and the Soviet Union. Each superpower considers nuclear weapons the ultimate insurance that the conflict will not get out of hand to its detriment. And the arms race, while certainly self-perpetuating and arational, is also the means through which each superpower strives for the ability to work its political will in the world unhindered by the opposition of the other.

When the case for nuclear disarmament is argued within the context of the existing superpower enmity, then the question logically arises, "What will replace the role of nuclear weapons in maintaining and managing that conflict?" And, "What will really prevent the other side from using a disarmament agreement as a ruse to finally attain a definitive upper hand?" The disarmament movement for the most part avoided the first question and answered the second with technical verification data. The American people rightly perceived that as no answer at all.

Ronald Reagan, on the other hand, dared to take up those questions directly and answer, "Star Wars." The "peace shield" may be a fantasy, but it is a fantasy that has the advantage of answering the question of how to eliminate the threat of nuclear war without making peace with the Soviet Union. As President Reagan said in the wake of the Iceland summit, "We will trust in American technology and not in agreements with the Soviet Union." And so far the American people are cheering.

It is now obvious, or should be, that to deal realistically with the threat of nuclear war, we must first come to terms with the U.S.-Soviet relationship. The abject failure of the Soviet test ban initiative and the Reykjavik summit demonstrates once and for all that as long as U.S. policy (mainstream Democratic and Republican alike) remains rooted in Cold War ideology with the Soviet Union permanently cast as the inhuman and intractable enemy, humanity will continue on a collision course with disaster.

We know and, with increasing frequency, we publicly argue that the Star Wars promise is an illusion. But we should also by now know, and begin to publicly demonstrate, that the only viable answer to the threat of nuclear war is a change in the nature of the U.S.-Soviet relationship.

As Freeze strategist Pam Solo has noted, what we have built in the last decade is a disarmament movement. And what we must build in the next decade is a genuine peace movement. We must become a movement for peace between the United States and the Soviet Union and a movement not just against a hypothetical war to come but also against the Cold War that rages here and now.

Nuclear disarmament that is durable and trustworthy can only be founded on the mutual interests of the two superpowers. That requires that our government recognize that the Soviet Union has a genuine interest in disarmament and peace. And it also requires recognizing their status as a world power equal to the United States. In the argot of President Reagan's beloved Western movies, we have to decide that this planet is "big enough for the both of us" after all. And in the midst of the many, and not insubstantial, differences between our two countries, we must find it within ourselves to recognize the common ground we share. We must recognize that the survival and security of each of our countries are inextricably linked and that for both of us long-term security can only be bought by lessening, not escalating, the threat we pose to each other.

That is not a particularly popular proposition in Ronald Reagan's America. Today such sentiments are regularly dismissed as naive, cowardly, or unpatriotic. But we don't have to accept a choice between surrender to anti-Soviet hysteria or self-marginalizing naiveté. A call for peace with the Soviet Union doesn't, and shouldn't, mean championing Soviet interests or proclaiming the goodness of the Soviet system. It can and should mean promoting our own country's truest national interests and appealing to our people's best and highest impulses.

In the past decade, the movement of conscience has been at its best when it has refused the logic of false choices imposed by the global powers-that-be and instead inserted fresh options into the debate from the grass-roots level. The need now is for new approaches that can open up discussion of the U.S.-Soviet conflict in fresh ways. In that discussion we should especially look for grass-roots peace initiatives that could speak to the deeply felt fears and aspirations, real or perceived, of ordinary citizens on both sides of the East-West divide.

To even begin speaking of a world in which the United States and the Soviet Union are no longer at war involves a mind-boggling task of theorizing and speculation, but most of all it will require the political will of the two superpowers to turn in a new direction. And the lessons of history, not to mention the existence of deeply entrenched interests on both sides with a political or economic stake in the status quo, would indicate that the political will for a new direction will have to flow from the bottom up. It will require fulfilling President Eisenhower's prophecy that "someday the people will want peace so much that the governments will have to get out of their way and let them have it."

That, of course, means something very different in the United States and the West than it does in the Soviet Union and the East. But there are a number of good reasons for first considering the American context. One obvious reason is that it is the one we can most directly affect. Another is the plain fact of history and current statistics that since Hiroshima the United States has initiated each new round of escalation in the arms race. But also important is the effect that U.S. policy has on the course of events in the Soviet Union and the Warsaw Pact countries.

Historically in the Communist societies, new social and political possibilities tend to open up in direct proportion to the relaxation of tensions with the West. And conversely the wall of militarism and repression tends to come down most decisively when the Soviet leadership feels itself most threatened by U.S. policies and rhetoric. This dynamic has played itself out at least twice in recent history.

During the late 1950s and early 1960s, the Eisenhower and Kennedy administrations made clear moves toward what was then called "peaceful coexistence" with the Soviet Union. This was a major factor in creating the context for Premier Nikita Khrushchev's post-Stalinist thaw in Soviet society. Then Khrushchev was perceived by Soviet hard-liners to have been humiliated by President Kennedy during the Cuban missile crisis—a confrontation that starkly illuminated the Soviet Union's military inferiority. Khrushchev was ejected from office, the loosening of domestic restraints was decisively reversed, and the much-vaunted Soviet arms buildup began.

A similar process can be detailed in the rise and fall of the détente policy over the course of the 1970s. Soviet Secretary-General Gorbachev's currently simultaneous moves toward domestic reform and nuclear disarmament reinforce this linkage. He knows he can only have change at home if he has peace with the West. The domestic changes Gorbachev contemplates are hardly what we would call democratic, but they do involve significant decentralization and broadened social participation and could sow promising seeds. Ironically, by refusing Gorbachev's disarmament initiatives, President Reagan may ultimately prove himself the greatest enemy of humane reform in the Soviet system.

Even in the current age of rough military parity, the United States' clear economic, political, and technological superiority makes it the dominant partner in the superpower relationship. For better or worse, we set the tone of the relationship and the terms of the conflict. If there is to be a turn toward peace, it will have to begin here. And it will have to begin with a change of heart among the American people.

That phrase "change of heart," with its emotional and even spiritual connotations, is chosen advisedly because the Cold War is much more than an ordinary bread-and-butter issue in American politics. It is more like an article of faith. It operates not so much at the conventional level of "interest group" politics as at the deeper level of values, myths, and feelings. So the battle to stop the Cold War must be waged at that level as well.

Most Americans give their tacit assent to the nuclear arms race in large part because they believe that the Soviet Union is a ruthless, totalitarian enemy that threatens our society and the freedom and prosperity it delivers. Americans' interest in having a "strong deterrent" stems from a worldview containing specific values about America and the Soviet Union. That worldview is based in part on an affirmation of the good that exists in our society but even more on fear of the Soviet Union and its perceived evils. Much of that fear is engendered by the gross exaggerations or downright falsehoods about the Soviet Union that are force-fed to us almost from the cradle. We have the picture in our minds of a cold, monochromatic land where political opinion, religious belief, and all human feelings are forcibly and brutally suppressed. And the dominant picture of this Orwellian land and its intentions toward us is defined by the popular analogy between the Soviet Union of the 1980s and the rapacious Nazi Germany of the late 1930s.

That popular conception is an almost unrecognizable caricature of the real, existent Soviet Union. But the uncomfortable fact is that the lies are mixed with just enough truth to make for convincing propaganda. The Soviet Union is not the Oceania of Orwell's *1984,* nor is it perceived as such by the vast majority of its people. But it is a closed society where political, social, and cultural options are severely, and sometimes forcibly, limited.

In the same way, the Soviet Union's international behavior is most decisively not analogous to that of Hitler's Germany. The Soviets suffered horror beyond most of our imaginations in World War II. Their desire to avoid another war is real and runs very deep. But the Soviet Union does maintain a repressive military occupation of much of Eastern and Central Europe, and it has been involved in a brutal interventionist war in Afghanistan.

These and other cruel facts about the Soviet system are, first and foremost, concerns for the peoples who live under it. Only their self-initiated efforts will create social change in the Soviet bloc. But the problems with the Soviet system are inevitably also our concerns because they rightly offend the democratic values held by the American people and thus contribute to the fear that feeds the Cold War. They do this in the same way that America's very real militarism, bellicosity, and international adventurism feed the fear of war and help keep the arms race going on the Soviet side.

All that only serves to point up the fact that knowing that the Cold War worldview is deceptively simplistic and the result of incessant propaganda won't make it go away. It must instead be confronted and replaced by a more appealing alternative vision of the world and America's place in it that can provide a credible and principled answer to the fears that are real. In the context of such an alternative, it will become more possible to dispel the fears that are false and destructive.

For us as Christians, the place to begin searching for that new worldview is with the gospel. As in every age, our task is to bring the Word of God to bear on the historical questions we face. That means we need to begin to forge a new theology of the Cold War to replace the one so clearly articulated by President Reagan.

The starting place for our theology of the Cold War must be with a "theology of the enemy." In Jesus' teachings we are, of course, flatly and unconditionally commanded not to hate, kill, or revile our enemies but to love them. This teaching is fleshed out with examples drawn from everyday experiences of "the enemy" faced by Jesus' contemporaries— the Roman occupation soldier, the rich and their courts of law, and the one who does physical violence. In each case study, Jesus puts forward an example of a creative response of love—walking the second mile, giving the cloak as well as the coat, turning the other cheek—that doesn't avoid or deny the reality of conflict between enemies but instead casts it in entirely new, unexpected, and humanizing terms.

The implications of this should be obvious for Christians living at the heart of the most dangerous enmity in human history. More than twenty years ago, in his book *The Nonviolent Cross,* theologian-activist Jim Douglass noted that with the advent of nuclear weapons the conventional politics of violence—the way humanity has done business since the time of Cain—has been rendered impotent. Violent force can no longer defend the nation or enforce order in the world. It can now only destroy itself and all who touch it. The serpent of violence has swallowed its tail, and the way of Jesus, the way of enemy-love we clumsily call nonviolence, has become not just a spiritual truth but a pragmatic necessity.

What remains is for contemporary followers of Jesus to take his way seriously at every level of our individual and communal lives and to translate it into the terms of contemporary history. As in Jesus' time, that means first and foremost that you do not deal with your enemies by killing them. Instead you approach situations of conflict and hostility with a posture that humanizes the enemy, recognizing that in addition to our differences we have some important and fundamental things in common. This should also make us able to empathetically comprehend that the enemy's posture toward us is rooted in much the same mix of feelings and fears as is our posture toward them.

And loving our enemy should eventually form the basis for political approaches that remove the threat of mutual destruction driving us ever deeper into our bunkers and instead open up new room for creative change on both sides, perhaps even to the point of reconciliation.

The command to love our enemies is the spiritual and practical foundation for a Christian theology of the Cold War. But the call to love our enemies can lead down a path of deception if it is not accompanied by a keen and equally biblical theology of the powers. The New Testament teaching on the powers and principalities (well amplified in the work of theologians Hendrik Berkhof, William Stringfellow, and others) should lead us to the recognition that, despite the best of intentions, real or proclaimed, both superpowers are fallen entities. And as such they are given to playing God by making absolute claims over their own citizens, over weaker nations, and, through their nuclear technology, over the whole of humanity.

Among other things, a biblical theology of the powers should provide us with a healthy measure of skepticism regarding the moral claims of both superpowers. It should make us wise as serpents, just as love for the enemy should make us gentle as doves. Christians should be among those who stand outside the authority and assumptions of the powers on both sides, holding both accountable to the values of the kingdom.

In addition to a theology of the enemy and of the powers, a Christian approach to the Cold War should also reflect a deep-rooted theology of solidarity. In a way, this is only an elaboration of the theology of the enemy, which asserts that all people, even our enemies, are children of God and the objects of God's compassion. But the biblical witness also calls us to a more specific solidarity that inevitably involves the making of choices. The God of the Bible is the one who actively chooses the side of the oppressed, the one who pleads their case before the powerful and acts for their deliverance. In accepting death on the cross, Jesus drew for all time a line between victims and executioners and demonstrated that God stands victorious with the victims.

In one rather obvious sense, nuclear weapons call us to God's universal compassion. In a nuclear war, even the executioners become victims. And our compassion for the potential victims of that unthinkable war is a primary spiritual foundation for Christian peacemaking. But that universal compassion becomes an empty, lifeless abstraction if it leads us to turn a blind eye to the suffering of the real and present victims before us. That means the homeless person on our city street, the unemployed worker, the abused woman, the displaced farm family, and our abandoned black or Hispanic communities. It means the Central American cities and villages under our guns, the Middle Eastern ones under the guns we supply, and the South African blacks under a system we and our allies finance. If we believe in a human future, we must demonstrate that aspiration and that belief in the here and now.

The same truth also applies in our relationship to the religious and political dissenters in Soviet mental hospitals and work camps and to the peoples under the Soviet gun in Eastern Europe and Afghanistan. We are irrevocably linked with them by our common humanity and common compassion; by our common aim of peace and life; and by our common participation in and victimization by a Cold War world system that makes the superpowers and their systems out to be as God. In our theology, our spirituality, and no less in our real-world politics, we must recognize and insist that acts of war and death on either side of the East-West divide are ultimately obstacles to peace and to life everywhere.

Any strategy for action that proceeds from these affirmations must begin by turning back what currently amounts to a unilateral U.S. assault on the Soviet Union. Probably the most important public policy element of the current assault is the Star Wars scheme. Its goal is either to gain a lopsided long-term military superiority over the Soviets or to force them to destroy the remains of their economy in a drive to catch up—or both. Either long-term prospect makes it the primary short-term obstacle to peaceful accommodation between the two superpowers.

At least as important as the technological manifestations of the Cold War is the incessant and often brutal anti-Sovietism growing in American culture. Ronald Reagan's Cold War mythology, with its brazen and manipulative appeal to the worst of human instincts, has trickled down with a vengeance to become a commonplace of American life in movies, television—news, entertainment, and commercials—and even children's toys. For the Christian churches, countering this wave of hateful propaganda with Jesus' teaching on the enemy is not solely, or even mainly, a political task. Though it is bound to have political implications, it has as much to do with the pastoral care of souls and with nurturing the survival of Christian faith in an overwhelmingly hostile environment.

Toward that end, we should engage at every possible level in programs aimed at fostering genuine understanding and friendship toward the people of the Soviet Union. Beginning at whatever level of political sophistication is appropriate in our context, we should move toward the declaration that we as Christians do not consider ourselves at war with the Soviet Union. And we should devise ways for Christians to act on that conviction.

Prayers for "the enemy," for the Soviet people and their leaders, should become a regular part of our worship life. People-to-people meetings between U.S. and Soviet citizens can be an especially significant experience for breaking down the barriers of fear. We should look for a wide range of traditions and rituals that can allow a spirit of reconciliation to grow among us.

In our current situation, almost any efforts aimed at fostering U.S.-Soviet peace, however small and limited they may seem, are worthy of our time and energy. Especially valuable are actions that grow from the recognition that change at the political level will only come as a result of changed attitudes and perceptions at the grass-roots level. Even in the current state of Cold War, we can begin charting a new direction that contributes to breaking down the East-West barriers and points toward, and helps lay the groundwork for, a human future beyond the Cold War. Rather than accepting the assumptions and restrictions of a bipolar universe, we can begin to act now on a vision of peace that is grounded in

respect for the human rights and self-determination of all peoples—
North, South, East, and West.

One way to begin doing this is by expanding our contacts, solidarity,
and alliance with those in the Soviet Union and the Soviet bloc who also
work for more humane, self-governing societies in a context of international peace and who see each of those goals as a necessary requirement
for the other. There are emerging throughout the Soviet bloc small but
brave and increasingly visible groupings of people who have declared
themselves for nonalignment and democracy and against militarization
and superpower hostility on both sides of the East-West divide.

In Europe over the last several years there has been a growing range of
contacts and even joint activities between these groups and the Western
peace movement. Together they have begun hammering out a vision of a
Europe that is no longer a battleground for the Cold War but is instead a
nonnuclear, nonaligned, and increasingly demilitarized and democratic
buffer zone between the United States and the Soviet Union. They see
themselves going under and around the superpower system to begin
creating a world free from it. Within that overarching vision, each group
carries on the specific immediate work within its own national context
that can create openings for that new possibility and contribute to the
slow dissolution of the Cold War bloc mentality.

It's not surprising that this vision and the work around it began in
Europe. There the unnatural separation of neighboring countries, the
division of Germany, and the military presence of both superpowers
makes the Cold War a concrete, unavoidable reality. But the vision of a
future that is dominated by neither East nor West will obviously require
the participation of the United States. And given a chance, that vision
should have great appeal to the American people as a principled and
practical answer to the Cold War stalemate, which dooms us to "little"
wars of intervention while constantly threatening us with the big war of
annihilation. That potential has already been demonstrated in small ways
by the efforts of the New York–based Campaign for Peace and Democ-
racy/East and West in garnering progressive American support for peace
and democracy activists in the Soviet Union and the bloc countries and in
initiating a trans-bloc initiative against U.S. intervention in Nicaragua.

So far the U.S. churches have lagged behind in this area of East-West
peace work, despite the fact that much of the activity in the East is based
in the churches and carried on by Christians. If we actually believe that

our first allegiance is to no earthly kingdom but instead to Jesus and the values of his kingdom, then standing with our counterparts on the other side of the lines of hostility is one clear way to demonstrate that belief. It is also an exceptionally clear and pointed way to offer hope for a future beyond the ironclad assumptions of line-drawers and warmakers.

Some within the peace movement, and even within the churches, have argued that involvement with so-called dissident groups in the East, which inevitably means drawing attention to their human rights struggles, can only contribute to Cold War hostility by reinforcing negative images of Soviet totalitarianism. It is certainly true that the U.S. government is most interested in using "human rights" as a club to beat the Soviet Union. For that reason it must always be made crystal clear that our statements and actions on those issues are coupled with clear, unmistakable opposition to the hostile acts of our government toward the Soviet Union. When approached in that light, an alliance for peace and democracy could help disarm our government's "human rights weapon" and offer a positive, constructive alternative to the digging of trenches and building of walls on both sides.

The brief history of what the Europeans call "détente from below" is not enough to suggest it as any sort of be-all and end-all panacea. It is still much more of a worldview or even a general attitude toward the world than it is a viable, fully worked out geopolitical option.

But as we've noted, it is in fact new attitudes toward the world and new morally rooted visions of a human future that are most needed to begin breaking the power of the Cold War. As such, the embryonic movement across the Cold War battle lines suggests at least the possibility of something genuinely new coming to pass. We've already had opportunities to observe the befuddlement of the powerful white men (and Margaret Thatcher) on both sides at the spectacle of people who renounce both the CIA and KGB and all of their works, who stand for self-determination in Poland and Nicaragua, and who demand nuclear disarmament and the dismantling of interventionary forces by both superpowers.

Even more threatening to the war systems of the West and East is the prospect of such people on both sides of the Cold War divide insisting that they and their concerns for peace, justice, and freedom belong together and can no longer be kept apart. Such a vision of peacemaking is consistent with our Christian values of both reconciliation and compassion. And it can draw on and appeal to the best American values of democracy and self-determination.

It offers at least one possibility of a creative response to the question of the enemy that meets the nonviolent criteria of not acquiescing to evil, recognizing the humanity of the other, and opening the way to reconciliation. It could offer the American people a constructive alternative to the Cold War religion by demonstrating that the values we claim to defend can really be best furthered by making peace. As such, it could offer hope where there is mostly what Daniel Berrigan has called "a grinding, low-grade despair." It could help fuel a spirit of cooperation and create new possibilities for openness and collaboration on both sides.

Perhaps we can even begin to discern the seeds of a still-imperfect world that at least no longer has "two sides" but is instead a kaleidoscope of human social experiments. Perhaps we can even begin to act now as if there is a future beyond the Cold War.

PART FOUR

Acts of Conscience: Civil Disobedience

BY WHAT AUTHORITY?
The Bible and Civil Disobedience
Ched Myers

Civil disobedience as a political tactic is of relatively recent genesis, but resistance to human sovereigns is as old as civilization itself. In the ancient world, this resistance usually took the forms of refusal to abide by the decrees of a king or a prophetic challenge to the legitimacy of a ruler's authority. Such disobedience was a serious undertaking.

Although democratic dissent and "free speech" were not unknown, the normal paradigm of political rule was that of the sovereign's absolute authority. Since the king was divine in the ancient Mediterranean world, disobedience meant transgressing the very order of the cosmos. The radical monotheism of the Bible—the belief that only God was sovereign—therefore accepts acts of resistance to ruling political authority as part of the fabric of the salvation history of Yahweh.

In surveying the biblical material for light on an essentially modern way of posing the question ("civil disobedience"), we must define what it is we are looking for. We are not, on the one hand, looking for a "doctrine of the state," though this impinges on the topic; nor are we, on the other hand, cataloging every form of subversive political action in the Bible. Rather, we are looking for biblical antecedents to our modern experimentation with civil disobedience. Thus, the focus is on instances of open and nonviolent acts of resistance to the structures of authority in a given biblical social formation.

There are two fundamental forms of resistance, which can be actions taken by individuals, small communities, or large, mobilized groups. The first we can call defensive disobedience: action aimed at protecting persons from aggression or injustice by the ruling structure, usually taking the form of noncooperation with law or policy. A modern example would be draft or tax resistance. The second is offensive disobedience: action intending to, through confrontation and engagement, expose moral, legal, or political contradictions in existing policy. Nonviolent direct action at nuclear weapons facilities would be an example of this.

In looking at disobedience to structures of authority first in the Old Testament, it is important to keep in mind the essentially negative view of kingship that formed the core of the original desert traditions. The Tower of Babel story in Genesis 11 is quite probably an ancient Hebrew polemic against the centralization of authority, technology, and political culture in imperial urban centers, such as ancient Babylon. Turning to Israel's self-rule, 1 Samuel 8 suggests that the founding of the monarchy was a rejection of the sovereignty of God in order to have a king "like all the other nations." The people here forfeited the decentralized tribal-charismatic polity of the era of judges—a political model that is still revered in the eschatological writings of the New Testament (Matt. 19:28; Luke 22:29–30).

French theologian Jacques Ellul sums up the political analysis of 1 Samuel 8: "Political authority rests on defiance; it is a rejection of God; it can only be dictatorial, abusive, and unjust." This attitude, at the core of the oldest traditions, is crucial in understanding the uniquely important role given to disobedience in the recitation of salvation history in the Hebrew Bible.

Classicist and rabbinic scholar David Daube writes in *Civil Disobedience in Antiquity:* "The oldest record in world literature of the spurning of a governmental decree occurs in the second Book of Moses. . . . This oldest instance of conscientious disobedience concerns a case of genocide." The reference is to the story of the birth of Moses (Exod. 1:8–2:10). Hebrew midwives defy an order by Pharaoh to kill all Hebrew males at birth and cover their tracks by lying to Pharaoh. The mother of Moses then takes her baby "underground" in order to save his life.

This story of defensive Old Testament disobedience is interesting for many reasons. First, it is highly political in nature, the backdrop being the oppression of the Hebrews and their threat to the social stability of Pharaoh's Egypt. The story, then, inaugurates the Exodus narrative.

Second, quite apart from the shock that many Bible readers in the United States may receive from discovering such bald-faced defiance of and lying to established authority, the disobedient act provokes greater repression on the part of the authorities. This response is very familiar in modern practice of civil disobedience.

Third, and most important to Christian readers, the story is closely paralleled in Matthew's birth narrative of the new Moses: Jesus. The second chapter of Matthew recounts that the infant Messiah is also threatened by royal infanticide, is saved by the civil disobedience and deception of a third party (the Wise Men), and goes underground to escape Herod. These stories reflect the bitter experience of power, pitting the genocidal political realism of kings against the divine hope borne by infants.

The book of Esther has a plot that similarly turns on a series of acts of noncooperation to a pagan ruler. This "historical novel," like the book of Daniel, is set in a Persian court but is meant to be instructive to the Jewish community at a later date. Esther contains three notable instances of noncooperation.

The narrative begins with the queen of Ahasuerus, Vashti, refusing to be put on show for the king's guests. This defiance, remarkable for the setting of an oriental court, opens the way for Esther, a Jew, to assume the role of queen and sets the stage for the Jewish leader Mordecai to refuse to pay homage to one of the king's governors, Haman. In order to save Mordecai and the entire Jewish community from retaliation for this noncooperation, Esther breaks the king's rules of visitation and manages to persuade him to overturn the edict for a pogrom.

The message of the story seems to be that Jews who find themselves in positions of access to power, like Esther, must act in solidarity with those who take positions of noncooperation on matters of principle, like Mordecai. The story may have been a kind of handbook for the persecuted Jewish community in its deliberations on concrete strategies of resistance.

This is certainly the case for the book of Daniel which, according to Daube, "may be described as a veritable charter of civil disobedience by a religious minority." At issue are Jewish dietary laws and, more important, the refusal to worship the oriental monarch. The account involves Daniel's solitary witness in chapter 6, as well as the group resistance of Shadrach, Meshach, and Abednego in chapter 3. These exemplary stories of faith in the first half of Daniel set the stage for the thinly veiled political criticisms of Antiochus IV Epiphanes in chapters 7 to 12.

The apocalpytic imagery in Daniel, according to Daniel scholar J. Collins, "may be understood as a political manifesto. . . . The mythical symbolism of the vision of Daniel is designed to inspire active but nonviolent resistance. . . . The wise man need not fight, but can express his resistance to the power of the king by noncompliance with his orders, and endurance of whatever suffering results."

This tradition of defensive civil disobedience for a persecuted community is later appropriated in the New Testament by Mark's apocalypse (Mark 13) and the book of Revelation.

There is an offensive disobedience tradition as well in the Hebrew Bible. The most massive action in defiance of a king of course is the Exodus event, which we can almost characterize as a "national cessation." But there is a strong tradition of dissent even within the Israelite theocratic/monarchial period, which we know as classical prophecy.

The court prophet Micaiah under Ahab defied the imperial expectation for favorable predictions on the eve of a military adventure (1 Kings 22) and was thrown in jail, after first mocking government-controlled forecasters and then discrediting the king's legitimacy in a parable. Likewise, Elijah refuses to tell a king what he wants to hear (2 Kings 1), despite attempts of military intimidation.

At the center of the tradition of Hebrew prophecy is the conviction that the Word of God must be spoken, especially when it portends bad tidings that will never be gladly received by the authorities. This is perhaps expressed most clearly in Ezekiel 33.

The notion of the prophet as "watchman" is not unlike the modern democratic idea that a "loyal opposition" must resist unjust laws and policies for the sake of the survival or integrity of the body politic. Thus, Martin Luther King, Jr., broke segregation laws to demonstrate the absolute incompatibility of apartheid with the U.S. Constitution.

Jeremiah is perhaps the greatest practitioner of this vocation in the Old Testament. His language is symbolic action, such as the purchase of the linen girdle in chapter 13 and the earthenware jar in chapter 19, that dramatizes the religious and social apostasy of the people. His actions more often than not land him in jail (chaps. 20 and 32).

Jeremiah's offensive engagements with the ruling caste of his time are highly political, such as his symbolic action of wearing a yoke to protest military alliances for purposes of national security (chap. 27), or his purchase of land on the eve of the Babylonian siege of Jerusalem to signal that hope lay not in futile resistance but in God's power to preserve the people through exile (chap. 32). Thus did the great prophet Jeremiah fulfill his vocation to "pluck up and break down" kingdoms (1:10).

As suggested in the story of Moses' birth, what is remarkable about "civil disobedience" in the Old Testament is how Israel perceived its salvation story as so often contingent upon acts of noncooperation with authority. Rahab the harlot is given a firm place in biblical history by her politically partisan resistance (Josh. 2, Heb. 11:31, James 2:25). David himself survives his contest with Saul the king only because Saul's son, Jonathan, and daughter, Michal (David's wife), give their loyalty to David in defiance of their father (1 Sam. 19–20).

It is worth noting how often women figure in roles of disobedience to achieve their aims. Daube notes that "a woman is the main figure also in the Greek prototype of civil disobedience": Sophocles' *Antigone*. From the early narratives on, there is a sense that the politics of noncooperation are the special weapon of oppressed sectors.

We have evidence from rabbinic writings that strategies and the political and moral ethics of resistance and noncooperation were the subject of serious deliberation within the persecuted Jewish community through the time of the emperor Hadrian. We can assume that the same discussions went on in the early Christian communities.

There were incidents of mass political civil disobedience in both Rome and Palestine under the Romans. Given the essentially defensive political posture of religious minorities in the Roman Empire, it is all the more impressive that the weight of New Testament evidence strongly indicates an offensive posture toward authorities.

The singular model for civil disobedience for the Christian is of course the ministry of Jesus, much of which can be understood as calculated confrontation with the structures of sociopolitical power of his day. We can briefly survey its two phases: his ministry in Galilee and his final days in Jerusalem.

Mark's narrative of Jesus' first mission around the region of Capernaum (Mark 2:13–3:6) presents us with a Jesus who systematically assaults the social order of first-century Jewish Palestine. Jesus takes on the rigid social caste system of clean and unclean by calling a tax collector into his discipleship community and underscores the point by sharing table fellowship with a variety of outcasts. By touching a leper, recorded in the first chapter of Mark, Jesus was already considered impure; by eating with "sinners," Jesus defies the Pharisaical codes of ritual purity.

Jesus' next act is to publicly decline to participate in a recognized fast day, an attack on the relationship between religious piety and the legitimation of leadership in Jewish society. Finally, Jesus assaults the symbolic center of synagogue Judaism, the Sabbath, by transgressing

Sabbath laws and boldly asserting, "The Sabbath was made for man, not man for the Sabbath" (Mark 2:27).

In each case, the act is public and carefully planned to address the various aspects of the social world of his time. Moreover, Jesus not only breaks regulations that were law in his day, but he asserts his perfect right to do so in every case (2:10, 17, 19, 28). The sequence, not surprisingly, culminates in one more public confrontation in a synagogue, where Jesus again breaks the Sabbath law by healing a man's hand (3:1–6). The response to these acts by the local Galilean authorities is a commitment to do away with Jesus.

This sequence is a dramatic and protracted "civil disobedience campaign" because the Law was the foundation of Jewish social order. There was no "secular realm," only a foreign colonizer, Rome, whose laws and religion were also inseparable. The sequence is characteristic of the whole of Jesus' ministry. He challenged the authority of kinship regulations (Luke 2:41–52; Mark 3:31–35), the dietary customs that gave Jews much of their social identity (Mark 7:1–5, 14–30), and the claim of the wealthy and the educated to their social and religious status (Mark 10:17–23; 12:28–34). Most important, Jesus' confrontation had a directly political thrust: his campaign was finally directed at the center of power, Jerusalem (Luke 9:51–56).

Luke's account of the Jerusalem section of Jesus' ministry is another sequence of highly symbolic and politically crafted actions. It begins with a messianic entry into the city and a lament over Jerusalem's imminent demise (Luke 19:28–44). Then comes perhaps the most dramatic and provocative of Jesus' actions, the "cleansing" of the Temple (19:45–48).

The Temple was both the political and economic heart of the Jewish social formation and the center of the symbolic order of Israel. To take action to shut down its commerce completely and denigrate its operation was a bold interpretation of the prophetic tradition of civil disobedience.

It is no wonder that the next episode in Luke's narrative is a direct challenge by the authorities, who are already plotting his arrest, to Jesus' authority to act in such a way (19:47–20:8). Civil disobedience is always most potent when it provokes a crisis of authority. As in many cases taken to court today by nonviolent resisters, Jesus responds to the challenge with a counterchallenge aimed at undermining the legitimacy of those who are in power. His counterchallenge is the parable of the vineyard (20:9–20).

The Jewish leaders, if not many modern interpreters, understand exactly the political point of the parable and proceed to press Jesus further. If he does not recognize their jurisdiction, will he acknowledge the authority of the colonial power, Rome? They thus throw back to him the infamous tribute question (20:21–26). In response, Jesus tells another parable, posing rhetorically the question as to the relative jurisdiction of Caesar in light of the rule of God. His opponents are stunned and perceive his answer as another instance of blatant defiance of the rule of Law, which they level at him later in his trial (23:2).

It is sufficiently clear from these two narrative sequences that Jesus is portrayed as deliberately choosing a prophetic style of confrontation with authority, at virtually every level of Law and custom in society, in order to underscore the new authority of the kingdom of God. It is inevitable that he would meet the cross, a form of capital punishment reserved by the Romans for political dissidents, and that the Jewish authorities would work in close collaboration with Rome to secure his condemnation.

Jesus expects his followers also to embrace this cross (Mark 8:34). They are to carry on his ministry of confrontation through the proclamation of the new order. They can expect that they too will be delivered up to councils, beaten in synagogues, and forced to stand before governors and kings (Mark 13:9)—a catalogue of the four levels of local and central Jewish and Roman authority in Palestine.

In the narratives of the early apostolic church, this continuation is precisely what we find. The post-Easter community takes up where Jesus left off: in the Temple, publicly challenging the order of sin and death, and being dragged before the authorities (Acts 3:1–4:18).

It is in the apostolic testimony that we have the clearest formulation, twice for emphasis, of the conflict. For preaching about Jesus, Peter and John are arrested and must answer to the high priest. "Whether it is right in the sight of God to listen to you rather than to God," they tell him, "you must judge" (4:19). In a similar situation recorded a chapter later, Peter answers, "We must obey God rather than human rule" (5:29).

Acts portrays the ministry of Paul as involving no less systematic conflict with the authorities (16:16–24; 19:23–41; 21:6–14), a fact confirmed by Paul's own Letters, many of which are penned from jail. Paul's Epistle to the Ephesians speaks of a mandate wherein believers are to "take no part in the unfruitful works of darkness, but rather unmask them" (Eph. 5:11).

The more defensive posture of disobedience to authorities is a very strong strand in much of the later New Testament literature. Similar to

Daniel, the book of Revelation is a resistance document, probably reflecting persecutions under the emperor Domitian in the last decade of the first century. Chapter 13 is particularly recognizable as a call to noncooperation with Roman authority and an exhortation to Christians to accept the consequences of their resistance.

John, writing as a political prisoner in exile, objects to Rome not only because of its persecution of Christians, but also because of its slave trade and oppressive economic structures (6:6; 18:3, 9–20) and military policies (6:2–4, 15; 16:13–21; 20:7–15). John insists that Christians must not only refuse to cooperate but also take steps to disassociate themselves from the imperial menace (18:4–5).

The well-known and much-abused teaching of Paul in Romans 13 must also be considered here. Numerous commentators have established that Paul is not advocating absolute and uncritical subordination to every authority, but rather exhorting conditional cooperation with the state that is "not a terror to good conduct" (Rom. 13:3). What is usually overlooked is that this teaching was needed at all; the implication is that the normal Christian practice was noncooperation. Ellul comments, "Paul's verses seem to me a reaction against the extremist of the antipolitical position."

Peter wishes to ensure that Christians are being put in prison for the right reasons: "Let none of you suffer as a murderer, or a thief, or a wrongdoer, or a mischief-maker: but if you suffer as a Christian, let you not be ashamed" (4:15–16). These words reflect genuine pastoral concern for the ambiguous public face and often mixed personal motives that are inherent in the practice of civil disobedience.

Both Romans and 1 Peter take a firm stance against the excesses of offensive disobedience and pastorally encourage defined and controlled defensive actions. No one who seriously proposes civil disobedience in our modern setting will deny that such political and pastoral guidelines are necessary to maintain public and personal integrity.

By the time of the writing of 1 Timothy, the "good fight of faith" is still conceived in terms of making a good defense before magistrates after the example of Jesus (1 Tim. 6:11–16). The writings of the time are full of concern about conduct in an era of persecution. This is not surprising, since as Daniel Stevick points out in his book *Civil Disobedience and the Christian,* "Such pleas reflect a time when, in the eyes and by the laws of the empire, to be a Christian at all was to be in a state of civil disobedience."

The early church struggled to form an ethic of obedience and disobedience because the nature of the kingdom seemed to radically contradict the atmosphere of imperial control in which the early Christians moved and lived. The Pauline gospel of freedom from the Law was especially potent politically. For Paul, the central metaphor for faith was the contention between the old and new order for the obedience of the believer.

The stance of the early church, with its recognition that conflict with the state was inevitable, made it imperative for a complementary set of teachings to be developed concerning subordination, in order that the freedom of the gospel not become an occasion for gratuitous or exploitative conduct (Rom. 6:1, Gal. 5:13). It is unfortunate that the latter set of teachings, originally conceived as a counterpoint, has become so often the one-dimensional ethic for a church no longer in collision, but rather in collusion, with the state.

Much can be gleaned for our modern practice of civil disobedience from this overview of biblical antecedents. First, we must be careful not to draw too many direct parallels. While we may find ourselves resisting for the same reasons as our biblical cousins, our sociopolitical setting is quite different, especially due to the influence of democratic ideology (if not reality). We should no more argue a reductionist position—no disobedience unless the Bible specifically stipulates it on a given issue—than we should a literalist one—every issue important to the biblical witnesses should be of equal importance to us. (We might, for example, have a hard time getting as excited about dietary fidelity as Daniel did.)

Second, we must affirm the pluralism of the Bible in matters of civil disobedience style. The Scriptures are full of both offensive and defensive modes of confrontation.

Third, the biblical pluralism regarding attitudes toward the legal system holds a lesson for us. On the one hand, there is a strong strand of repudiation of the courts as a vehicle for gaining a hearing for truth: Jesus remains silent before Pilate, and Paul doubts the justice to be gained in Roman courts (1 Cor. 6:1). On the other hand, Paul took advantage of many opportunities to testify before the rulers of his day (Acts 23–26), even to the point of insisting upon the rights of "due process" (Acts 16:37–39; 22:25–29; 25:11). Prophetic silence and prophetic speech before the law both have biblical precedent.

It is clear enough that civil disobedience in many forms is biblically justified and at times even imperative. The failure of most Christians to acknowledge that is a hermeneutic problem, not an exegetical one. For too long, Christian teaching has been entrenched on the side of "law and order"; perhaps there needs to be more theological attention given to the contemporary meaning of "freedom from the law."

The U.S. church has historical as well as biblical roots to draw upon, given the rich precedents of nonviolent direct action and noncooperation. Only by more seriously developing a politics of noncooperation and nonviolent engagement with authority will the church begin to embody a truly hopeful alternative to the spiral of violence and repression in our time. Then "through the church the manifold wisdom of God might be made known to the principalities and powers" (Eph. 3:10).

WITH ALL DUE RESPECT:
A Historical Perspective on Civil Disobedience
Richard K. Taylor

Unless we are philosophical anarchists, most of us probably believe that it is right to obey most laws most of the time. (I say "most" because of that 30 m.p.h. we've driven in a 25 m.p.h. zone.) We recognize that law is a valuable and necessary ordering force in human affairs. It has the potential to help make life both more peaceful and more just in everything from traffic regulations to protecting the civil rights of minorities.

Many people become so enraptured by the majesty of law, however, that they oppose breaking law under any circumstances. Society, they say, must be governed by the rule of law. Law creates structures of authority and justice, which, while admittedly imperfect, are much to be preferred to any lawless alternative. No one has the right to place themselves above the law, for to do so is arrogantly to become a law unto oneself. To pick and choose which laws one will obey or not obey leads to social disorder and, if widely practiced, to a chaos in which everyone's rights and liberties will be sacrificed.

Many Christians join in opposing any disobedience to law. They draw upon Paul's teaching in Romans 13 and other biblical passages, which they interpret as making unqualified claims for "civil disobedience." According to this view, to resist the authorities and their laws is to resist what God has appointed. But how does this absolutist view of obedience to law stand up when we look at history?

What if you had lived in the United States in the mid-1800s, for example, when the draconian federal Fugitive Slave Law required that all citizens assist in returning escaped slaves without delay to their owners? Would you have gone along with prominent Americans, like Daniel Webster, who supported passage of the slave law as part of the Compromise of 1850 and who branded resistance to the law as "treason"? Or would you have been more drawn to the views of the Quaker poet and abolitionist, John Greenleaf Whittier, who called slavery a "hateful hell" and said, "I would rather die than aid in that wicked law"?

If you had refused to aid in the law and in fact helped fugitive slaves to escape, you would have risked fines, arrest, and imprisonment, as did the hundreds of Christian abolitionists who set up the famous "underground railroad" to shuttle slaves to their freedom. You would have been a lawbreaker *par excellence.* Yet looking back on the mid-1800s, I think most reasonable people would agree that those who broke the Fugitive Slave Law, enabling an estimated hundred thousand slaves to escape to freedom, acted with greater moral integrity than those who obeyed the law and helped return the slaves to bondage.

Or what if you had lived in Germany in the 1930s and 1940s, when Hitler was in power and passing laws requiring Jews to be rounded up and shipped off to the death camps? The vast majority of Germans went along with Hitler's edicts, often using as their justification the need to obey the law and duly constituted authority.

Would you have been part of this law-abiding majority? Or would you have been among the minority who disobeyed Hitler's decrees and whom history now judges as heroes? Would you have acted as did Franz Jagerstatter, the young Austrian peasant farmer, married father of three daughters, who was called to active duty in the Nazi army in 1943 and urged to serve by his pastor, other priests, and his bishop, but refused and was beheaded by the Nazis because he saw Hitler's philosophy as diametrically opposed to his Catholic faith? Or would you have acted as did Adolf Eichmann, who said at his trial that he had no personal hostility toward Jews, but participated in the "final solution" only out of a desire to do his "duty," to obey orders and "the law"? Surely there is hardly a more telling historical example than that of Nazi Germany to show that obedience to law must not be absolutized.

Human history gives many examples of times when people of integrity had to put conscience or faithfulness to God ahead of obedience to human law. Often these people were derided, imprisoned, even killed in their own time, but they are now revered.

Christian history contributes heavily to this saga of principled civil disobedience to human law. In its earliest days, the primitive church came up against the Roman custom of performing acts of worship to the emperor. To the Romans the Christian affirmation of Christ as Lord seemed seditious, a contradiction of the supremacy and divinity of the emperor.

When Polycarp, bishop of Smyrna, was arrested in A.D. 156, the

Romans told him that he would be freed if he would simply take the legal oath of allegiance, burn the incense on the altar in the prescribed manner, and show his devotion to Caesar by cursing Christ and affirming, "Caesar is Lord." Polycarp replied, "For eighty-six years I have been his [Christ's] slave, and he has done me no wrong; how can I blaspheme my king who has saved me?" Moments later, he was burned to death.

In A.D. 202, Septimus Severus issued an edict forbidding conversions to Christianity. If Christians had obeyed it (they of course did not), they would have had to cease all missionary activity. In A.D. 249 the emperor Decius ordered that all citizens must sacrifice to the gods, an edict that led to the imprisonment and death of Origen, bishop of Rome, and countless other Christian lawbreakers. The persecutions by Emperor Valerian, which began in A.D. 257, threatened Christians with the death penalty if they so much as went to any church meetings or services or even visited a Christian cemetery.

Early Christian civil disobedience also included refusal to fight in the emperor's wars. One example of this refusal is recorded in the case of a centurion named Marcellus, martyred in A.D. 298, of whom it is written, "After throwing down his soldier's belt in front of the legionary standards which were there at the time, he bore witness in a loud voice: 'I am a soldier of Jesus Christ, the eternal king. From now I cease to serve your emperors and I despise the worship of your gods of wood and stone, for they are deaf and dumb images.'"

It is no wonder, then, that civil disobedience has strong roots in Christianity. If early Christians had been totally law-abiding, they would have had to conform to Roman laws, which would have made a mockery of their faith and probably driven it out of existence.

In later centuries, when Christianity became the religion of the empire, there was no longer a need to defend the persecuted church against the hostile state. Christian theologians continued to teach, however, that rulers can betray their trust and that citizens have a right to disobey.

The greatest medieval theologian, St. Thomas Aquinas, wrote that unjust laws do not bind one's conscience and that a law that contravenes the divine law ought not to be obeyed. "Man is bound to obey secular rulers to the extent that the order of justice requires," Aquinas wrote. "For this reason if such rulers have no just title to power, but have usurped it, or if they command things to be done which are unjust, their subjects are not obligated to obey them."

After the Protestant Reformation, civil disobedience was often the response of persecuted sects in order to survive and affirm their right to free exercise of their faith. This practice of "Godly dissent" helped to secure a number of freedoms we now cherish.

To give one example, if you were a Quaker trying to hold a meeting for worship in Massachusetts in the 1650s, the law would have made you liable to heavy fines and banishment from the colony. If you tried to return, a law passed in 1658 could impose the death penalty on you. Several Quakers were in fact hanged under this law, and others were beaten, branded, or had their ears cropped.

Controversy around this conscientious defiance of law was the fertile ground out of which grew many of the freedoms and democratic concepts that we take for granted today, such as freedom of worship, the separation of church and state, and the right of people of all persuasions to participate fully in civic affairs. The Quakers in England and the United States, with the Anabaptists of Germany and Switzerland, also revived the Christian tradition of refusing military service.

Civil disobedience is sometimes the deeply inward stance of individuals who are simply trying to remain true to personal convictions that obedience to a particular law would make them violate. At other times, it is a more conscious tactic designed to bring about desired social change. Often it is a mixture of inward faithfulness and an outward yearning for social change. In any case, it is important to note that conscientious civil disobedience often has far-reaching social impact.

As Daniel Stevick notes in his book, *Civil Disobedience and the Christian:*

It is well to remember that such gains as the achievement of religious liberty, the elimination of slavery, the granting of the franchise to women, the recognition of the rights of organized labor, the acknowledgment in law of conscientious objection to military service, the securing of the civil rights of minority groups— not to speak of the very existence of the American nation itself—were all accomplished in part by acts which were at the time illegal.

This beneficial result of civil disobedience is another reason why obedience to law cannot be absolutized.

Take, for example, the question of women's suffrage. Since most American women living today have never in their lifetimes been denied the right to vote, it is easy to forget that women have had the franchise for only a little more than sixty-five years. And many Americans are not aware of how important a role civil disobedience played in the struggle to secure this basic right.

Alice Paul, a women's suffrage leader, explained her strategy simply: "If a creditor stands before a man's house all day long, demanding payment of his bill, the man must either remove the creditor or pay the bill." Thus, women "creditors" began to stand before the White House in picket lines in 1917, much to the embarrassment of President Woodrow Wilson, who opposed the vote for women but was trying to rally the nation in a war to "make the world safe for democracy." Unready to "pay the bill," the government "removed the creditors" by arresting the women.

Undeterred by increasingly lengthy prison sentences, the women returned again and again to the White House. Hundreds were arrested and scores jailed. Julia Emory alone was arrested thirty-four times. Other similarly dedicated women toured the country, relating their harrowing experiences in jail. When President Wilson continued to refuse to work for the suffrage amendment, the women highlighted his hypocrisy by publicly burning speeches in which he said he was for freedom.

At first this civil disobedience was widely criticized. The *Washington Post* noted soberly that the White House picketing had probably blocked passage of a New York state equal suffrage law for five to ten years. The women were criticized as politically naive and "unwomanly"; their banners were called an insult to the president.

In the heat of war fervor, the women's slogans provoked hostility from onlookers, many of whom were servicemen. "Kaiser Wilson!" a banner said, "Have you forgotten how you sympathized with the poor Germans because they were not self-governed? Twenty million American women are not self-governed. Take the beam out of your own eye!" Such banners were grabbed and destroyed. Picketers were knocked about and bruised. In jail, women went on hunger strikes to protest the prisons' substandard conditions.

Slowly sympathy for the women's courage grew. Newspaper editorials began to change in tone. Congressmen reversed their opposition when they realized that only passage of the suffrage amendment would make the women stop escalating their protest. Even President Wilson eventually gave in and included suffrage in his war aims. The women's right to vote was finally secured with the passage of the Nineteenth Amendment in August 1920.

Perhaps the advocate of civil disobedience who best articulated the link between conscientious conviction and practical social change was Mohandas Gandhi. He went to India from his successful campaign in

South Africa at about the same time that American suffragettes were beginning their demonstrations in front of the White House. Jawaharlal Nehru, a disciple of Gandhi who became first prime minister of an independent India, wrote of Gandhi's method:

Gandhi had placed it before the country not only as the right method but as the most effective one for our purpose. . . . It was a dynamic method, the very opposite of meek submission to a tyrant's will. It was not a coward's refuge from action, but a brave man's defiance of evil and national subjection.

Gandhi acknowledged his indebtedness to the American writer Henry David Thoreau for coining the expression "civil disobedience" in what Gandhi called his "masterly treatise" on the subject. (Thoreau's essay, published in 1849, was called, "On the Duty of Civil Disobedience.") Gandhi described civil disobedience as the necessary resistance a good person must give to an evil government or law. It was both a way for the individual to draw closer to God, the source of all goodness, and a way for a whole people to remove the "consent of the governed" from an unjust government, thus setting in motion vast forces of positive social change.

Gandhi went beyond Thoreau and made an especially important contribution by stressing both halves of the expression civil disobedience, making it a synthesis of civility and defiance. Disobedience was a necessary part of Gandhi's philosophy of political power, for he believed that people could be governed only as long as they consented to be governed. The maintenance of an unjust or undemocratic regime (in his case, British rule in India) depends on the cooperation, submission, and obedience of the people who obey the government's laws and rules, however grudgingly.

Disobedience meant to remove consent and thus force the government to change, to give in, or even to dissolve. But Gandhi believed that even greater value must be given to the adjective "civil" than to the noun "disobedience." He wrote: "Disobedience without civility, discipline, discrimination, [and] nonviolence is certain destruction. Disobedience combined with love is the living water of life."

Gandhi's campaigns against the British, then, attempted to withdraw all voluntary association with the British government and its laws, while still maintaining goodwill toward the British as individuals. In his 1930–31 civil disobedience campaign, which began with the famous twenty-six-day "salt march," the British faced a mass nonviolent revolt that involved tax refusal, boycotts, nonviolent raids, strikes, illegally raising the Indian flag, refusal to buy British cloth, resignations from government schools and offices, enormous parades, seditious speeches, and other defiance of British rule.

The colonial government responded by arresting some hundred thousand Indians, including Gandhi, and subjecting others to beatings, shootings, censorship, fines, and other forms of intimidation. Although the campaign did not win immediate independence, it showed the Indians the strength of nonviolent civil disobedience and laid the groundwork for further actions that did eventually free India from British rule.

Just as Gandhi, the Indian, learned from Thoreau, the American, so Martin Luther King, Jr., the American Christian, drew enormous inspiration from the Hindu Indian, Mohandas Gandhi. King first learned of Gandhi while still a student at Crozier Theological Seminary, and he read avidly about his life and work. Later, in February 1959, he made a month-long pilgrimage to India to meet with Gandhians and to see firsthand the results of the independence movement.

In Gandhi's example, King found specific tactics for social change that resonated deeply with the biblical Christian faith of the black American churches. Gandhi, King said, "was probably the first person in history to lift the love ethic of Jesus above mere interaction between individuals to a powerful effective social force on a large scale." The truth of this discovery was borne out throughout the fifties and sixties as black Christians, especially in the South, became the core of a movement whose willingness to suffer harassment, beatings, and imprisonment for the sake of justice moved the conscience of the nation.

King never claimed that nonviolent civil disobedience would cure all ills or bring in the kingdom of God. What he did claim was that it was a powerful force for uprooting the three-hundred-year-old pattern of segregation that denied black people the vote, exposed them to vicious lynch mobs, confronted them day in and day out with humiliating signs reading "white only" and "colored," and denied them simple amenities like ordering a hamburger at a lunch stand. In a decade of nonviolent struggle, in which civil disobedience of segregation laws was a key tactic, the black movement totally shattered that centuries-old pattern that no other strategy had been able to touch.

The civil rights movement was in turn both the inspiration and the breeding ground for the massive popular resistance to the U.S. war in

Vietnam. Many of the Gandhian tactics used in the South were carried over to the antiwar struggle.

Civil disobedience played a crucial role in the antiwar movement, with hundreds of thousands of young men refusing conscription into an unjust war. Ever since the early Christians, there have been those who choose suffering and prison rather than take up arms. There is a uniquely American tradition of draft resistance, especially in this century as both world wars and Korea brought successive generations of resisters into the federal prisons. But the United States had never seen draft resistance on the scale practiced during the Vietnam War.

Again the connection between deeply personal acts of conscience and public policy was clear. Documents later made public in *The Pentagon Papers* showed that the level of draft resistance had a very practical effect in limiting the possible scope of U.S. military action in Vietnam. While the struggle to get the United States out of Vietnam went on entirely too long, without public resistance here, including civil disobedience, the suffering of the Vietnamese people would probably have been immeasurably worse. Today the commitment of some eighty-five thousand people, through the Pledge of Resistance, to engage in nonviolent direct action if the United States escalates its intervention in Central America is having a similar effect in warning our leaders of the pitfalls of sending U.S. troops into countries such as El Salvador.

Civil disobedience, conducted mostly by Christians, has also played an important part in the formation of the current public outcry against the nuclear arms race. Prophetic acts of civil disobedience at various nuclear facilities have alerted many to the danger of the arms race, often for the first time.

Two of the Catholic bishops who have become the most outspoken in urging noncooperation with the arms race, Bishop Leroy Matthiesen of Amarillo, Texas, and Archbishop Raymond Hunthausen of Seattle, Washington, have said that their consciences were first stirred on the nuclear issue by acts of civil disobedience committed by other Christians at nuclear facilities in their dioceses. The stands taken by these two bishops have in turn had a ripple effect in raising the level of debate and concern about the arms race throughout the church and the nation.

As the movement against nuclear weapons continues to gain strength, the growing number of people participating in civil disobedience has become an important indication to the government of the deep commitment of those opposed to its policies.

WITH ALL DUE RESPECT / 255

Civil disobedience, whether practiced as conscientious principle or conscious social change strategy, has a long and illustrious history. It has been basic to the success of the worldwide labor movement, which probably could not have arisen had it not been willing to use strikes and boycotts in defiance of laws that prohibited union formation and activity. It has been used in successful movements to overthrow brutal dictators, for example, the general strike that in 1944 removed from power Gen. Maximiliano Hernandez Martinez of El Salvador. It has even been part of effective nonviolent battles against Nazism, as when the Danish people's illegal smuggling operation during World War II made Adolf Eichmann admit that "the action against the Jews of Denmark has been a failure."

Civil disobedience is being widely used in Latin American movements for human and political rights, as in Brazil, where major figures in the church hierarchy not only speak out for nonviolent struggle, but place their bodies alongside peasants and workers in risky confrontations with the police and military. And the women of Greenham Common in England wrote a new page in the history of civil disobedience with their encampment protesting the placement of cruise missiles in Britain.

Should we always obey the law? Theoretical discussions of the subject rage on. But a look at history strongly suggests that obedience to law cannot be made absolute. To absolutize obedience to law would mean in history innumerable instances where conscience would be crushed, where evil would triumph through unjust law, and where needed social change would not be achieved.

Law has immense value. It should be given all due respect. But law is like the Sabbath. It was made for us, not us for it. If the choice is between following the law and following what is right, we must be willing to be lawbreakers.

THE CLEANSING OF THE TEMPLE:
Jesus and Symbolic Action
Bill Kellermann

So the disciples went off and did what Jesus had ordered; they brought
the ass and the colt and laid their cloaks on them, and he mounted. The
huge crowd spread their cloaks on the road, while some began to cut
branches from trees and lay them along his path. The groups preceding
him as well as those following kept crying out: "Hosanna to the Son of
David! Blessed is the one who comes in the name of the Lord! Hosanna in
the highest!" As he entered Jerusalem the whole city was stirred to its
depths, demanding, "Who is this?" And the crowd kept answering, "This
is the prophet Jesus from Nazareth in Galilee."

Jesus entered the temple precincts and drove out all those engaged
there in buying and selling. He overturned the money changers' tables
and the stalls of the dove-sellers, saying to them, "Scripture has it, 'My
house shall be called a house of prayer,' but you are turning it into a den of
thieves."

MATT. 21:6–13

The events of the Gospels concerning Jesus in Jerusalem are the
most political in all the Bible. Yet growing up in American Christendom,
you would hardly know it. The church's habitual ways of reading and
responding to the Bible have all but stripped these passages of "political" content.

These Gospel events are rendered innocuous not only by the piecemeal
and disconnected fashion with which we read Scripture but by the
narrowness of our political understanding. My first seminary paper in
New Testament was on the triumphal entry. Having devoured the
commentaries, I concurred with the conventional scholarly opinion that
Jesus was an apolitical messiah. After all, he rejected the Zealot option
of violent revolution. After all, he wasn't interested in Caesar's job, or
Pilate's. Therefore we conclude: apolitical. The problem with this
conclusion is that the varieties of political action are wider than we are
taught to imagine.

I contend that Jesus' primary political method was dramatic symbolic action. He was, by all accounts, a walking public drama, not in the sense of fabricated or cheap theatrics, but in the manner of visible and acted truth. He offered signs that revealed and pointed and unmasked, actions that seeded the imagination and staked out the presence of the kingdom.

Johoichim Jerimias, in a well-known book on the parables, describes the Jerusalem walk and the Temple cleansing as an "acted parable." That could be said of many of Jesus' doings, from healings to feedings to raisings. They are more than simply incidents recounted through the eyes of this or that Gospel poet. They are Jesus' way of being in the world and the method he chose to encounter death and its power.

The triumphal entry into Jerusalem might best be conceived as an inspired bit of street theater. Time and place and person come together in a dramatic and revealing way. Jesus walks into a militarily occupied city on the eve of a liberation festival during which images of freedom and faithful history are at the surface of public consciousness. He taps those symbols by beginning this walk at the Mount of Olives, the traditional site of judgment for Israel's enemies, and ending up at the Temple: today that's called "making a connection."

One can't help thinking of connectional walks in more recent non-violent history: Gandhi's march to the sea, the San Francisco to Moscow disarmament walk, or Selma to Montgomery.

Jesus rides into town on the colt of an ass, an ironic and self-consciously messianic act, in line with the prophetic words from Zechariah 9:9:

> Rejoice greatly, O daughter of Zion!
> Shout aloud, O daughter of Jerusalem!
> Lo, your king comes to you;
> triumphant and victorious is he,
> humble and riding on an ass,
> on a colt the foal of an ass.

Jesus is explicitly intentional in his planning. His careful instructions to his disciples concerning the donkey and his foreknowledge of their conversation with the owner may have more to do with preparation than with clairvoyance.

John's Gospel makes it clear that the disciples did not understand either the entry or the Temple cleansing (John 2:22; 12:16). It was only in retrospect, after the resurrection, that they fully comprehended the meaning and truth of these events. This is often the case with symbolic actions; they may not be received at the time, or may even be grossly misunderstood. Those who take part in them must trust in the transcendent character of truth, resting in the hope that in time the meaning and power of events will be released.

Entering the city on the back of a donkey may be as much for Jesus' own sake as for the crowd or the authorities. The day may have been one of temptation for Jesus. The Gospels make clear that following the early temptations to power in the wilderness, the tempter leaves Jesus to await a more opportune time. Here, the tempter's time and opportunity may well be ripe. If the march built as we imagine in bandwagon fashion, with a surging and cheering crowd, the option of a sudden Zealot-style revolt may have been quite tempting. I wager that Jesus struggled to keep his spiritual and political balance. And the colt helped.

Riding a donkey is a preeminently nonviolent posture, an act of humility, and a contemplative reminder of spirit and intent. The Gospels link it with the drastic and confrontational action at the Temple, for which it is preparation. The two actions complement and illuminate one another: nonviolence, humility, and bold, strong action.

In Matthew, Mark, and Luke, it is the Temple cleansing that finally precipitates the arrest of Jesus. While the charges at the trial (inciting revolt, advocating tax resistance, and claiming authority to establish an alternative government) do not explicitly mention the action, Jesus' ironic words about "destruction of the Temple" are brought to bear as evidence.

Herod the Great had refurbished and expanded the Temple. It stood out on the Jerusalem skyline like the World Trade Center. The Temple was truly the economic mainstay of a city whose primary business was religious tourism.

Passover was the commercial equivalent of the Christmas rush. At Passover time, Jerusalem's population of thirty thousand could be doubled or even quadrupled. That's a lot of rooms at the inn. As many as eighteen thousand lambs would be slaughtered as sacrifices. We're talking about powerful economic interests.

The Temple had received special permission from Rome to collect its own tax. This half-shekel tax may have a modern equivalent in the tax-exemption of the churches, by which their silence and complicity with the state is effectively purchased. Pilate was able to dip into that half-shekel treasury on occasion without objection from the Temple bigwigs. He built his aqueduct in part with such funds.

The Temple functioned as a bank; it was not only a source of loans for those with proper credit but also the depository for records of indebtedness. High taxes and runaway interest rates had forced many small farmers into sharecropping and indentured slavery, making the Temple instrumental in an oppressive system.

By the time of Jesus, the high-priesthood had become so entangled with the Roman occupation that it was all but a political patronage job, appointed by Pilate and subject to purchase and bribe. A position once solitary and lifelong became temporary and vulnerable to whims and changes in the regime. The Gospels often speak of high priests in the plural, which includes those who had been deposed; they also refer to Annas as "high priest that year."

The Sanhedrin, before whom Jesus and, eventually, the disciples were tried, was made up substantially of the Sadducean party, landed Jews whose economic interest in the status quo made them backers of the *pax Romana* military order.

When, therefore, Jesus goes to the front porch of the Temple, where the money changers have set up shop, he's not simply annoyed with the inflated price of doves. He has chosen the public place that is the most visible symbol of complicity between the occupying forces and the religious authorities. The Temple represents the intersection of the Roman money market and the local economy, the spiritual idolatry of status quo power; it is the place of prayer that has been invaded by the clink of Roman coins changing hands. In driving the money changers out, Jesus performs a kind of material exorcism.

Jesus' words as he overturns tables are a thoughtful combination of a phrase from a potent discourse of Isaiah's and a line from Jeremiah's fiery Temple sermon. Jesus does his theological homework with his eyes open: Jeremiah was also soon thereafter arrested and imprisoned.

Jesus is not engaged in civil disobedience in the classic sense of breaking an unjust law in order to change it. He had often been taken to task for violating the Mosaic law, particularly around the Sabbath, but here he is not interested in improving the letter of law, either Roman or Jewish, one jot or tittle. He is simply doing a strong action of visible truth in a place protected by law and authority. The question posed to him is: by what authority do you do these things?

Later when the disciples take to the streets after Pentecost and head for the Temple portico to preach the resurrection, the scene is loaded. It is like returning to the scene of a crime. Arrested repeatedly by the authorities, the disciples are warned not to preach in Jesus' name, but they keep going back to the Temple. Once again the question posed to them is one of authority; and in court the disciples respond: "We must obey God rather than human rule."

Jesus' act, like the disciples', places him in personal jeopardy and risk. That risk is not incidental to the action. Indeed it was so integral that in the early church the risk became, for some, a thing in itself, to the extent that the active pursuit of martyrdom needed to be declared a heresy. Of course, such temptations linger even today.

Still, the risk is crucial, and it hangs over not only the action but all the events in Jerusalem. Jesus has staked his life on being there. His words about Caesar's coin, the teaching in the Temple, even the private contemplative symbolic acts in the upper room—everything is against the background of being in trouble. The words are therefore loaded, and the disciples listen hard. The church must acknowledge that the risk of the cross hangs over Jesus' whole life and teaching.

A friend of mine once reflected that a more concrete, modern translation of Jesus' call would be: "If you would be my disciples, face your electric chair and follow me." I have a strange picture of electric chairs replacing crosses over altars and on church walls. Such a tack would surely bring the cross home from pious sentimentalism and abstraction.

Jesus was not ignorant or naive about the risk; he freely chose it. Beginning with his announcement to the disciples that they were headed for Jerusalem, he spoke openly about the consequences. It is not surprising that Peter and friends tried to talk him out of it.

Jesus' risk is one with its consequences. His submission to death is a faithful public act that is one with the Temple action. In fact, it is in the cross that Jesus' confrontation with the powers (spiritual, economic, political) is finally realized, revealed, and resolved.

Paul says that if the powers had known what they were doing, they never would have crucified Christ. Jesus drove the powers into the public arena and made a spectacle of them, unmasking and overcoming their ultimate source of authority: death. Whenever and wherever believers act today, it is under the freedom of that faith.

These reflections are offered as a contribution to the continuing, and often heated and strained, conversation within the church and biblical communities concerning resistance, symbolic action, and civil disobedience.

Some of the questions that arise whenever symbolic action and civil disobedience are contemplated could be directed toward Jesus and his action. These questions include: why does Jesus have to be so confrontational? Won't he turn people off? Does Jesus really want to communicate? Isn't this violence against property? Couldn't Jesus stand outside the Temple and get his point across just as well? Why doesn't Jesus work within the system, go through Pilate or the Sanhedrin? Or even become high priest? Wouldn't he have a greater impact from a position of public power? Why does Jesus risk his life and freedom? Think how much more good he could do staying in Galilee quietly preaching and healing. After all, you can't do ministry while sitting in jail or hanging on a cross.

These questions are put with some irony, but if they are real questions for ourselves, then let's not hesitate to ask them of Jesus as well.

DIVINE OBEDIENCE:
A Letter to the Minister of Justice
Allan Boesak

In July 1979 the South African Council of Churches (SACC) held a meeting with the theme "The Church and the Alternative Society" with Rev. Allan Boesak as the keynote speaker. At that meeting the SACC adopted a resolution encouraging Christians to engage in acts of civil disobedience against apartheid laws, a step Boesak had called for in his address.

Subsequent to that meeting, South African Minister of Justice Alwyn Schlebusch issued a warning that the South African government was becoming impatient with statements like the SACC resolution that "posed a threat to the stability of South African society." In response Allan Boesak wrote the following letter to Minister Schlebusch. The letter is included in Boesak's book *Black and Reformed* (Orbis Books, 1984).

—The Editor

The Honourable A. Schlebusch
Minister of Justice
Union Buildings
Pretoria

Dear Sir,

A short while ago you thought it your duty to address the South African Council of Churches, as well as church leaders, very sharply and seriously over radio and television and in the press in connection with the SACC resolution on civil disobedience. Although the resolution was not taken as a direct result of my address, I did express my point of view openly on that occasion, and I am one of those who support the SACC in this respect.

You are the minister of justice, and it is in this capacity that you have issued your serious warning. I take your words seriously. Hence my reaction, which I express to you respectfully and which I ask you to read as a personal declaration of faith.

Your warning has become almost routine in South Africa: the government continually says to pastors and churches that they must keep themselves "out of politics" and confine themselves to their "proper task": the preaching of the gospel.

However, on this very point an extremely important question emerges: what is the gospel of Jesus Christ that the churches have been called to preach? Surely it is the message of the salvation of God that has come to all peoples in Jesus Christ. It is the proclamation of the kingdom of God and of the lordship of Jesus Christ. But this salvation is the liberation, the making whole, of the *whole person*. It is not something meant for the "inner life," the soul, only. It is meant for the whole of human existence. This Jesus who is proclaimed by the church was certainly not a spiritual being with spiritual qualities estranged from the realities of our human existence. No, he was the Word become flesh, who took on complete human form, and his message of liberation is meant for persons in their *full humanity*.

Besides, the fact that the term "kingdom" is such a political term must already say a great deal to us. For example, this fact brought Reformed Christians to believe (and rightly so) and profess with conviction throughout the centuries that this lordship of Jesus Christ applies to all spheres of life. There is not one inch of life that is not claimed by the lordship of Jesus Christ. This includes the political, social, and economic spheres. The Lord rules over all these spheres, and the church and the Christian proclaim his sovereignty in all these spheres. Surely it is the holy duty and the calling of every Christian to participate in politics so that there also God's law and justice may prevail, and there also obedience to God and God's word can be shown.

The Dutch Reformed Church professes this in its report "Race Relations in the South African Situation in the Light of Scripture." The report states plainly that in its proclamation the church must appeal to its members to apply the principles of the kingdom of God in the social and political sphere. When the word of God demands it, the church is compelled to fulfill its prophetic function vis-à-vis the state *even in spite of popular opinion*. The witness of the church with regard to the government is a part of its essential being in the world, says the report. This is sound Reformed thinking, and the Dutch Reformed Church accepts this because it wants to be Reformed. Why, then, are you refusing to grant other churches and Christians (also other Reformed Christians!) this witness and participation?

But there is still another problem. Through its spokesmen your government has often warned that those of us who serve in the church must "keep out of politics." Yet at the same time it is your own colleagues in the cabinet who want to involve the clergy in political dialogue!

The only conclusion that I can come to is that you do not really object in principle to the participation of the clergy in politics—as long as it happens on *your* terms and within the framework of *your* policy. This seems to me to be neither tenable nor honest. In addition, are you not denying your own history by holding to this viewpoint? Did not the Afrikaner clergy speak as leaders of their people, and did they not inspire their people in what you saw as a just struggle? Did not the churches of the Afrikaner, even in the Anglo-Boer War, stand right in the midst of the struggle? Why, then, do you reject today with a sort of political pietism that which yesterday and the day before you accepted and embraced with thankfulness to God?

But, Mr. Minister, there is even something more in your warning I cannot ignore. It has to do with the exceptionally difficult and sensitive issue of the Christian's obedience to the government.

It is important that you understand clearly that I have made my call for civil disobedience as a Christian, and that I was addressing the church. The context and basis of my call may thus not be alienated from my convictions as a Christian addressing other Christians upon that same basis.

It surprises me that some have tried to interpret this as a call for wanton violence. It is precisely an *alternative* to violence! And I turn to this alternative because I still find it difficult to accept violence as an unobjectionable solution. Or perhaps there are some who fear that should Christians in South Africa perform their duty in being more obedient to God than to humans, the idolized nature of this state will be exposed. Surely a state that accepts the supreme rule of Christ should not have to be afraid of this?

I believe I have done nothing more than to place myself squarely within the Reformed tradition as that tradition has always understood sacred Scripture on these matters.

Essential to this is the following: it is my conviction that, for a Christian, obedience to the state or any earthly authority is always linked to our obedience to God. That is to say, obedience to human institutions (and to human beings) is always relative. The human institution can never have the same authority as God, and human laws must always be subordinate to the word of God. This is how the Christian understands it. Even God does not expect blind servility; Christians cannot even think of giving unconditional obedience to a government.

Our past experience has taught us that this is exactly the kind of obedience, blind and unquestioning, that your government expects. I want, however, to be honest with you: this I cannot give you. The believer in Christ not only has the right, but also the responsibility, should a government deviate from God's law, to be more obedient to God than to the government. The question is not really whether Christians have the courage to disobey the government, but whether we have the courage to set aside God's word and not obey *God*.

Over the years, nearly all the Christian churches in this country have condemned the policies of your government as wrong and sinful. My own church, the Dutch Reformed Mission Church, last year at its synod condemned apartheid as being "in conflict with the gospel of Jesus Christ," a policy that cannot stand up to the demands of the gospel. I heartily endorse this stand my church has taken. Your policy is unjust; it denies persons their basic human rights, and it undermines their God-given human dignity. Too many of the laws you make are blatantly in conflict with the word of God.

I have no doubt that your policies and their execution are a tremendous obstacle to reconciliation between the peoples of South Africa. There are laws that are most hurtful, or more draconian than others, and these especially have been condemned by the churches. Now the churches have reached a point where we have to say: if we condemn laws on the grounds of the word of God, how can we obey those laws?

In my view, Christians in South Africa today do not stand alone in this decision. Scripture knows of disobedience to earthly powers when these powers disregard the Word of the living God. Daniel disobeyed the king's law when he refused to bow down before the graven image of Nebuchadnezzar (Dan. 3:17–18), because he regarded the king's law as being in conflict with the demands of his God. Peter's refusal to obey the commands of the Sanhedrin not to give witness to Jesus has always been the classic example of disobedience to a worldly authority. To this day his answer still resounds like a bell in the church of Christ: "We must obey God rather than human rule" (Acts 5:29). There are other examples. Paul displayed nothing of a servile obedience when the magistrates of Philippi wanted to release him from prison after having confined him unlawfully (without a trial!): "They gave us a public flogging, though we are Roman citizens and have not been found guilty; they threw us into prison, and are they now to smuggle us out privately? No, indeed!" (Acts 16:37).

In the case of Peter and John, the Sanhedrin was the highest authority, not only in religious matters, but in everything that did not lie directly in the sphere of the Roman procurator. In the case of Paul, the magistrates were the highest officials in the Roman colony of Philippi. For both Peter and Paul it was clear that occasions could arise where disobedience to unjust authority was the only honorable way for the Christian.

Furthermore, Luke 23:6–12, Mark 15:1–5, and John 18:8–11 teach us that Jesus himself did not always demonstrate obedience to state authority. Before Herod, on one occasion, "he answered him not a word." Also before Pilate there were those moments when he chose to give reply neither to the questions of Pilate nor to the charges of the high priests and scribes. John tells us something else of great significance. He tells us that Jesus reminded Pilate of something that every bearer of authority must remember or be reminded of: "'You would have no authority over me at all,' Jesus replied, 'if it had not been granted you from above'" (John 29:11).

I am not arguing that there is "proof" from these actions of Jesus, Peter, and Paul that violent, revolutionary overthrow of a government is justifiable. That is a completely different issue. I am saying, rather, that blind obedience to civil authorities is alien to the Bible and that, for the Christian, loyalty and obedience to God are first and foremost. May I also point out, parenthetically, that the issue on which everything hinges and the lesson that South Africa has to learn is that what is needed is *not* servile submissiveness of citizens to the state, but *rightful corresponsibility* for the affairs of the state? And this is precisely what your policy denies millions of South Africans.

This is not the place to present a full treatment of Romans 13. However, I would simply point out that the first verse of Romans 13, which is often taken as unconditional legitimization of a government's contention that its authority can never be challenged by Christians, is in fact a very serious criticism of that very authority. A government wields authority because, and as long as, it reflects the authority of God. And the power of God is a liberating, creative, serving power. Thus Paul can refer to civil authority as "a servant of God [*diakonos!*] for your good." Thus, throughout the years, it has been taken for granted in Reformed thinking that a government has authority as long as there is evidence that it accepts responsibility for justice, for what is right.

Put another way, the definition of government in Romans 13 does not simply point out that civil authority exists. It also suggests that there is proper authority only where there is a clear distinction between good and evil, so that it is not only important whether a government is "Christian" or not, but really whether it is still truly *government*—that is, understands the difference between good and evil. Where there is no justice and no understanding, the authority of the government is no longer derived from God, but is in conflict with God. Resistance to such a government is both demanded and justified.

Even Augustine, one of the respected fathers of the church, who was concerned particularly with protecting the state and who defended political authority with extraordinary energy, had this to say: "Justice is the only thing that can give worth to a worldly power. What is worldly government if justice is lacking? It is nothing other than a bunch of plunderers."

Calvin echoed this sentiment when he wrote to King Francis in the letter published as the prologue to his *Institutes:* "For where the glory of God is not made the end of the government, it is not a legitimate sovereignty, but a usurpation." And Calvin added, "Where there is no vision, the people perish." Calvin also stated clearly that "worldly princes" lose all their power when they rise up against God. Christians should resist such a power, not obey it.

When, precisely, do the actions of a government collide with the demands of the word of God? In deciding this, the church should be led by the word itself, knowing the demands for justice and peace, and also by the actual experience of the people. It is in the concrete situations of actual human experience that the word of God shows itself alive and more powerful and sharper than any two-edged sword.

In making this decision, the church should look for criteria not among those who make the laws and who have political and economic power, or among those who are favored by unjust laws, but rather among those who are disadvantaged by these laws, who are hurt at the deepest level of their being: those who suffer, those who have no voice—the oppressed, the "least of these my people." And in the eyes of the least of the people in our country, your government and your policies stand condemned. I need not repeat these accusations; I simply want to draw your attention to them and to the truth that is in them.

The untold suffering of men, women, and children, the bitterness of too many, the wounds caused by your policy through the years can never be forgotten or compensated for by the "concessions" your government is apparently willing to make. The superficial adjustments to apartheid already initiated do not touch the root of the matter. It is as one of your colleagues has said, "The fact that a black man is allowed to wear a *Springbok* emblem (as he participates in multiracial sports) does not give him political rights." Indeed, and we may add it does not give him his God-given humanity either.

You complain that the churches are "against the government." But it is because of your policies that so many churches and so many Christians find themselves against you. In this, we really have no choice, because the church of Christ in South Africa *must* obey God rather than you. I plead with you: stop your disastrous policies.

May I end with a personal word? I am not writing this letter in order to be brave or arrogant. I must honestly confess that I am afraid of you. You are the minister of justice. As such, you have at your disposal awesome powers such as only a fool would underestimate. The victims of these powers are sown across the path of the past and recent history of South Africa.

I, like any other South African, want to live a normal life with my wife and children. I want to serve the church without fear. I want a country where freedom is seen as the right of every citizen and not as a gift to be given or withheld by the government. I want, along with millions of our people, to have coresponsibility for government in our native land, with everything you want for yourself and your children. I too want peace, but authentic peace, which is the fruit of active justice for all. However, my longing for a "normal" life must not undermine the service to which God has called me. That would be intolerable. And my service is also to you. That is why I write this letter. I shall surely stand guilty before God if I do not witness against this government.

I think the time has come for your government to make a choice: you are either the "servant of God" of Romans 13, or you are the "beast from the abyss" of Revelation 13. Unless and until the right choice becomes *evident* (through the wholehearted and fundamental change of your policy), Christians in South Africa shall be called upon, *for the sake of their faith,* to resist you as we would the beast of Revelation 13. For the Christian, obedience to God and God's word must be the first priority.

I am aware that the decision to resist the forces of government cannot be an easy one. That is why the synod of the Dutch Reformed Mission Church made this so clear last year: "If a Christian is bound by his conscience to follow the way of criticism, which brings him into conflict with the state, then he should obey God more than humans. In this case, however, he must be prepared to accept suffering in the spirit of Christ and his apostles."

Once again, this is not a matter of being brave. Rather, I should like to use this occasion to urge you to realize that peace and salvation, indeed the future of South Africa, do not lie in more "security laws," in more threats, or in an ever-growing defense budget. They lie, rather, in the recognition of the human dignity of all South Africans, in the pursuit of justice, and in respect for the God-given rights of all.

You as whites are not in a position to achieve this on your own. That is why the churches have pleaded for a national convention where the people could be represented by authentic, chosen leadership. We demand the right to have the vote, so that our citizenship in South Africa may become meaningful. Give us the right to express ourselves and our political will. We need to have the opportunity to participate fully and meaningfully in the political processes in South Africa. Is this not the fundamental thing you grant yourself?

I plead that you make use of the offer and the opportunity to have discussions. Honest negotiations with the intention genuinely to share together in South Africa is always better than to stand against each other as enemies.

I am using this letter as an open witness, and I thus will make it available to the press.

I thank you for giving me your time.

May God give you wisdom in everything.

Sincerely,
Allan Boesak

Hope

IN THE COMPANY OF THE FAITHFUL:
Journeying Toward the Promised Land
Vincent Harding

But recall the former days when, after you were enlightened, you endured a hard struggle with sufferings, sometimes being publicly exposed to abuse and affliction, and sometimes being partners with those so treated. For you had compassion on the prisoners, and you joyfully accepted the plundering of your property, since you knew that you yourselves had a better possession and an abiding one. Therefore do not throw away your confidence, which has a great reward. . . .

Now faith is the assurance of things hoped for, the conviction of things not seen. For by it the men and women of old received divine approval. . . .

By faith Enoch was taken up so that he should not see death. . . . By faith Noah, being warned by God concerning events as yet unseen, took heed and constructed an ark for the saving of his household. . . .

By faith Abraham obeyed when he was called to go out to a place which he was to receive as an inheritance; and he went out, not knowing where he was to go. By faith he sojourned in the land of promise, as in a foreign land, living in tents with Isaac and Jacob, heirs with him of the same promise. For he looked forward to the city which has foundations, whose builder and maker is God. By faith Sarah herself received power to conceive, even when she was past the age, since she considered him faithful who had promised. . . .

These all died in faith, not having received what was promised, but having seen it and greeted it from afar, and having acknowledged that they were strangers and exiles on the earth. For people who speak thus make it clear that they are seeking a homeland. If they had been thinking of that land from which they had gone out, they would have had opportunity to return. But as it is, they desire a better country, that is, a heavenly one. Therefore God is not ashamed to be called their God, for he has prepared for them a city. . . .

By faith Rahab the harlot did not perish with those who were disobedient. . . . Women received their dead by resurrection. Some were tortured, refusing to accept release, that they might rise again to a better life. Others suffered mocking and scourging, and even chains and imprisonment. They were stoned, they were sawn in two, they were killed with the sword; they went about in skins of sheep and goats, destitute . . . wandering over deserts and mountains, and in dens and caves of the earth.

And all these, though well attested by their faith, did not receive what was promised, since God had foreseen something better for us, that apart from us they should not be made perfect.

Therefore, since we are surrounded by so great a cloud of witnesses, let us also lay aside every weight, and sin which clings so closely, and let us run with perseverance the race that is set before us, looking to Jesus the pioneer and perfecter of our faith, who for the joy that was set before him endured the cross, despising the shame, and is seated at the right hand of the throne of God.

HEBREWS 10:32–35; 11:1–2, 5–16, 31, 35–40; 12:1–2

I need to reflect with you on some of the meaning for me and my life—and perhaps you and your life—of this great passage that has been so rich to so many of us, this statement of faith and hope from the Letter to the Hebrew believers.

But before getting to that, I need to say that there is a set of experiences that has placed the Hebrews passage in a new and even more powerful setting for me. Over the past months my wife, Rose, and I have been very conscious—partly through the death of my mother—of the writing and thinking that's been going on in our times concerning "near-death experiences," the experiences that people have had as they approached the threshold of death and then moved back again.

One of the most powerful testimonies that occurs again and again in the words of those who have been on that threshold is the description of great, warm, welcoming light surrounding, suffusing, giving them a sense that there is nothing to fear at all. And then in the midst of that light, almost uniformly, they tell of the appearance of women and men and children, loved ones who have been important to them in their life, and who now stand in the light, in the midst of the threshold, to welcome them and to help them make the passageway through.

There is something marvelous about such scenes, partly because they bring us back to this great New Testament document that was written for those who, because of the dangerous commitment they had made to the way of Jesus, often had to face that threshold of death and new life. But what I also realize again is that not only is there this tremendous, magnificent, welcoming, loving host of folks who are prepared to welcome us into the light beyond this life, but also they are available to us now, on this side of death. Yes, the same cloud of witnesses is here now to help us live in the light, here to help us walk in the light, here to help us be enlightened in the fullest and deepest sense of that word, to help us walk in the truth.

And if there's anything I want to share, it is my conviction of how important it is that we get past any sense of spookiness, strangeness, or fear about the reality of this great cloud of witnesses whose fulfillment cannot take place without our own. I would call us to see and appreciate these folks who are like a great cheering squad for us. In the midst of everything that seems so difficult, that seems so powerful, that seems so overwhelming, they are saying to us: "We are with you," and "There is a way through; there is a way to stand; there is a way to move; there is a way to hope; there is a way to believe. Don't give up!"

To know them, to know that they are present, is to know that regardless of how alone we feel sometimes, we are never alone. We are *never* alone: nowhere, no how, in nothing. Never.

First of all I want you to remember to whom this letter was written: the Hebrew believers in Jesus, those who had come to the new way out of the Jewish experience. This letter was written to those men and women who had likely been good, upstanding members of the Jewish faith community. They were, in our terms, the ones who had been in the mainstream church for generation after generation after generation. Most of them probably knew their pedigree and their family's pedigree in that church, members from the very beginning.

But at some moment in that strange transformative time of history, these were the ones who had heard the call, had seen a vision, had been told that there is another city, there is another way to go. They had learned that "the way that my family and my family's family and their family have been going for all this time may not be the way for me, and this madman Jesus may have something to say to my life." They had heard the call of Jesus. They had heard the call of the kingdom. And what it meant was that they had to turn away from all that had been comfortable, from all that had been reasonable, safe, secure, and respectable. They had stepped out in a direction that was totally unpredictable, following a leader who had ended up on a cross.

So the writer speaks to them in loving, understanding, challenging ways, reminding them about when they first saw that light. He says, "Remember the former days when, after you were enlightened, you endured a hard struggle with sufferings" (Heb. 10:32). You can just imagine what they must have gone through to take that step out of the mainstream into the wilderness—into the wilderness with no assurance but the presence of God.

"Sometimes being publicly exposed to abuse and affliction, sometimes being partners with those so treated" (Heb. 10:33). What a marvelous image! Not only were these people themselves publicly vilified and accused and called fools and stupid and subversive and all kinds of other names, but not being satisfied with that, some of them apparently—when they could have been relatively safe—went and stood with other people who were being accused in the same way. For they saw no real escape, no real safety for themselves as long as there was anyone who was under that kind of persecution.

The writer continues, "For you had compassion on the prisoners, and you joyfully accepted the plundering of your property (10:34). Yes, they are reminded, that when you went this way, some people said you were no longer under the protection of the law, and anybody could take what you had. And then you had to decide what was more important to you, your property or the way to which you were called. The Letter says, not only did you accept the plundering of your property, but you all must have been crazy in the eyes of the world, because "you *joyfully* accepted the plundering of your property, since you knew that you yourselves had a better possession and an abiding one. Therefore do not throw away your confidence, which has a great reward. For you have need of endurance, so that you may do the will of God and receive what is promised" (Heb. 10:34–35).

After fifteen, twenty, thirty years some of them were tired of this strange way. Some of the Hebrew Christians were surely wondering if they should not go back into the familiar way of their fathers and mothers. Everything was much clearer in the old way; everybody knew exactly what should be done in that way because people had been doing it for thousands of years. Compared to this Christian business, it seemed a safe way, and there must have been in many minds a tremendous temptation to escape all this vilification and abuse and strangeness and "walking-on-the-edge-ness."

So the loving writer says, "I understand all that, but what is needed now, more than anything else, is endurance. Don't give up. Hold on. Hold on. Keep your eye on the prize and hold on." (You may not see that in the text, but I see it. Some black folks added it to the canon in their own times of suffering.) And then to try to encourage the sufferers, he says to them, what you need most is faith, defining that faith as "the assurance of things hoped for, the conviction of things not seen" (Heb. 11:1).

Here the writer begins going through a list of folks who had lived in faith: Abraham, Enoch, Sarah, Noah—just running through the line-up, including a prostitute in the list of people who had lived by faith in God, making it clear that faith in God is available to everybody who is open to it.

Then the writer stops and picks up certain people, such as Abraham: "Abraham obeyed when he was called to go out to a place which he was to receive as an inheritance; and he went out, not knowing where he was to go" (Heb. 11:8). That's a powerful image, important not only for the lives of those Hebrew folks, but for our lives: the call to go out to a place that does not fit into the computer program, where there is no predictability, where there is only wildness and unpredictability. That was Abraham, called to go out to a place, and he went out not knowing where he was to go.

For all those who believe that the Christian faith is a life of security, just chew on Abraham for a little while, and hear the believer who taught us that the Christian faith is not meant to lead to a life of security; rather, it is meant to be a life of "creative insecurity." If you are secure, you don't need grace. If you are secure, you don't need prayer. If you are secure, you don't need brothers and sisters. If you are secure, you don't need the power of God. You've got it all made.

But faith, the life of faith, is a life of walking, teetering, always not being quite sure whether or not you've made the right decision, but still enduring and calling out, "Where the hell am I, Lord? Hey! Hold my hand while I run this race, 'cause I don't want to run this race in vain."

Then we're told, "By faith [Abraham] sojourned in a land of promise, as in a foreign land, living in tents with Isaac and Jacob" (Heb. 11:9). This is a marvelous way of telling us something about the way that we are called to live for this time. We are living in an age in which all the old sureties are falling apart, in which all the old structures that gave so much promise of security are breaking down and there is nothing to do but set up tents and say, "Hey! I see something else."

Set up the tents, as it were, in Washington, D.C. and say, "I see a city that is not separated by color or class, but I see a city where men and women and children of every color and every class are living and loving and working together to create a new society—a compassionate and just society, a beautiful city." Say to yourself, say to the world, "I see that, and I'm not just going to sing about it. I'm not just going to talk about it. I'm not just going to create beautiful liturgy about it. I'm going to bet my life on it. I'm going to be out there with my tent, ready for the time when the new city comes. As a matter of fact, I'm going to help make it come."

Thinking about that, saying that, doing that, we can remember that Rosa Parks didn't say, "Oh, I do believe the Lord wants us to live together as black and white and just have happy times together, and I'm going to sing about that in my church every night." No, she said, "I think the time has come now. The Lord wants us to live in a different way. I don't know why, but it looks like God's starting with me. So I'm going to stay sitting down on this seat until the Lord takes me and does what the Lord wants to do with me."

That's how things get started, by people taking wild bets with their lives, and saying, "I'm going to set up my tent here until the time comes for the real buildings to be built, and when they're built, I'm going to be right in the midst of them because I'm going to be among the builders, seeing things that nobody else sees, envisioning new ways of living, seeing cities that people say are crazy, totally unrealistic, not in the plan." That happens when we are able to testify out of our dreams, in our tents, "I believe in holiness. I believe in righteousness. I believe in justice. I'm ready for a new kind of city, for a new kind of coming together of men and women and children who can really celebrate the love and the grace of God." That's what the Letter was talking about here, saying that all these crazy visionaries and tent-dwellers from long ago "died in faith, not having received what was promised, but having seen it, and greeted it from afar" (Heb. 11:13).

We know some of those folks, too. You remember the black young man who on that last night said, "I've been to the mountain top. I've seen the promised land. I may not get there myself, but you will get there." That's what it means to live a life of faith, not trying to gobble everything that you can get your hands on, not saying that if I can't see it, if I can't have it myself, then I don't believe in it. It means knowing that there is a city set out there, within here, for God's people, for all people, a city that is better than anything we have known. Living in faith means knowing that this is not someplace in the sky, but that it is in the hearts and lives of the women and men who will work for it, who will seek to create it.

Living in faith is knowing that even though our little work, our little seed, our little brick, our little block may not make the whole thing, the whole thing exists in the mind of God, and that whether or not we are there to see the whole thing is not the most important matter. The most important thing is whether we have entered into the process. Like Martin King talking to the old woman in Montgomery, Alabama, during the long bus boycott, asking, "Mama, why are you walking like this, walking miles and miles to work? I mean, you're not even going to benefit much from this new situation yourself." And she said, "Dr. King, I'm not doing this for myself. I'm doing this for my grand-children." That's why she could also say to him then, "Yes, Dr. King, my feets is tired, but my soul is rested."

That's how your soul gets rested, when you stop being selfish, when you stop thinking, working only for yourself, and start dreaming, as the Native Americans do, for seven generations beyond us. Your soul gets rested when you realize that your life is not meant to be captured just in your skin, but that your life reaches out to the life of the universe itself. And the life of the universe reaches into us and demands of us that we be more than we think we can be, demands that we live out these dreams.

So we look again at the Letter to the Hebrews, the Letter to us, and realize that this is living by faith. For people who speak and act in this way make clear that they are seeking a homeland, going to the homeland, bringing in the homeland. If they had been thinking of that land from which they had gone out, the land of safety, the land of security, the land of doctrinal clarity, then they would have had the opportunity to return. But these crazy, wild sojourners desire a better country, which is a heavenly one. Therefore, we are told, God is not ashamed to be called their God, for God has already prepared for them a city.

Then the writer goes on to talk about all the other folks who are moving toward that city and, as they move, building, creating, adding to the city the quality, the truth, the integrity, the faith of their own lives. We are not allowed to forget them. The Hebrew Christians are not permitted to forget them. Here are the heroes of the faith. Here are the people. Here are the beautiful, suffering, overcoming people: women receiving their dead by resurrection; faithful ones tortured, refusing to accept release; the people suffering mocking, scourging, chains, imprisonment; and some stoned, some cut in two, some going around in caves and in deserts.

What a wild company we belong to! I mean, do you understand?

These are our foreparents. Do you understand? These are the founders of our faith. Do you understand? These are the old alumni. These are the ones who established the "institution"—these wild people, persecuted people, afflicted people, impractical people, going-out-not-knowing-where-they're-going people.

If this is our ancestral faith community, then what is it that we are now called to be, to do in this day, in this hour? Has the work all been done, so that we can now sit down in quietness, safety, and security because the crazy part, the dangerous part is all over now? That doesn't seem to me to be what the writer was saying then, and I don't think that any of us living in the United States of America at this time can really believe that.

So the text speaks again to our hearts, speaks to our lives, as if to say, "Listen, sisters and brothers, we are surrounded by such a great cloud of witnesses. Sisters and brothers, do you see, do you know why we are surrounded by such a powerful community of struggle? Not so that we can admire them and talk about them and sing about them and pray about them. All of that is okay, beloved ones, but not sufficient. No, they are here so that they can fill us with courage and strength and life, in the great tradition of the wild baptizer by the Jordan, in the company of the lover on the cross. They are here so that we can move right on into the struggle that they helped to establish." Therefore, "let us also lay aside every weight, and sin which clings so closely, and let us run," let us run, let us run, "let us run with perseverance the race that is set before us, looking to Jesus the pioneer and perfecter of our faith" (Heb. 12:1–2).

Jesus the Word was the pioneer of our faith both before and after Jesus of Nazareth. It was this compelling Word who drew all those long-ago people out of their safe places, out of their quiet places, out of their easy places, and said there is a city that needs to be created, and I want you to put your hands, your hearts, your minds to work.

And now we come in a place like this, we come in a city like this, we come in a nation like this, and we are tempted, almost before we begin, to be overcome. We are tempted to think there is no way that we can possibly deal with this imperial behemoth in which we are lodged. We come thinking that the powers of this world are just too much for us: multinationals, State Departments, Soviet and U.S. military jugger-nauts. There is just too much conflict, poverty, biting away, grinding away at the lives of our brothers and sisters, and we are tempted to run into a carpeted hole someplace and call that Christian faith, call that the church.

But it is very clear by now that that is not the way of our forebears. Rather, their way, and our way, is to get out of the hiding places, and to stand up, and to be afraid, with our knees knocking, with all kinds of tears coming to our eyes, with all kinds of unclarity about what even the next step is, but to stand and to know that we are not alone. It is to know that we are surrounded by a company, by a gathering, by a whole bunch of folks who care about us, who care about us because we're a part of the same company, part of the same wild community, citizens of a country that does not yet exist—and yet does.

Among us now are folks caring about us, crowding around the table of the Lord, leaving space for us. No one can tell you what you should say to them, but I would urge you to say something to them, because they're here, *presente*, present and accounted for. I know what I want to say to them, maybe the same as you, maybe something different, but let us welcome them.

Dorothy Day, thank you for being with us, you magnificent old curmudgeon! You beautiful, strong, determined woman, you old lover of the poor, thank you for being here. Teach us how to live creatively with the poor. Teach us how to live for the poor. Teach us how to make the poor the center of our concerns, Dorothy. And don't let us excuse ourselves with anything about being women, about not being married, about being old, about anything. Teach us, Dorothy. I don't know what you want to say to her, but that's what I want to say.

And Fannie Lou Hamer. "This little light of mine, I'm gonna let it shine." Thank you, Fannie Lou. People said you had only a fourth-grade Mississippi education, which they claim was no education at all; therefore, they said you were unqualified for anything. But, Fannie Lou, you taught us that life does not begin at Harvard or Princeton or Yale, but that it begins where women and men determine that they must lead a new life, and they must take on the powers of oppression, and they must not give in to injustice, and they must not allow anybody to press them down into the dirt.

Fannie Lou, teach us how not to let even poverty become an excuse for failing to enter into the process of creating God's kingdom. Thank you for your music. Sing it to us. Thank you for your life. Live it through us, Fannie Lou Hamer. Well, well! Something good *can* come out of the Delta of Mississippi! Thank you.

I need to deal with brother Clarence Jordan. For what Clarence showed me and showed us was that there ain't no sense in making all kinds of generalizations about white Southerners, and white Southern Baptists, and what they are and what they ain't, 'cause Clarence was white, and Southern, and Baptist, and Christian, and one of God's great heroes of this generation, who loved in such a way that all of the old hindering stuff could not only be overcome, but could be transformed into a gift of life.

Clarence needs to talk to us about something else, too. That is, how can you, after you have seen the light, after you have been led into the light, how can you—as he did—go back to your mama's and daddy's native soil and deal with those people there, and let them know that you have seen something else and that you're going to have to be something else, not in defiance, not in self-righteousness, but in love?

Clarence, it's hard to know how you did it, except through amazing grace and that great sense of humor. Now, brother Clarence, some of us ain't got much of that humor at all, especially when it comes to laughing at ourselves. So help us with that. That's right, you're the patron saint of the sense of humor. Help us. Help us to laugh our way to the table.

And how can we come to the table and not know that brother Tom Merton is right here, with his old, beat-up, longshoreman's wool cap on, looking like anything but a monk, but being an ultimate servant of God. Stand with us, Tom. Teach us how in the strangest, most isolated places you can let the pain of the world come into you, how you can feel black people in the monastery in Kentucky. How you can feel poor people, how you can feel them so much that you have no peace in your peaceful setting. Teach us, Tom, how to live in peace out of peace, how to stand in that paradox—and write poetry!

Of course, I want you to understand that you can't come to this table and have Tom Merton, Fannie Lou Hamer, Dorothy Day, and Clarence Jordan here without somebody who used to be called Detroit Red walking up to the table, too. Yes, I know Malcolm X is here. Whatever else anybody thinks, thank God Malcolm is here, caring about us, knowing how to go through brutal, terrible, and desperate valleys of experience, and to keep moving with endurance, to keep running the race until the poet could say of him, "He became much more than there was time for him to be."

Malcolm, teach us how to become much more than we have time to be. Detroit Red. Oh, brother of the faith. El-Hajj Malik El-Shabazz. Oh, companion of Jesus in the hard way. Thank you. *Assalam 'alaikum.*

And I know that A.J. is holding him, old A.J. Muste. I don't know if he's still smoking his perennial cigarette, but if he is, then he's holding Malcolm with one hand, and saying, "Malcolm, I understood you all the time. I knew what passion for justice you were coming out of, and I'm so glad that we are here together."

The last time I remember seeing A.J. in any fullness was back in 1963 when John Kennedy was assassinated, when the Peace Walkers were traveling from Quebec to Guantanamo Bay, Cuba, and when they got stopped in southern Georgia, and people were ready to kill them there. They came into our house to find refuge and quiet, and they were all upset, and some were a little crazy because they were under such stress and such pressure. Old A.J. came down from New York—or some-where—and just calmed them, just said, "Now let's sit and talk about this. What are we going to do? What should be done?"

I want in my life A.J.'s grace under pressure, A.J.'s capacity to be calm and quiet facing the guns. In the midst of climbing over fences to get into missile sites, in the midst of holy disobedience, refusing to give his assent to the ways of war, in the midst of war itself, I want to be like A.J., so that when they're taking me off to jail, I'd want to, like him, know what the score is in the Yankee's game that day. Thank you, A.J.

There are so many. As the writer says, "Tongue can hardly name them." Barbara Deming—sure, she's here. I don't understand all of Barbara Deming. I don't understand how she put together so many parts of her life. But I know that Barbara was in that Albany, Georgia, jail with black people and white people, just calling upon Jesus in her own agnostic way. And I want the Barbara Demings to know that I know that they are here, and that we need their courage; and that some of us need to know how to be woman—how to be woman tough, how to be woman loving, how to be woman compassionate, how to be woman courageous, how to be woman. I think Barbara knows something about that.

Do you know, do you sense, do you feel Martin here? Thank God for Martin Luther King, Jr. Let him teach us whatever he will. Let him teach us how to choose, how to make hard choices for peace and freedom, even, as he did, against the fears of his parents and his friends. Let him teach us how to choose even against the ways of his tribe. Let him teach us how he got on the case for the poor, and once that scent was in his nostrils, how he was never to be turned aside from his total conviction that the poor must find life and power in our society. Martin, help us.

Gandhi, help us. Thank you, thank you, brother Gandhi. Teach us the way of self-discipline. Teach us the way of fasting. Teach us the way of prayer that we may run with perseverance the race that is set before us.

Bishop Oscar Romero. *Presente*. Thank you for being here. Teach us how to change our minds. Teach us how to face our own sons with the guns in their hands. And teach us to speak to them of love and compassion and the way of Jesus, which is not the way of guns. Teach us how to stand with the people, for the people, no matter what comes.

And then in this time there are witnesses who are very fitting for just this American hour, like Bonhoeffer, like the Confessing Church of Germany. What you taught us is that the time comes again and again in Christian faith when Christian people must go against their own government in order to go for life. Dietrich Bonhoeffer, help us to know how to do that without self-righteousness, without fear, without recrimination, and, if you have learned, without being overwhelmed by the temptation to violence.

In a time when our own government is moving against the compassion of God's love for the world, teach us how to speak and live truth, no matter what the cost. Teach us how to love America and its people so much that we will risk our lives in the struggle for transformation, for the new city, for the new land. Thank you.

Of course, each of us has some of our own most personal and cherished witnesses to deal with, to talk and listen to. I've got Mabel and Gordon and Dock and Fred and Howard and Sister Viola. Thank you for your love. Thank you for your light.

Well, here we are, all present and accounted for. What a gang! What a table! What a host! What a chance for holding and being held, for feeding and being fed, for giving, receiving, and being the light.

No excuse for drooping—at least not for long. No excuse for not running—or at least walking strong. No excuse for staying down. 'Cause we are surrounded, folks. So, let's straighten up, and shuck off; let's get refreshed at the table, and then get down with some real long-distance walking and running—and maybe even some flying, like eagles, in due time. That's our tradition. That's our destiny. That's our hope. So go right on, sisters and brothers, people of the tents: walk in the light, run with the cloud, mount up on your wings, follow the Pioneer. There is a city to build.

Now, until we meet again, until we meet again in love and struggle and hope, may God bless you and strengthen you and keep you—and give you at least a few good laughs along the way. Amen. Amen.

LIVING IN HOPE:
Remembering the Resurrection
Jim Wallis

In December 1983 I received a letter that read in part:

Since 1978 my husband and I have been doing research on what nuclear arms and nuclear war mean and on how to stop this madness. We are members of various church and political groups that are involved in education and in applying political pressure toward bilateral disarmament. We don't know what else to do.

A type of paralysis is beginning to creep into us and those around us. I find my young friends to be particularly stuck in this problem. The specific problem is a loss of a sense of the future. We had planned to get pregnant in April or so. We wonder now if we should. Given the present course of things, a war seems inevitable.

I never realized how much I lived in the future. I try to live in the present, but I catch myself not bothering to do little things because I don't want to waste my time on a future that seems to be already nonexistent. I imagine that this is baldly a form of despair. We are still fighting and we haven't given up, but we have lost a sense of the future, especially for our children, and it is eerie to live without it.

I have received more than one letter like this. In these difficult times, where do we find hope? Among many this is becoming a frequent and heartfelt question.

There are countless good reasons to give up hope. But hope is not an abstract theological issue; it is the substance of the faith necessary for survival. We have all known the agony and loneliness of despair. We have all had to find the kind of hope that is not destroyed by the failures, defeats, and sufferings of the moment.

The powers that be are counting on our losing hope. That is their hope. Some people, especially in places of high political authority, are just waiting for us to wear down and out. It is the persistence of hope, even in the midst of their seeming domination, that is the single greatest threat to their absolute authority. To hope against their power is to undermine the illusions and control they depend upon.

The poor of the world, on the other hand, are hoping we don't give up. Their very lives are at stake in keeping hope alive. Our despair and resignation do them no good at all. Only in hope can we join with them in the quest for justice and freedom. For the poor and for those who take their side, hope is not a feeling or mood, it is a necessary choice for survival.

Hope means more than just hanging on. It is the conscious decision to see the world in a different way than most others see it. To hope is to look through the eyes of faith to a future not determined by the oppressive circumstances of the present. To hope is to know that the present reality will not have the last word. It is to know, despite the pretensions and cruelties of idolatrous authorities, that God rules. It is God who will have the last word.

We need more than resistance; we need hope. A radical judgment upon the present situation is not enough; we need a positive vision of where we are going. To dig in our heels and say no to the present madness is a good thing, but to walk a new path and say yes is a better thing. If we are just holding out and hanging on, we will not last long. But if we are beginning to live out new possibilities, we can spark a movement of hope.

That is why it is particularly important for people who are trying to build a different future to live now in a way that demonstrates real hope for that future. I'm not speaking of the kind of false optimism and denial of reality that so many still hang on to. I'm speaking of the concrete choice to live in hope, despite harsh and dangerous realities. That choice is an act of faith. It can only come out of the deepest confidence that God is still God and that, come what may, nothing will separate us from the love of God.

In the days ahead, the world will desperately need people who can demonstrate that kind of faith and exemplify a radical hope in the face of many reasons for discouragement. It is precisely because the times are so bad that we need to plant, build, and create new life. It could be that the most appropriate response to the growing storm clouds of war is to have and raise children with the determination that they will have a future. To give up is to succumb to despair; to act in hope is to live in faith.

The resurrection stands as the most radical sign of hope we have. The authorities who killed Jesus were trying to kill hope. They tried desperately to prevent the resurrection, and they failed. Their plans were undone, and hope was alive forevermore.

Only forgetting the resurrection can kill hope now. That is exactly what those in power have always wanted us to do. But we will not forget. Though sometimes discouraged, we will not forget. Though often defeated, we will not forget. Though even in despair, we will not forget. We will remember, and because we remember, we will live and act in hope.

CONTRIBUTORS

Daniel Berrigan is a priest, poet, and peace activist and the author, most recently, of *The Mission: A Film Journal* (Harper & Row, 1986).

Allan Boesak is a black Dutch Reformed minister and president of the World Alliance of Reformed Churches. He is the author, most recently, of *Comfort and Protest: Reflections on the Apocalypse of John of Patmos* (The Westminster Press, 1987).

Danny Collum is associate editor of *Sojourners* and a member of Sojourners Community.

Jim Corbett is a retired rancher from Tucson, Arizona, who was found innocent in May 1986 of charges that he conspired to smuggle Central American refugees.

Sarah Corson is co-founder of SIFAT (Servants in Faith and Technology), located in Wedowee, Alabama, which offers practical training in meeting basic human needs.

Gordon Cosby is the founder and pastor of Church of the Saviour in Washington, D.C.

Jim Douglass is cofounder of the Ground Zero Center for Nonviolent Action in Bangor, Washington, and the author of *Lightning East to West: Jesus, Gandhi, and the Nuclear Age* (Crossroad, 1983).

Walter Fauntroy is the delegate to the U.S. House of Representatives representing the District of Columbia and is pastor of New Bethel Baptist Church. He is a long-time leader in the black freedom movement and is a central figure in the Free South Africa Movement.

John Fife is pastor of Southside Presbyterian Church in Tucson, Arizona, and was one of eight sanctuary workers convicted in May 1986 of conspiracy to smuggle and transport Central American refugees.

Vincent Harding, the author, most recently, of *There Is a River: The Black Struggle for Freedom in America* (Harcourt Brace Jovanovich, 1981), is professor of religion and social transformation at Iliff School of Theology in Denver, Colorado.

Joyce Hollyday is associate editor of *Sojourners* and a pastor of Sojourners Community.

Bill Kellermann is a United Methodist pastor in Detroit, Michigan, and a long-time activist in peace and social justice movements.

Vicki Kemper is news editor of *Sojourners*.

Karen Lattea is managing editor of *Sojourners* and a member of Sojourners Community.

Elizabeth McAlister is a member of Jonah House in Baltimore, Maryland, and a mother of three children. In the summer of 1986, she was released after serving a three-year sentence at the Federal Correctional Institution in Alderson, West Virginia, for her role in the Griffiss Plowshares civil disobedience action in November 1983.

Catherine Meeks is an instructor and director of Afro-American studies at Mercer University in Macon, Georgia.

Stacey Lynn Merkt works with Central American refugees at Projecto Libertad in the Rio Grande Valley of Texas.

Ched Myers is a longtime activist against the nuclear arms race in the Pacific region and the author of a commentary on the gospel of Mark, to be published by Orbis Books in 1987.

Ronald J. Sider is president of Evangelicals for Social Action and co-author, with Richard K. Taylor, of *Nuclear Holocaust and Christian Hope: A Book for Christian Peacemakers* (Paulist Press, 1982).

Ginny Earnest Soley is assistant pastoral coordinator of Sojourners Community.

Rob Soley is a Montessori teacher, a poet, and a member of Sojourners Community.

Richard K. Taylor has worked on many peace efforts including Witness for Peace and the Pledge of Resistance, and is co-author, with Ronald J.

Sider, of *Nuclear Holocaust and Christian Hope: A Book for Christian Peacemakers* (Paulist Press, 1982).

Desmond Tutu, winner of the Nobel Peace Prize in 1984, is archbishop of the Anglican Church in Capetown, South Africa, and former head of the South African Council of Churches.

Philip Willis-Conger is former director of the Tucson Ecumenical Council's Task Force on Central American refugees. He was one of eight sanctuary workers convicted in May 1986 of conspiracy to smuggle and transport Central American refugees.

Jim Wallis is the editor of *Sojourners* and a pastor of Sojourners Community. He is the author of *Agenda for Biblical People* (Harper & Row, 1984), *Revive Us Again* (Abingdon, 1983), *The Call to Conversion* (Harper & Row, 1981), and editor of *Peacemakers* (Harper & Row, 1983) and *Waging Peace* (Harper & Row, 1982). He is also an itinerant preacher who is deeply involved in the movements that make up the rise of Christian conscience.